DEDICATION

With love to Emma Muller;
my guardian who gave me
love and guidance
when I most needed them

Contents

Acknowledgments

The author wishes to extend his appreciation to Mara Musciano for foreign research and translations; John W. Conrad and Fred Muller for their assistance in translating German documents and letters; A. E. "Ed" Ferko and Lorenz Rasse for contributing photographs and biographical information; French Armee de l'Air; German Fighter Pilots' Association; U.S. Air Force; Royal Air Force; General Adolf Galland; General Hannes Trautloft; Robert Roland Stanford Tuck; Clive "Killer" Caldwell; Walker Mahurin; American Fighter Pilots' Association; Bruce Reynolds and the San Diego Aero-Space Museum; Günther Rall; Gerhard Barkhorn; Aladar de Heppes; Robert S. Johnson; Douglas Bader; and Walter Boyne, Curator of Aeronautics, National Air and Space Museum, Smithsonian Institution, for photographs and historical biographical information. To all, a sincere thank you. Plus a special thanks to Diane M. Jenkins for her tireless stenographic efforts preparing the manuscript, which made this volume possible.

Introduction

"War was once cruel and magnificent; now war is cruel and squalid." This astute observation, made by the renown soldier/statesman/historian Sir Winston Churchill, is generally correct with one exception: fighter planes in aerial combat. The magnificence to which Churchill alluded was the hand-to-hand, face-to-face combat of ancient and medieval warriors, while he considered modern, impersonal warfare with sophisticated weapons as squalid and without dignity. Shortly after the fighter plane made its appearance in World War I, tactics evolved into a form of hand-to-hand combat reminiscent of the knights of old. Outstanding aces such as William Bishop, Rene Fonck, and Manfred von Richthofen became the contemporary counterparts of Achilles, Horatio, Roland, Tancred, and other legendary warriors. After the Armistice, through the twenties and thirties, military theorists generally agreed that the era of "romantic" dogfighting was over. However, the Second World War proved them wrong. True, contact between adversaries was of much shorter duration because of greater aircraft speed and rapid-fire guns of larger caliber, but it was still comparable to Churchill's "magnificent" war.

The Second World War was waged with an unsurpassed human effort and material expenditure by both sides. Its most important and decisive activity was the war in the air, which decided the outcome of battles, campaigns and the war itself. The air forces of the principal combatants were developed under diverse tactical and strategic philosophies which, it will be seen, placed an incomparable burden upon the German fighter pilots, forcing them to perform Herculean tasks. It was the superhuman and astonishing achievements with which the Luftwaffe's fighter aces are credited that inspired the author to enter into the serious research necessary to dispel numerous myths, inaccuracies, and vicious wartime propaganda spread about these brave men. When examined with academic seriousness, cool head, and calm heart, we will find the World War II German fighter pilots to be fair opponents and more than qualified to take their places with those legendary warriors of bygone, romantic eras.

The Luftwaffe's five top-scoring fighter pilots accumulated a total of 1,453 victories: Erich Hartmann, 352 victories; Gerhard Barkhorn, 301; Günther Rall, 275; Otto Kittel, 267; and Walter Nowotny, 258 victories! If this astonishing number of downed Allied aircraft were parked end-to-end on an open field, they would cover over 25 acres and equip more than 50 Allied fighter squadrons with a full complement of aircraft: a veritable air force!

"Ace" was an unofficial term used only by Allied air forces, given to any pilot who shot down five or more enemy aircraft. The German Luftwaffe did not use the term ace; they called proficient pilots "Experten," or experts, and it required more than a mere five victories to earn that title. To become an Expert, a pilot must prove, through continuous performance, that he was worthy of that coveted and exclusive title.

If we use the Allied method (RAF/USAAF) of bestowing the ace title, then the German Luftwaffe produced over 3,000 aces during the Second World War! When this is compared to the number of Allied aces fighting in the European and Mediter-

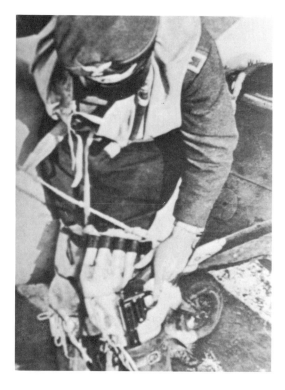

A Jagdflieger prepares for a freie Jagd, or fighter sweep, over southeastern England. Notice the signal flares and flare pistol strapped to his leg. He wears an inflatable vest because much of the flying and fighting will be over water. Next, a ground crew member assists with the parachute.

Erhard Milch became managing director of Lufthansa Airline in the mid-'20s and secretly trained his pilots in air combat techniques.

Hermann Göring, himself an Alte Adler with 22 victories and holder of the Blue Max, was able to attract numerous WWI veterans to help him organize the Luftwaffe.

This rare photo shows the four WWI Jagdgeschwader or Wing Leaders together in late 1918. From left to right are Oskar von Bonigk, Eduard Ritter von Schleich, Bruno Lörzer, and Hermann Göring. All contributed to the development and the operation of the Luftwaffe.

Alte Adler General Oberst Hans-Jürgen Stumpff was appointed Luftwaffe Chief of Air Personnel and then became Chief of Staff. During Operation Barbarossa, he commanded Luftflotte 5 in the far north.

Ernst Udet and Hermann Göring flew in the same unit in World War I and, although never friendly, worked together in developing the Luftwaffe.

Eduard Ritter von Schleich was known as the Black Knight during the First World War. The Alte Adler was an organizer of the Hitler Youth Aviation Program and did much to stimulate interest in aviation in Germany. He was one of the first to answer Göring's call for assistance in organizing the Luftwaffe.

Luftwaffe Chief of Staff General Walther Wever proposed a balanced force of fighters and bombers in 1936. He was ignored. Wever is at extreme left with General von Blomberg (center) and Erhard Milch (right).

Italian air power prophet Lt. Col. Giulio Douhet predicted the coming importance of the airplane as a decisive weapon and proposed a well-balanced air force for tactical and strategic roles as early as 1909. The Luftwaffe planners ignored his theories and the Jagdwaffe paid the price.

Gen. Kurt von Döring, an Alte Adler who flew in the Richthofen Jagdgeschwader and scored 11 victories in World War I, also contributed his talents in the formation of the Luftwaffe. In 1943 he was in command of No. 1 Flieger Division in the Netherlands.

Another Alte Adler who joined in the formation of the Luftwaffe was Gen. Joachim-Friedrich Huth. Despite losing a leg in World War I, he led combat units in the Battles of France and Britain! After serving as Jafu 2, he was placed in command of various Jagddivisions and finally Jagdkorps I.

General Werner Junck scored 5 victories in World War I and became one of the first Inspekteur der Jagdflieger in 1939. In 1943, he was in command of No. 3 Flieger Division or Jafu 3.

ranean theater, we begin to realize the outstanding record of the German Jagdwaffe or "Hunting arm": Royal Air Force, including Canada, Australia, and New Zealand, 868 aces (top ace—40 victories); USAAF (8th Air Force), 262 aces (top ace—24 air-to air-victories); USSR, 162 aces (top ace—62 victories); France, 130 aces (top ace—33 victories); South Africa, 23 aces (top ace—15 victories); Americans in the RAF, 20 aces (top ace—25 victories); Poland, 47 aces (top ace—18 victories); Norway, 16 aces (top ace—16 victories); and Czechoslovakia, 12 aces (top ace—28 victories) for a grand total of 1,540 aces.

There are 2 German fighter pilots who scored over 300 victories, 13 who scored between 200 and 300 victories, 92 who scored between 100 and 200 victories, and about 360 who scored between 40 and 100 victories. These figures become quite believable when we discover that the Luftwaffe's fighters were caught up in the remorseless grind of the 1939–1945 war as were the pilots of no other nation.

The armor and infantry in the Spanish Civil War; the Polish Invasion; the overrunning of Denmark and Norway; and the invasion of the Netherlands, Belgium, and France would never have been successful had it not been for the Luftwaffe's fighter arm and its advanced state of tactical fighter aviation, which reached its zenith just prior to the Dunkirk evacuation. The heavily publicized Luftwaffe fighter assault on Britain was a minor event compared to the incessant, years-long aerial pounding inflicted on Germany by the British and U.S. air forces. The valiant British fighter pilots who fought off the very brief and almost half-hearted German air offensive called the "Battle of Britain" have become the "immortal few," and yet the equally valiant Luftwaffe fighters who tried to halt the huge Allied air assault have remained in obscurity. This despite the fact that the Jagdwaffe lost more fighters in one month during the Allied air offensive than it did throughout the entire Battle of Britain!

Outnumbered during the most of the war, the German fighter pilots were forced to fly up to five missions a day and from 500 to 1,000 missions or sorties during their combat career. It is questionable if more than a few of the most active Allied pilots even carried out one hundred missions during the entire war. This feverish uninterrupted activity gave the Jagdwaffe pilot more opportunity to score victories; conversely, it also increased the possibility that he would fall victim to an Allied pilot's guns. Many were, in fact, shot down a dozen or more times, only to return to action and score even more victories!

The brilliant fighting achievements of the Jagdwaffe pilots contrasted sharply with the poor decisions made by the inept leadership of the Oberkommando der Luftwaffe (Luftwaffe High Command). Despite the Ob. d. L. incompetence and lack of vision, the German fighter pilots fought on with skill and bravery in the finest military tradition.

The German fighter pilot was a chivalrous soldier; he fought hard but, in the best knightly tradition, was a passionate believer in fair play. His orders included: never shoot a parachuting flyer nor to strafe an enemy who is forced to land. There are no records that prove these instructions were ever violated.

As impartial investigation reveals, Germany's fighter pilots fought valiantly for their country as do the fighting men of all nations. The Luftwaffe, especially the fighter pilots, will always occupy a special place in the imaginations of those who are keenly interested in the history of men under arms. This is their story.

MESSERSCHMITT
A·C·E·S

PART ONE

The Battleground — Air War on Three Fronts

THE LUFTWAFFE BEFORE WORLD WAR II

When the Central Powers lost the 1914-1918 war, the resulting Treaty of Versailles prohibited Germany from having an air force and forbade the construction of powered aircraft of any type. Four years later, the Allies relented and granted Germany the construction of nonmilitary aircraft only. Having been stripped of all military aircraft and permitted only a small army for defensive purposes, the nation experienced a strong desire to overcome this military helplessness by any means at her disposal. The aircraft manufacturers of Focke-Wulf, Heinkel, Dornier, and Junkers, as well as eager and talented designers such as Willy Messerschmitt, Kurt Tank, Ernst Heinkel and Claude Dornier, applied much thought and ingenuity to the problem of producing civil aircraft designs that could be readily converted to military purposes. Obviously, this half-way measure resulted in designs that fell short of full-fledged military aircraft. However, an undercover air force was becoming a reality.

The Reichswehr (as the post-war token army was called) Chief of Staff General Hans von Seeckt was the individual most responsible for the resurrection of a German air force. In the early spring of 1920 he instituted a series of conferences with the Soviet Russian Commissar for War, Leon Trotsky. The Russian revolution had destroyed the officer corps and now the USSR sorely needed highly trained military leaders and technicians. Germany possessed a nucleus of well-trained military leaders, but required a suitable base for secretly testing military equipment and training pilots, away from the prying eyes of the Allied Armistice authorities. Germany

and the Soviet Union had much to offer each other, and an agreement was soon reached whereby the Germans would train a Soviet officer corps in exchange for the use of Russian real estate for developing a new German air arm. By the fall of 1922, almost 400 German technicians and aerial warfare experts had arrived in Russia, many of whom eventually attained prominent positions in the Luftwaffe. The Soviet/German air training school at Lipetsk, about 200 miles south of Moscow, was set up to train German pilots, but the shared base provided the Russians with the ability to study the German training methods, tactics, and organization that were being refined after the World War I experience. The Germans, in turn, had the opportunity to learn the Soviet problems and their air-war philosophies.

During this time, Germany granted Lufthansa, the civil airline, a monopoly in exchange for about one-third of the company's stock. This enabled von Seeckt to slip key men into strategic positions in the airline. One of these was Erhard Milch, a former executive of the Junkers firm, who became the Lufthansa managing director. By working closely with von Seeckt, Milch saw to it that the four Lufthansa pilot training centers included air combat techniques, bombing operations, and other military skills.

When, in 1933, the extremely anti-Communist National Socialist or Nazi party, under the leadership of Adolf Hitler, came to power in Germany, the secret training of German airmen in the Soviet Union naturally came to an abrupt end. The Fascist Italian government came to Germany's assistance, and Benito Mussolini invited the German airmen to conduct their advanced training with his Regia Aeronautica. Disguised as Tyroleans and tourists, the

1

General Hugo Sperrle was a key commander from the time he joined the Luftwaffe to the end of the war. In 1937, he was placed in charge of the Condor Legion in Spain and then led Luftwaffe 3 from the Battle of Britain to the Allied mass bombing of the Continent in 1944/45.

After serving as head of the Luftwaffe Technical Department, Alte Adler Wolfram von Richthofen was selected as Sperrle's Chief of Staff in the Condor Legion. He later served in a wide variety of assignments, including command of VII Flieger Korps during the Battle of Britain.

This Messerschmitt Me 109B-2 was one of the first to arrive in Spain, during April, 1937. Note the St. Andrew's cross insignia.

With their Messerschmitts waiting in the background, pilots of JG 88 review their mission prior to takeoff. One of the JG 88 aircraft is caught diving on its objective.

This unusual photo is of a Schwarm (four aircraft) made up of two Rotte (aircraft pairs). The formation is called "finger four" by the RAF and "double-attack" by the USAF. The nearest plane at the top and the plane at the right form one Rotte while the distant plane at the left and center aircraft form the other Rotte. Observe the large distance between planes.

With 14 confirmed victories, Werner Mölders was the top German Expert of the Spanish Civil War. He is seen here emerging from his Messerschmitt after a mission.

Reichsmarschall Göring is flanked by Gen. Albert Kesselring (left) and Gen. Bruno Lörzer during a meeting at the Pas de Calais.

Gen. Robert Ritter von Greim was another Alte Adler who helped organize the Luftwaffe. After leading Flieger Division No. 5 in 1939 and many subsequent commands, he flew into flaming Berlin in 1945, landed in the streets, and visited Hitler in his Bunker. The Führer was furious at Göring for trying to usurp his position and named von Greim commander in chief of the tattered Luftwaffe. The Alte Adler commited suicide on that May 24.

Alte Adler Gen. Alfred Keller was Commanding Officer of Bombengeschwader No. 1 in 1918, and was quick to answer Göring's call. Among his many commands were Flieger Division No. 4 in 1939 and Luftflotte 1 in the northern sector of the Russian front during Operation Barbarossa.

most enthusiastic Lufthansa personnel—air-minded young men—and promising pilots poured over the Alps into Italy, where they donned Italian Regia Aeronautica uniforms and flew Italian planes during the advanced training courses. The famous Italian long-distance flyer Italo Balbo and German World

War I Ace Hermann Göring had worked out the basic arrangements for the three-month course that trained many future aces for the Luftwaffe.

Germany repudiated the Versailles Treaty in March, 1935. With universal military service, a 36-division army and a 20,000-man Luftwaffe (as the new air force was called) became a reality virtually overnight, because of the secret training during the previous 13 years. Hermann Göring had established the new Luftwaffe as an independent service, equal to the German army and navy, at a time when the United States air services were still divided under separate army and navy control. Göring was promoted from his civilian job of Commissioner for Air to a ministry appointment, similar to a U.S. Presidential cabinet post, as Reichsluftfahrtminister, or Air Traffic Minister. Göring quickly ordered all flying and gliding clubs, of which there were many, to consolidate into one official government-sponsored aerial club. This became an excellent source of potential Luftwaffe pilots. He also organized a clandestine technical department in the Luftwaffe, known as C-Amt, to evaluate and select aircraft for the new air service.

One of Göring's most useful activities was maintaining contact with his World War I air service comrades, and now he called upon these former flyers to contribute their experience to the new Luftwaffe. Just before the 1918 Armistice, the German navy had mutinied; the shattered army revolted and many units joined Bolshevik causes, while riots infested many cities. Only the Luftstreitkrafte, as the Imperial Air Service was called, remained loyal and in fact, scored decisive victories during the last days of the war. These men could not understand why they were ordered to surrender when they had not suffered defeat in the air.

Eager to resurrect their beloved air service, many World War I aces and other leading air personalities flocked to Göring's call and were given key positions in the new Luftwaffe. Some of those who formed the roots of the new German air arm were Theodore Osterkamp, 32 victories; Alfred Keller, commanding officer of Bombengeschwader No. 1 in 1918; Eduard Ritter von Schleich, 35 victories; Kurt Student, 5 victories; Werner Junck, 5 victories; Bruno Lörzer, 45 victories; Hans Klein, 22 victories; Friedrich Christiansen, 21 victories; Wolfram von Richthofen, 8 victories; Hugo Sperrle, Kommandeur der Flieger VII Army; Robert Ritter von Greim, 25 victories; Hilmer von Bülow-Bothkamp, six victories; Kurt von Döring, 11 victories; Oskar von Bonigk, 26 victories; Joachim Friedrich Huth, who lost a leg in the 1914-18 war; Karl-August von Schönbeck, eight victories; Erich Mix; and others. Hermann Göring, himself an ace with 22 victories and the recipient of Imperial Germany's highest award, Pour le Mérite, selected Walther Wever as Chief of Air Staff, Hans-Jurgen Stumpff as Chief of Air Personnel, and reassigned Erhard Milch as Secretary of State for Air.

Hilmer von Bülow-Bothkamp led JG 2 Richthofen and other units in action and later became Kommandeur of Jagd Division No. 5 and Jafu 4.

General Hans Jeschonnek, a veteran of the Imperial Air Service in World War I, played an active role in the secret training of German flyers in Russia. He replaced Kesselring as Luftwaffe Chief of Staff in 1939.

Gen. Kurt Student, an Alte Adler with 5 WWI victories, was given command of the German Paratroop Corps, which was part of the Luftwaffe. His expertise came to the fore in the aerial invasions of Norway and Crete.

These Alte Adler, or Old Eagles, were extended all the homage they well deserved. Their appearance in the Luftwaffe was far more than mere tradition however, for many served as leaders right down to *geschwader, gruppe* and *staffel* level, and were truly in command of the air arm. Several, including Erich Mix, Harry von Bülow, and Theodore Osterkamp actually went on combat patrols during the World War II and scored victories over Allied pilots young enough to be their sons! The Luftwaffe was the only air force in which World War I pilots engaged in aerial combat during World War II.

Despite the abundance of talent that responded to Göring's call, there was one World War I ace who wanted nothing to do with the new Luftwaffe. This was Ernst Udet, the highest-scoring German ace to survive World War I (62 victories), second only to Manfred von Richthofen, the legendary Red Baron. Since the Armistice, Udet had done what he loved best: fly. He demonstrated his flying ability at international air shows and worked as a film stunt man, which earned him the title of the finest stunt pilot in aviation. Udet also manufactured airplanes for a while, which gave him some technical aeronautical experience. Although he was immensely successful as a fighter pilot and served under Baron von Richt-

hofen and Hermann Göring, Udet disliked killing and war and ridiculed the pompous Göring. Despite his continued refusals, Göring persisted in offering Udet key posts in the new ministry.

By 1934, the Luftwaffe leaders were divided about which type of aircraft to develop. One argument centered on the dive bomber, a type of aircraft that had stimulated Udet's interest ever since he had observed U.S. experiments with the steep-diving aircraft. Erhard Milch and Major Wolfram von Richthofen, the Chief of the Technical Department, were against it, while General Walther Wever wanted dive bombers as well as long-range bombers developed and produced. Fearful that the dive bomber would probably not be adopted unless he was there to defend its cause, Ernst Udet finally agreed to join his comrades in the Luftwaffe and replaced von Richthofen as Chief of the Technical Department with the rank of Oberst. When he took over von Richthofen's department, he found a directive in his file, prepared by von Richthofen, canceling further dive bomber development! Udet quickly negated the order and pressed ahead with dive bomber, or Sturtzkampflugzeug (Stuka), with a passion.

While on the subject of Lufwaffe equipment selection, it is important to illustrate how the great powers who were destined to be involved in World War II were influenced by three respected airpower prophets regarding the application of the airplane in warfare.

Lt. Col. Giulio Douhet, Italian Staff Officer, stated in 1909: "The sky is about to become another battlefield, no less important than the battlefields on land and sea. In order to conquer the air, it is necessary to deprive the enemy of all means of flying: by striking at him in the air, at his bases of operation, and at his production centers. We had better get accustomed to this idea and prepare ourselves." Col. Douhet had the foresight to visualize the need for fighter planes to strike "at him in the air," for short-range tactical bombers to attack "at his bases of operation," and for long-range strategic bombers to assault "his production centers." Douhet envisioned a well-balanced air force, but his views were not accepted by his contemporaries. He was imprisoned for a year as a troublemaker in 1916.

His prediction of the Caporetto disaster, where German troops devastated the Italian army in October, 1917, earned him a release from prison, though he remained unrepentant. In 1918, Douhet was named to the Italian Directorate of Aviation, and two years later the conviction of 1916 was officially reversed. He retired from the military in 1920 and devoted his life to his writings about his

During the campaign in Poland, JG 2 Richthofen was assigned to protect Berlin against a possible bombing raid. Here, the defending Messerschmitt Me 109B-2 fighters are shown undergoing general maintenance and gunsight alignment.

theories that future wars would be decided in the air. The key, he wrote, would be the massave heavy-bomber offensive. These could be stopped, he said, only by the fighter plane, which must attain and maintain control of the air. Giulio Douhet died in 1930, one of the most respected and widely-read prophets of air power.

Captain Bertram Dickson, the first British military officer to fly, stated in 1911: "Both sides will be equipped with large corps of aeroplanes, each trying to obtain information of the other. The efforts which each would exert in order to hinder or prevent the enemy from obtaining this information would be by armed aeroplanes against each other." Dickson claimed that fighters were the most important combat aircraft, and that they would control the air.

Brigadier General William "Billy" Mitchell, U.S. proponent of air power, stated in 1920: "The most important branch of aviation is pursuit (fighters) which fights for and gains control of the air." Gen. Mitchell was court-martialed because of his insistence that the U.S. Army recognize the need for a strong air arm.

The Luftwaffe ignored the prophets and suffered the consequences.

Luftwaffe Chief of Staff General Walther Wever was an enthusiastic exponent of a well-balanced air force. He had embarked on a program of creating a strategic force of long-range bombers for distant missions, which could reach any point on the European continent. He called it the "Ural Bomber," referring to Russia's Ural Mountains, which he considered the prime strategic target in the event of war with the Soviet Union. But tragedy struck for the Luftwaffe on June 3, 1936, when General Wever was killed in a plane crash in Dresden. Albert Kesselring succeeded Wever and promptly argued against further development of the long-range four-engine bomber. Obsessed with the Stuka and tactical bombers, Udet joined forces with Kesselring and, together, they scrapped the big-bomber program, despite the fact that both Junkers and Dornier had already constructed prototypes. Kesselring and Udet offered the following reasoning: Large bombers would consume too much raw material; two or three smaller bombers could be built for the cost of one four-engine giant; only close-support, tactical, high-speed, lightly-armed bombers, fast enough to outrun enemy fighters, were needed to pave the way for the Army's advance. This would enable the Panzers (tanks) to move ahead so rapidly that they would overwhelm the enemy troops and reach production centers before the enemy could produce sufficient war material to halt the German progress. Germany's enemies were on her borders and long-range bombers were, therefore, not necessary. Slower, long-range bombers would require the production of more fighter aircraft for escort purposes, thereby adding to the long-range bomber cost!

A majority of the Luftwaffe's founders were former fighter pilots, as was its leader, Hermann Göring. Fighter planes were initially given considerable attention in the Nazi armaments program with Göring leading the way, but he lost interest and let others make decisions that altered the Luftwaffe's procurement path. The principal interest turned to bombers and while controversy raged over the types of bombers to develop, fighters played a decidedly secondary role in the minds of high-level Luftwaffe personnel.

The Royal Air Force never underestimated the fighter plane. Both the United States and Britain, contrary to the German war philosophy, continued the development, started in 1936, of long-range four-engine bombers. Their development culminated with the Flying Fortress, Liberator, Stirling, and Lan-

caster, aircraft which virtually won the war in the European theater. Germany's decision to abandon the long-range, four-engine bomber was a major factor in her defeat in the Second World War, and imposed an impossible task on the neglected Luftwaffe fighter arm, unlike that imposed on any other fighter force. This will become evident as we examine the decade of intense activity of the Jagdwaffe.

THE SPANISH CIVIL WAR—A TESTING GROUND

Members of the new Luftwaffe entered combat for the first time during 1936 in the Spanish Civil War. The Republic was established in February, and the new government consolidated its controls, retiring many recalcitrant officers early, sending others to assignments outside Spain. By July the Army revolted, led by General Francisco Franco and other disenchanted officers. Germany lent the rebels several Junkers Ju 52 troop-transport planes to ferry 1,000 black rebel troops from Morocco to Spain, 22 at a time. When the rightist rebels scored some early victories, the leftist government asked for help from foreign governments. France and Russia responded: France with small arms, and the Soviets with tanks and planes. The strictly anti-Communist governments of Germany and Italy reacted by sending help to Franco and his Nationalists, as the rebels called themselves. Italy sent planes and tanks as well as troops, while Germany, sensing the chance to test the new Luftwaffe in actual combat, made arrangements to send planes and pilots to Spain.

It was an open secret at the time of 1936 Olympic Games that the Axis powers were taking an active part in the Spanish conflict, although the Germans expended much effort to camouflage their participation. The Luftwaffe personnel who were selected for service in Spain were sent to Special Branch "W" in Berlin, where they were given civilian clothes, papers and Spanish money. The initial contingent was made to appear that it was going on a "sunshine cruise" as part of the "Strength through Joy" movement. On July 31, the volunteers were given a fiery speech by General Erhard Milch, and on the next day they boarded the 22,000-ton Wörmann Line freighter *Usaramo*, which had already been loaded with six Heinkel He 51 biplane fighters, 11 Junkers Ju 52 transport planes, and spare parts and ammunition. Upon their arrival in Spain on August 7, the men were issued olive-brown uniforms that resembled the outfits worn by the Nationalists. All mail to the airmen was addressed in care of the fictitious "Max Winkler, Berlin SW 68" and then forwarded to the men. As the six Heinkel fighter pilots disembarked, they were identified as Oberst Leutnant Herwig Knuppel; Leutnant Freiherr von Houwald; Leutnant Ekkard Hester; Oberst Hannes Trautloft; a Leutnant Kleine and an Oberst Eberhard.

The Heinkels were based on Tablada, the military air field near Seville, with the intention of training Spanish air force pilots when the Germans were not using the aircraft. Leutnant von Houwald was in charge of the training. Under Oberst Eberhard's command, the six-man fighter air force first flew on August 25, when Trautloft opened the scoring by shooting down a French-built Breguet. Eberhard also scored during this encounter, as well as on the following day, on which Oblt. Knuppel also destroyed a Russian-built Chato biplane, a feat he repeated on the 27th. On September 5, the tiny force scored two more victories, but on the 28th, Lt. Hester crashed to his death for the unit's first fatality. From August through October, this small fighter force, plus poorly trained and equipped Spaniards, bore the brunt of aerial fighting for General Franco's revolutionary forces.

The arrival in Spain of scores of Russian-built I-15, I-153, and I-16 fighters, often called Chato, Chaika, and Moska, proved the obsolescence of the German Heinkels. Despite the fact that six more Luftwaffe pilots arrived with more Heinkels in late October, several members of the group were killed in dogfights with the superior Soviet equipment. Included in the losses was the unit commander, Oblt. Eberhard, who collided with a Chato. Even with the arrival of more Heinkels in November, the Germans were still outclassed and outnumbered by the equipment sent by a determined Russia. Aware that something more had to be done, the Luftwaffe command sent a new Messerschmitt Me 109B fighter to Spain for combat evaluation. This modern fighter arrived on December 9 and was assigned to Hannes Trautloft for evaluation. He prepared reams of reports with recommendations on how to improve the design for combat readiness.

Early in 1937, a complete German expeditionary force was assembled. Drawn mostly from the Luftwaffe, this organization was called the Condor Legion. The Legion consisted of a fully integrated air force with bomber, fighter, and ground-attack units, plus transport, liaison, and reconnaissance ele-

ments, all under the command of General Hugo Sperrle with Oberst Lt. Wolfram von Richthofen as his Chief of Staff. Richthofen, who had recently been replaced as head of the Luftwaffe Technical Department by Ernst Udet, was a cousin of Manfred von Richthofen, the famous Red Baron of World War I. Wolfram had been a member of his cousin's Flying Circus in World War I and now held a doctorate of engineering. The fighter complement of the Condor Legion consisted of four Staffels, or squadrons, that formed J 88, or Jagdgruppe 88 (Fighter Group 88). The staffel leaders at this time were: I/J88 Oblt. Lützow; 2/J88 Oblt. Galland; 3/J88 Oblt. Harder; and 4/J88 Oblt. Pitcairn. Still flying the Heinkel biplanes, J88 proved successful in action over the Madrid area, but when transferred to the northern front in February, 1937 it met stiff resistance from the Loyalists' Soviet aircraft. In April, the first Messerschmitt Me 109B-2 fighters were delivered to No. 2 Staffel, and the new fighter quickly gained air superiority over the Russian aircraft and demonstrated its formidable performance when in the hands of a capable pilot. While the Messerschmitts of 2/J88 escorted Heinkel bombers on high-altitude raids, the Heinkel fighters were relegated to troop-support duties, strafing, and other tactical activities. During an action west of Madrid, J88 is credited with halting a powerful Loyalist offensive with Olympic Gold Medal winner Major Gotthardt Handrick in command. More Messerschmitts arrived in August and by the spring of 1938 only 3/J88, now led by Adolf Galland, was left with the obsolescent Heinkels.

The Messerschmitts of the Condor Legion were painted overall in a flat medium gray. In addition, some aircraft had a black streak on the fuselage side, starting at the exhaust openings and widening as it ran aft to about half the fuselage height. Its insignia was a round black spot near the tip of the wings with a white St. Andrew's Cross on the spot. The round black spot also appeared on the fuselage sides, but with a smaller cross. All Messerschmitts of J88 displayed a black number "6" to the left of the fuselage spot, with the plane indentification number appearing to the spot's right. The rudder was white with a black St. Andrew's Cross.

Condor Legion practice dictated that the pilots serve in strict rotation in order that as many Luftwaffe personnel as possible could take advantage of this combat experience during peacetime. On May 24, a new arrival in Spain, Werner Mölders, replaced Adolf Galland as commander of 3/J88, and Galland returned to Germany without having the chance to lead a Messerschmitt Staffel. The long-awaited Me 109C fighters arrived in July, and the entire Jagdgruppe was finally equipped with Messerschmitts. With 48 of the modern fighters in action, the men of J88, led by master tactician Mölders, began to develop new fighter formations. These were more adaptable to the new, all-metal, low-wing, high-powered fighter planes then being developed by every major air force. The existing tactical formations had been formulated for slow-flying biplanes, for which they were well suited.

Virtually every air force at that time favored large, unwieldy armadas. The basic element was a tight arrangement of three planes flying in a "V" formation, with the leader at the apex. When this was multiplied six to ten times to form a squadron, it was found that the average pilot paid more attention to avoiding collisions with his fellow pilots than he did to the combat situation itself. In the Luftwaffe, the three-plane flight was called a Kette. Mölders replaced the Kette with a "Rotte," which consisted of only two aircraft flying about 600 feet apart. This distance gave them room to maneuver and enabled them to cover a larger expanse of sky. In each Rotte, one pilot assumed the primary attack role, with his Rottenflieger, or Wingman, protecting his tail. Naturally, the leader of each Rotte would be the abler and more experienced pilot and marksman. With the assurance that his Rottenflieger was on guard, he could give much of his attention to attacking the enemy. Two Rotten combined to form a Schwarm and, as in the Rotte, one Rotte assumed the primary attacking role of the Schwarm, while the companion Rotte protected it from enemy attack. The four planes flew alongside each other at varying altitudes, and when viewed from above, each plane flew in the location of the four fingertips of a horizontally extended hand, palm down, with fingers straight and slightly spread. With this loose and flexible formation, large expanses of sky were no longer cut off from view by friendly aircraft in tightly-packed formations. Now that every modern fighter plane was equipped with radio equipment, it was no longer necessary to remain close to the flight leaders to see visual hand signals. With such obvious advantages, it is not surprising that a man with Mölders' ability would eventually develop this formation. It is a tribute to the excellence of his idea that every air force in the world has adopted this formation. In the Royal Air Force it is known as the "finger four" formation, and in the United States Air Force the "double-attack system."

The combination of modern fighter aircraft and superior formations and tactics brought the German fighter pilots accelerated success in the Spanish conflict. By the time Werner Mölders' tour of duty in

Spain had expired in November, 1938, he had 14 kills to his credit as the top German ace of the Spanish Civil War. Other successful Luftwaffe fighter pilots in this conflict included: Wolfgang Schellmann, 12 victories; Walter Ösau, 8; Hans-Karl Mayer, 8; Adolf Galland, 7; Walter Grabman, 6; Günther Lützow, 5; Herbert Ihlefeld, 7; and Wilhelm Balthasar, who shot down 4 Moskas in 6 minutes, 7 victories. Although outnumbered, the Condor Legion J88 scored a total of 314 acknowledged victories.

The Nationalists captured Tarragona in January, 1939, and reached the French border February 9. This signaled the end of the Spanish Civil War and Franco and his Nationalists emerged as victors.

The Jagdwaffe of 1939 was considered the most efficient, the most battle-worthy, and best-led force of its kind in the world. The lessons learned in the Spanish conflict helped make the Luftwaffe an effective weapon, and many military and aviation experts, including Charles A. Lindbergh, tried to warn their countries of this fact. The High Command, as well as politicians, overestimated the Luftwaffe's success by overlooking the fact that the Condor Legion, although numerically inferior, was pitted against relatively second-class aircraft once the Messerschmitt was placed in service in Spain. It had not yet been tested against modern British, French, or U.S. fighters. The Condor Legion's outstanding success with ground-support activities converted the Luftwaffe leaders to such an extent that they thought only in terms of tactical air power, and neglected the philosophy of a balanced air force.

THE EVE OF WORLD WAR II

As during the years immediately preceding the 1914-1918 war, there existed considerable unrest and friction between the small East European political and ethnic groups during the months prior to the 1939-1945 war. It is important to review the situation briefly to understand why these countries fought alongside Germany on the eastern front.

Bulgaria, Serbia, and Greece revolted against the Ottoman Empire in 1913 and were victorious in what is called the First Balkan War. Greece and Serbia annexed Macedonia, but denied Bulgaria her share. This precipitated the Second Balkan War, in which Bulgaria was beaten by her two former allies. Bulgaria joined Germany in the 1914-1918 war expecting to be on the winning side with hope of getting a piece of Macedonia, but lost again. She always gazed southward longingly, waiting patiently for her next opportunity.

During the First World War, Romania seized Bessarabia, northern Transylvania, and Bukovina from revolution-torn Russia. The eastern giant wanted their return.

When Austria-Hungary lost the 1914-1918 war, the Treaty of Trinon stripped Hungary of 75% of her land and 50% of her population. With this territory, the countries of Yugoslavia and Czechoslovakia were formed. Hungary was, therefore, also eager to recapture some of her lost territory.

In the Munich Conference of September 30, 1938, Britain and France agreed that Germany could take the German-inhabited Sudetenland from Czechoslovakia. Within a few days, Poland had seized Czechoslovakia's Teschen area while Hungary annexed sections of Ruthenia and Slovakia. On March 15, 1939, the Germans occupied Czechoslovakia, which became the protectorates of Moravia and Bohemia, while Slovakia declared her long-awaited independence under German sponsorship. Units from Luftflotte II, III, and IV were involved in this operation, and while the Czech air force consisted of 1,200 aircraft, there was minimal resistance. Eight days after the German occupation, Hungary took the rest of Ruthenia from Slovakia in what was called the Carpathian War, which included considerable air action.

Much of this activity and accompanying anxieties escaped the notice of many historians because the attention of the world was occupied with Germany at that time.

The pre-World War II Luftwaffe was organized into four Luftflotten, or Air Fleets, each covering a geographic area: 1. East—headed by Gen. Albert Kesselring; 2. West—Gen. Felmy; 3. South—Gen. Hugo Sperrle; 4. East Prussia—Gen. Wimmer. The Luftwaffe units in Austria were under the command of Gen. Löhr. These Luftflotten consisted of the following Flieger divisions, or air divisions. No. 1— Gen. Grauert; No. 2—Gen. Bruno Lörzer; No. 3— Gen. Putzier; No. 4—Gen. Alfred Keller; No. 5—Gen. Robert Ritter von Greim; No. 6—Gen. Deszloch; No. 7—Gen. Kurt Student. Gen. Oberst Hans-Jurgen Stumpff, who had replaced Gen. Kesselring as Luftwaffe Chief of Staff, was now replaced by Gen. Maj. Hans Jeschonnek, himself a veteran of the 1914-1918 Luftstreitkrafte, as well as one of the organizers of the secret training in Russia. By 1939, the Luftwaffe had accepted delivery of about 850 Messerschmitt Me 109E fighters. These were distributed to twelve Jagdgruppen, or fighter groups, as part of Jagdgeschwadern, or fighter wings. The Gruppen were dis-

tributed throughout Germany, Czechoslovakia and Austria as follows: I/JG1 at Jessau; I/JG2 and II/JG2 at Döberitz under Hilmer von Bülow-Bothkamp; Stab/JG3 at Bernburg; I/JG3 at Zerbst; I/JG26 at Cologne; II/JG26 at Düsseldorf; and III/JG26 at Ostheim under Eduard Ritter von Schleich; I/JG51 at Aibling under Theodore Osterkamp; I/JG52 at Böblingen; I/JG53 at Wiesbaden; and II/JG53 at Mannheim under Hans Klein. Many select Geschwadern were also given names in honor of German heroes or names describing their unit insignia, e.g.: JG 2 Richthofen after the Red Baron; JG 53 Pikas (Ace of Spades) to describe the geschwader insignia.

It is quite obvious from the above that the veterans of World War I aerial combat were in charge of the Jagdwaffe on the eve of World War II. About 230 older models of the Messerschmitt Me 109 were distributed to ground-support and other units that were not yet intended for the first-line, fighter-to-fighter role, such as: I/JG 20 at Döberitz; I/JG21 at Jessau; I/JG71 at Böblingen; 2/JG71 at Fürstenfeldbruck; I/JG76 at Vienna; I/JG77 at Breslau; and II/JG77 at Pilsen.

THE WAR BEGINS

When Germany was preparing for its assault on Poland, Slovakian President Tiso permitted Luftwaffe units to move into the Slovak airfields of Nova Ves, Piestany and Spisska in July, 1939. This placed the Luftwaffe closer to the south of Poland, thereby forming giant pincers around the country.

On September 1, 1939, the German 3rd, 4th, 8th, 10th and 14th armies crossed the Polish border with the support of Luftflotten I and IV. Within a few days, I/JG 1 and I/JG21, plus I/LG 2, had eliminated most Polish fighter resistance. Slovak air units assisted the Luftwaffe with a few scattered attacks on Poland, including a bombing raid on Tarnopol, apparently in retaliation for Poland's seizure of land in March, 1938. The Polish air force fought stubbornly with its antiquated equipment, and inflicted a loss of 285 planes on the Luftwaffe, 109 of which were bombers. About 745 German airmen were killed in this lightning campaign of approximately three weeks. JG 2 had been assigned to defend Berlin against possible bombing raids.

Three future Me 109 aces flew with distinction in Poland: Gordon Gollob, flying with 1/ZG 76, a bomber destroyer unit, scored the first of his 150 victories; and Karl-Gottfried Nordmann of I/JG 77 scored the first of his 78 victories; while Adolf Galland utilized the ground support experience he learned in Spain to lead a Staffel or squadron of II(S)/LG 2 in a troop-supporting capacity, giving him no opportunity to score a victory.

Britain, Australia, New Zealand, and France declared war on Germany on September 3; Russia invaded and occupied eastern Poland two weeks later.

At the time of the Polish Campaign, the Messerschmitts were colored a very dark green overall except for the undersides of the wing, horizontal tail, and fuselage, which were a very pale sky blue. The standard black Latin-cross national insignia with white outline appeared on the fuselage sides and near the wing tips. A black swastika or Hakenkreuz political insignia appeared in a circular white background on each side of the fin. Geschwader, gruppe and staffel markings had just been developed and began to appear on the aircraft.

Now that a state of war existed between Germany and the West European Allies, both sides exercised extreme caution and forbade any bombing of enemy territory. All aerial activity was therefore restricted to reconnaissance flights and attacks on enemy shipping. During the month of September, the Germans sank 26 British merchant ships. Similarly, the RAF concentrated on German naval units, but did not meet with equal success. From the first RAF raid against the German fleet on September 4, to the September 29 attack, in which 11 Handley–Page Hampden bombers raided the naval base on Helgoland and 5 were shot down, British losses were high. JG 1, based on the islands off the German coast, and JG 77, distributed around Bremen and Hamburg, harassed the British raiders unmercifully. The commander of these Messerschmitt-equipped interceptor forces was Oberstlt. Carl Schumacher who, with his headquarters at Jever, was the Jafu Deutsches Bucht, or Fighter Leader of the German Bight. The raids continued along the northwestern German coast until December 14th, when 12 Vickers Wellington bombers raided the German naval bases north of the Elbe estuary and, again, only 6 returned to Britain. Four days later, 24 Wellingtons from Nos. 9, 37, and 149 Squadrons, RAF, raided the German Cruisers and battleships off the naval air base of Wilhelmshaven, and were engaged by Messerschmitts of III/JG 77 and JG 1. Again, the unescorted British bombers received a mauling and half of the raiding force was destroyed. Two German fighters were shot down and several others severely damaged by the bombers' four-gun rotating tail turrets. JG 77 Staffelkapitan Lt. Johannes Steinhoff accounted for two of the downed Wellingtons, the first

of his 176 victories. Because of these reverses, the Royal Air Force attempted no further unescorted daylight raids over Germany during the remainder of the war!

The Luftwaffe Technical Section issued orders at this time to revise the aircraft color scheme to light and dark green patches on all surfaces except the bottom, which remained very light sky blue. The division lines between the colors was a zigzag pattern with straight lines changing direction abruptly. This differed a bit from the curving division lines used on French and British aircraft. This new camouflage scheme was not instituted overnight, and therefore many aircraft that were very dark green all over were still in service.

During this period, the Jagdwaffe reorganized some of its Geschwadern: JG 2 Richthofen, JG 3, JG 26 Schlageter, JG 52, and JG 53 Pikas were all increased in strength to three Gruppen each, while JG 70, JG 71, and JG 72 were disbanded entirely. JG 51 received a second Gruppe, and three new Gruppen were formed: I/JG 27 Afrika and II/JG 27, and I/JG 54 Grünherz (Greenheart).

While Royal Air Force bombers and Luftwaffe fighters were battling high above north German waters, Russia attacked Finland on November 30 to enforce territorial demands. The sturdy Finns stood firm against large-scale Soviet assaults and, although greatly outnumbered, the little nation did well, especially in the air, where they used U.S, Dutch, and German aircraft. Overwhelmed, Finland finally lost this "Winter War" and ceded 10% of its territory to the Soviet Union in March, 1940.

Germany, which was not too well endowed by nature with raw materials, purchased considerable quantities of iron and other minerals from neutral Sweden. This was transported westward across Norway to the port of Narvik, where it was loaded into ships bound for north German ports via the North Sea. This iron formed an essential part of Germany's war effort, so naturally the British made plans to cut it off. An amphibious operation was to be launched against Norway during the spring of 1940, not only to stop this flow of iron, but also to outflank the Germans in the north.

When German intelligence learned that the British preparations were nearing completion, the Luftwaffe was given the job of getting to Norway before the British. A special task force was quickly assembled and designated "X Flieger Korps" with Gen. Geisler in command. April 9, 1940 was the date specified for occupation, and the code name for the entire operation was "Weserübung." The force consisted of transports, paratroopers, dive bombers, medium bombers, and twin-engine heavy fighters with about 30 Me 109E-3 fighters from II/JG 77 to provide the invasion force with fighter cover. The Messerschmitts encountered only brief, but determined, resistance from Norwegian and British Gloster Gladiator biplane fighters, which focused their attention on the German bombers. The Luftwaffe did beat the British invasion force, and Germany secured its supply of iron while protecting the northern flank. The Norwegians surrendered on May 1, 1940.

The Luftwaffe units that were now assigned to standby alert for western operations were: Luftflotte 2 under Gen. Kesselring with I and IV Flieger Korps; Luftflotte 3, under Gen. Sperrle with II, V and VII Flieger Korps or Air Corps. Gen. von Richthofen, who had been strongly against the adoption of dive bombers, now found himself in command of VII Flieger Korps which consisted mainly of Junkers Ju 87 Stukas! The 860 operational Messerschmitts were distributed to: JG 1 and JG 77, guarding northwestern Germany; JG 2 Richthofen protecting Berlin; and JG 3, JG 26 Schlageter, JG 27 Afrika, JG 51, JG 52, JG 53 Pikas, and JG 54 Grünherz. This force faced the French Armee de L'Air fighter arm of just under 600 aircraft distributed into five groupements, or wings, consisting of 24 groupes de chasse, plus an RAF expeditionary force equipped with 10 squadrons of Hawker Hurricane fighters. The diminutive Belgian Aeronautique Militaire had only 11 Hurricanes based at Diest, 27 Italian Fiat CR 42 biplanes based at Nivelles, plus 15 Gloster Gladiator biplanes also based at Diest.

THE BATTLE OF FRANCE

At the break of day on May 10, 1940 the German armed forces opened their assault on France with the Luftwaffe striking in a coordinated attack on the Armee de L'Air bases at Lyon, Nancy, Metz, Dijon and Romilly. Numerous French and Belgian aircraft were destroyed on the ground by the bombing raids, and any Allied fighters that were able to take to the air were quickly dispatched by the Jagdwaffe. The six weeks that followed the German onslaught were to prove the worst in the history of French military aviation. Under the Messerschmitts' protective umbrella, the Stukas paralyzed communications and paved the way for the ten invading Panzer Divisions. The rapidity of the advance was such that the Messerschmitt units were moving their bases for-

ward daily, and conversely the Armee de L'Air fighter units were forced to fall back at the same rate. Countless French fighter planes were abandoned when returning pilots discovered that while they were engaging the Luftwaffe, German troops had captured their airfield!

The Messerschmitt color scheme was altered slightly just before the French Campaign by extending the very light blue color of the fuselage bottom up the side to the cockpit. This was done because, it was reasoned, the fighters would be in the air more than on the ground, therefore sky colors were more important than earth colors.

Gen. Alfred Keller directed the German bomber crews in attacking a total of about 70 French, Belgian, and Dutch airfields, which destroyed about one-quarter of the Hurricane strength on the Continent. This effectively reduced Allied resistance by cutting the number of fighters that could meet the Messerschmitt on virtually equal terms.

Luftwaffe successes increased steadily, rising to a crescendo on May 14, 1940. This day was called "Tag der Jagdflieger," or Fighter Pilots' Day, because it was the most active and successful day for the Jagdwaffe in the Battle of France. The 814 fighter sorties launched on that day accounted for over 90 victories over Sedan. I/JG 53 was the top scoring unit, with 39 Allied aircraft shot down. This success paved the way for the Panzer breakthrough at Sedan on the following day, and by the next week Allied air power over France had been considerably weakened.

The most successful German fighter pilot of the French campaign was Hauptmann Wilhelm Balthasar, who had scored seven victories in Spain. The Staffelkapitan of 7/JG 27 was awarded the Ritterkreutz or Knights' Cross for shooting down 23 Allied aircraft, and destroying 13 more on the ground in strafing attacks during the Battle of France.

After scoring 16 victories during the Franco–German hostilities as Kommandeur of III/JG 53 Pikas, Hauptmann Werner Mölders was surprised by a French fighter pilot over Compiegne on June 5 and forced to bail out of his damaged Messerschmitt. He was quickly captured and spent the next few weeks in a French P.O.W. camp.

The Netherlands capitulated on May 15, and by the 26th, 300,000 French and British troops had been pushed onto the beaches at Dunkirk, as Belgium surrendered. It was here that the Spitfire, flying from bases in England, made its initial combat appearance, having been carefully husbanded by not being committed in the Battle of France. The sleek British fighter soon showed itself to be the equal of the Messerschmitt during the early encounters, and evened the balance of power in the air to some degree; however, it is important to consider that many Messerschmitts were unable to reach the beaches of Dunkirk due to a lack of fuel. The major disadvantage of the Me 109 was its extremely short range which, as we shall see, was its Achilles heel. The rapid, airfield-hopping advance to the French coast caused the supply columns to fall behind, forcing many Messerschmitts out of action because they could not reach the coast from those airfields which had fuel. This was an important factor in the Dunkirk escape.

During the remainder of May and throughout June, the French and British squadrons fought continuously, but they were doomed to defeat under the weight of German combined air and ground offensives. Retreating from airfield to airfield, the air crews were often forced to abandon their ground personnel, leaving them to become prisoners of war. The Allied air units managed to destroy 350 Luftwaffe aircraft before they were themselves annihilated. The French losses were enormous, and the Royal Air Force alone lost over 450 planes. The remnants of the RAF flew back to England as France surrendered on June 22, 1940.

THE BATTLE OF BRITAIN

Having vanquished the larger and better-armed half of the Allied forces, Germany now turned towards Britain. Reasoning that the British would be helpless without the RAF Fighter Command, the German High Command, believing Hermann Göring's boast that the Jagdwaffe could render the RAF impotent in six weeks, decided to send the Jagdgeschwadern across the English Channel to meet the British squadrons in mortal combat. The Germans remembered the mauling they gave the unescorted RAF Hampden and Wellington bombers and therefore knew that, without Fighter Command to escort their bombers, Britain could neither raid Germany nor intercept Luftwaffe bombers over Britain.

The Luftwaffe was extremely optimistic, because the lightning destruction of the Polish, Norwegian, Belgian, and French air services had generated a feeling of invincibility. By securing air superiority over quantitatively, qualitatively and tactically inferior fighter forces, the Jagdwaffe had paved the way for the bombers and full-scale use of the tactical air forces. Now, the German fighter pilots were

suddenly elevated from their secondary role and thrust into stardom with a mission to destroy a well-equipped, well-organized fighter force located 20 to 50 miles away. However, this adversary was across open water and not adjacent to the German-held borders, as had been the case with past conquests. The Jagdwaffe was designed for a continental war and not for an assault on a less-accessible nation.

This handicap would soon reveal itself in the forthcoming Battle of Britain. This was the moment of truth.

In preparation for the Battle, another change in coloring was ordered for the Messerschmitts. The two shades of green on the fuselage above the cockpit were changed to light gray, blending into the light blue of the fuselage side. Additionally, dark gray hazy spots were distributed on the light gray and light blue, down the middle of the fuselage. This was done to make the camouflage more effective when the plane was airborne, where the Luftwaffe planned to have the Messerschmitts most of the time during their attack on Fighter Command.

Although there are many aspects of the Battle of Britain still to be agreed upon by aerohistorians, it is generally accepted that it began during July, 1940 with raids on British shipping in the England Channel. While much of the Luftwaffe rested, waited, and watched, an antishipping group was formed under the command of Oberst Johannes Fink, consisting of his own bomber force, KG 2, two Stuka Gruppen, and JG 51, which was still under the leadership of Theodore Osterkamp. This was to be a preliminary activity to the main assault on Fighter Command, which was scheduled for mid-August. The sinking of British shipping, although crucial to the German war effort, was of secondary importance in this operation. The primary objective was to lure Fighter Command over the Channel, where a downed pilot had only a slim chance of rescue and, more importantly, the short-range Messerschmitts could be sent into battle over the adjacent waters in greater numbers and for longer periods of time. A brief description of the opening action of the Battle of Britain follows.

A large British coastal convoy was sighted by German reconnaissance aircraft off the coast of Folkestone late in the morning of July 10. In response to the alert, II/KG 2 under Maj. Adolf Fuchs, based at Arras, and III/JG 51 under Hptm. Hannes Trautloft, based at St. Omer, made rendezvous in the early afternoon, flying between 3,000 and 6,000 ft. As the 20 Dornier Do 17 bombers and 20 Messerschmitts neared the convoy, Trautloft sighted 6 Hurricanes of 32 Squadron from Biggin Hill protecting the convoy, and waiting for a chance to pounce on the Dorniers.

Trautloft kept his Gruppe on station, protecting the bombers as they unloaded their lethal cargo on the ships. As they did so, four full squadrons of British fighters suddenly appeared, flying at 15,000 feet. Göring's tactic had worked! The interceptors consisted of No. 56 Squadron with Hurricanes from Manston; No. 64 Squadron with Spitfires from Kenley; No. 74 Squadron with Spitfires from Hornchurch; and No. 111 Squadron with Hurricanes from Croydon. There were 32 British fighters against 20 German fighters, as the bombers sped for home over the water at wave-top level. At the onset, Oblt. Walter Ösau, Staffelkapitan of 7/JG 51, scored two Hurricanes and was after his third when the diving Hurricane smashed onto one of the bombers. When the melee was over, six British aircraft had been shot down while two seriously damaged Messerschmitts were forced to belly-land on the French coast near Calais and Boulogne. One of these was piloted by Trautloft's Rottenflieger, Fw. Dau, who emerged unhurt.

The Channel attacks continued throughout July until, by July 16, Hannes Trautloft's 40 Messerschmitts of III/JG 51 had been reduced to 15 serviceable fighters. Only a few were shot down; the majority had been seriously damaged in combat or had broken landing gears. JG 51 bore the brunt of this initial contact phase of the Battle of Britain, with considerable assistance from III/JG 3 under Hptm. Walter Kienitze. The remainder of the Jagdwaffe was in need of rest and reorganization, and new bases and logistics. On July 19, Trautloft's pilots attacked a dozen new Boulton–Paul Defiants near Dover. This was a new two-seat monoplane whose four machine guns were concentrated in a rotating turrent over the rear cockpit. The initial attack sent 5 of the Defiants plunging into the Channel and, by the time the battle was over, 11 Defiants had been destroyed. Four Messerschmitts were damaged in this action. This brought the score for III/JG 51 to 157 victories, of which Osterkamp scored 6, versus a loss of 29 German aircraft.

A few days later, Oberst Osterkamp led his entire Geschwader on a series of fighter sweeps over southeast England, in an attempt to lure the British fighters into combat. Air Marshal Sir Hugh Dowding, the chief of Fighter Command, refused to accept the challenge, because every day's delay in all-out confrontation would give him time to repair his force's striking power from the damage of the French Campaign and Dunkirk.

During July, prior to launching its all-out attack on Fighter Command, the Jagdwaffe underwent reorganization, and by August I/JG 1 became the third Gruppe of JG 27; I/JG 20 became the third Gruppe of JG 51; and I/JG 76 became the second Gruppe of JG 54 Grünherz; I/JG 21 became the third Gruppe of JG 54 Grünherz. The German fighter-unit organization for battle against Britain included Luftflotte 2 under Gen. Albert Kesselring based in northwestern France and the Low Countries, with headquarters in Brussels, and Luftflotte 3 under Gen. Hugo Sperrle based in western France with headquarters in Paris. Gen. Wolfram von Richthofen's VIII Flieger Korps in Luftflotte 3 included JG 27 under Oberst Max Ibel, while the independent Jagdführer (Jafu 3), or Fighter Leader of Luftflotte 3, Gen. Werner Junck, directed JG 2 under Oberst Hilmer von Bülow-Bothkamp and JG 53 under Oberst Lt. von Cramon-Taubadel. The Jagdführer of Luftflotte 2 (Jafu 2) was now Gen. Theodore Osterkamp who directed JG 3 under Oberstlt. Viek, JG 26 under Maj. Gotthardt Handrick, JG 51 under Oberst Werner Mölders, JG 52 under Oberst von Merhart, and JG 54 under Maj. Mettig, a total of 22 Gruppen. This was the force assigned to smash the RAF Fighter Command.

This Jagdwaffe task force possessed a combat strength of 878 Messerschmitt Me 109 fighters, while RAF Fighters Command strength consisted of 29 Hawker Hurricane squadrons with 527 aircraft, and 19 Supermarine Spitfire squadrons with 321 aircraft; a difference of only 30 single-engine fighters between Fighter Command and the Jagdwaffe.

One of the first major engagements of the Battle took place on July 28 when JG 27, JG 51, and JG 53 lost eight Messerschmitts including one piloted by Oberst Werner Mölders. The very first day, after assuming command of JG 51, Mölders' plane was seriously damaged by the famous RAF ace, Squadron Leader Adolf "Sailor" Malan. Although wounded, Mölders nursed the plane across the Channel and made a belly landing near Wissant, France.

These initial operations not only reaffirmed that the Me 109's range was insufficient for the task it was assigned to perform, (after deducting the time necessary to get to the battle area and return to base, the Messerschmitt was left with a maximum of 20 minutes for action over England), but also revealed that every Luftwaffe formation crossing the Channel was being tracked by British radar. Fighter Command's unbroken chain of radar stations forewarned of every Luftwaffe attack and made a surprise raid virtually impossible. This never-before used method of detecting an enemy's presence was developed by Sir Robert Watson-Watt, and installed for operation in 1939. To complement the radar, Air Marshall Dowding carefully organized a sophisticated arrangement of ground-based fighter direction and control. This combination gave the British ample warning of German raids and enabled the Fighter Command pilots to wait on the ground for a take off signal. Once airborne, they were guided into proper position for the intercept. In contrast, the German pilots flew unguided and virtually blind until they visually sighted intercepting British aircraft. When the chief of the Luftwaffe's signal and communications system, Gen. Wolfgang Martini, learned of British radar with its reporting and directing network, he related his discovery to the Luftwaffe Chief of Staff, Gen. Jeschonnek, who immediately issued orders that the radar stations be destroyed by "special forces of the first wave" of raiders.

Starting on August 3, Stukas, Junkers 88, twin-engine dive bombers, and Messerschmitt Me 110 twin-engine fighters raided the coastal radar stations with 500 to 1000-lb. bombs. Although the raids destroyed assorted buildings, the aerials and towers appeared virtually indestructible because of their complex structure. The raids were a bitter disappointment to the Germans because the stations were often repaired and in operation within a few hours after a Luftwaffe bombing raid. The worst hit was the Ventnor station on the Isle of Wight which required 11 days to rebuild and return to operation. The inability to destroy this network was the Luftwaffe's first failure.

Besides the Me 109's short range, and the use of radar, Fighter Command fought with a third advantage: By engaging in air battles over their own territory, the British pilots were invariably able to bail out and parachute to safety or nurse their damaged fighter's to a belly landing living to fight again another day. Not so for the Jagdwaffe pilots.

Adler Tag, or Eagle Day, was the code name for August 13, when the Luftwaffe decided it would begin attacking Fighter Command airfields to destroy the British fighters on the ground. The plan also involved the bombing of British engine and airplane manufacturing plants to destroy Fighter Command's supply of aircraft. This new tactic arose because the Luftwaffe had begun to realize that Fighter Command could not be destroyed through aerial confrontation alone. Now the primary targets were Fighter Command in the air, its ground organization, and the industry that kept it supplied with weapons.

Select bomber and fighter units were poised for take-off on Luftflotte 2 and 3 airfields in France and the Low Countries, to make landfall over the English coast at 7:30 in the morning of Adler Tag. Although the weather appeared promising the evening before,

August 13 dawned with heavily overcast skies, fog on most airfields, and a thick layer of clouds over the Channel. Luftwaffe High Command quickly issued orders to postpone the attack until that afternoon. However, several formations had already taken off before the orders filtered through the Luftflotten chiefs to the units involved. A few raiders reached Eastchurch Airfield while others returned to base with all bombs in place. Confusion reigned over England as the escorting Messerschmitts became separated from the bombers because of the foul weather while Hurricanes attacked! The afternoon raids fared a bit better. Gen. Bruno Lörzer's II Fleiger Korps Stukas were escorted by I/JG 26 under Hptm. Fischer and II/JG 2 under Hptm. Ebbighausen, whose Messerschmitts cleared a path to Detling Airfield near Maidstone. The Stukas left it in ruins. Other raiders struck at Andover Airfield with the same results. Despite the late start and bad weather, over 480 German bombers and almost 1,000 single and twin-engine fighters made it across the Channel, damaging five airfields. The Luftwaffe was unaware at the time that the most seriously damaged airfields—Eastchurch, Detling and Andover—were not Fighter Command bases! This error may have been caused by the poor visibility and flying conditions, or it is possible that Luftwaffe intelligence personnel were ignorant of Fighter Command airfield locations. Not only did Adler Tag fail in it's primary objective, but the day's activity cost the Luftwaffe 34 aircraft in contrast to the 13 British fighters shot down.

Though the weather worsened on August 14, curtailing activity considerably, Adolf Galland's III/JG 26 did see action. As it escorted Stukas over England, the Gruppe shot down six intercepting British fighters, with Galland, Oblt. Beyer, Oblt. Müncheberg, Oblt. Schöpfel, Lt. Müller-Dühe, and Lt. Bürschgens scoring.

The following day saw the Luftwaffe launch 800 bombers and Stukas, plus over 1,100 single and twin-engine fighters from Luftflotten 2 and 3, and another 170 aircraft from Norway-based Luftflotte 5 against England. The day started much the same as the two previous; however, the sun burned through the cloud cover in the early afternoon and the attack began. Handrick's JG 26, Mölders' JG 51, Trübenback's JG 52, and Trautlofts' JG 54 of Luftflotte 2 crossed the Channel early with escort work and fighter sweeps. While Stukas raided the airfields at Lympne and Hawkinge, and Junkers Ju88 twin-engine dive bombers pounded the Driffield base, the Jagdgeschwaders flew high above in a Freie Jagd, or free chase, just after noon. By four o'clock, Dornier

Do 17 bombers, with fighter escort, struck the airfields at Eastchurch and Rochester and severely damaged the Short bomber factory. Production of the Stirling bomber was thereby delayed for months.

Major Gotthardt Handrick's JG 26 Schlageter was involved in heavy fighting on August 15: Haupt. Fischer's I/JG 26 operated west of Calais and Oblt. Henrici shot down a British fighter; II/JG 26 swept the Dover, Folkestone, and Tonbridge triangle; three British fighters fell before the guns of Hptm. Ebbighausen, Oblt. Ebersberger and Lt. Krug. Maj. Galland's III/JG 26 was one of the most successful units, and shot down 18 interceptions in four separate sorties while escorting the bombers of KG 1 and KG 2 in raids on Hawkinge and Maidstone. Seven of the 18 victories were scored by 7/JG 26; bringing that Gruppe's total to 119.

Then it was quiet over southeastern England.

Apparently, cooperation between Luftflotten 2 and 3 was virtually nonexistant in the planning of raids, because Sperrle's Luftflotte 3 did not become active until almost six o'clock in the evening. This tactical timing error gave Fighter Command almost two hours to rest, re-arm and refuel their Hurricanes and Spitfires, insuring their state of "immediate readiness" by six o'clock. Had Sperrle launched his raiders simultaneously with those of Kesselring, his pilots would have met little or no resistance from from Fighter Command.

Oberst Ibel's JG 27 and Maj. von Cramon-Taubadel's JG 53 of Luftflotte 3 assisted the twin-engine Me 110 fighters of ZG 2 in escorting Stukas and Ju 88 dive bombers. The 250 planes reached England landfall shortly after six o'clock and were immediately attacked by 14 squadrons of Spitfires and Hurricanes—a total of 170 fighters, a record interception for Fighter Command! While some Spitfires kept the Messerschmitts busy at the higher altitudes, others dived through the bombers formations, wreaking havoc with the Ju 88 and their Me 110 escort. Five of the seven Ju 88 bombers in Hptm. Jochen Helbig's 4/LG 1 were quickly shot down by Spitfires attacking from astern and, of the 15 Junkers in his Gruppe, only 3 survived to reach the target, Worthy Down airfield, near Southampton. Despite this disaster, Me 109's escorting I/LG 1 under Hptm. Kern destroyed two Fighter Command squadrons plus hangars and runways as the 12 Ju 88's screamed across Middle Wallop Airfield. Only a few 609 Squadron Spitfires were able to take off in time to escape destruction and engage the attackers.

As Luftflotte 3 aircraft began returning to their bases, Luftflotte 2 was readying another raid. This time it was a Jagdbomber (Jabo), or fighter-bomber raid, in which bomb-carrying fighter planes would fight their way back to the continent after jettisoning their load. The Jabo force consisted of 15 twin-engine Me 110 fighters and 8 Me 109 single-engine fighters, all escorted by Me 109s from JG 52. The Jabo's target was the very important Kenley airfield, just south of London. As previously mentioned, the German raiders flew unguided and virtually blind, resulting in frequent navigational errors and attacks on wrong targets. Somehow, the escorting Messerschmitts fell behind, and it was eight o'clock when the Jabos reached their target unescorted; only it wasn't Kenley! An error in navigation had brought the force closer to London than planned, and when the London aircraft of Croyden appeared below, it was mistaken for Kenley. The order to attack was given. At that moment 111 Squadron Hurricanes appeared overhead and began to dive; however, the heavily laden Jabos remained ahead of their pursuers by diving at a higher speed. The first bombs were well placed and crashed into hangars, destroying 40 planes. Others slammed into an aircraft factory and engine works, while the last severely damaged an aircraft radio factory; a successful attack, but on the wrong airfield. The Luftwaffe had been given very strict instructions not to bomb the enormous area of Greater London and Croyden lay within this area. The Jabos, relieved of their load, sped home as 111 Squadron and newly-arrived 32 Squadron from Biggin Hill began to take their toll of the invaders. As the battle approached the English coast, 66 Squadron Spitfires joined the fray. By the time the Jabos returned to base in twilight, they had lost 6 of the 15 Me 110 fighters, but only one Me 109 single-engine fighter.

So closed the third day of the Battle of Britain, considered by many aerohistorians to have been its most active day. Both sides exaggerated their victories and minimized their losses. Fighter Command claimed it destroyed 182 German aircraft and another 53 probably destroyed. Most of these were bombers and Me 110 twin-engine fighters. Luftwaffe records indicate that it suffered the loss of only 59 planes. The Germans claimed that 111 British fighters were shot down and another 14 probable victories. This total did not include those British aircraft destroyed on the ground. Fighter Command admitted to only 34 aircraft losses. The final tally for losses seems to have been 34 British fighters to 75 German bombers and twin-engine fighters, including a few Me 109s. Regardless of the statistics of this summer Thursday, the fact was the unescorted multiengine bombers, fighters, and Stuka dive bombers were defenseless against determined single-seat fighters. Despite the dual role given the Jagdwaffe of destroying Fighter Command in the air and protecting the bombers and Stukas from the British fighters, Luftwaffe fighter production was half that of the Royal Air Force during the summer of 1940. The airfield attacks continued, and the key Fighter Command bases of Tangmere, Kenley, and Biggin Hill were severely damaged.

On Sunday, August 18, four Stuka Gruppen of VIII Flieger Korps crossed the Channel for raids on the Ford, Gosport, and Thorney Island airfields, and the radar station at Poling. Before they could re-form for the return flight after completing the strike, the unescorted Stukas were intercepted by 152 Squadron Spitfires and 43 Squadron Hurricanes. The ensuing carnage sounded the death knell for the vaunted Stuka in the Battle of Britain. The slow and ungainly bomber was revealed to be virtually defenseless and desperately in need of a fighter escort to function successfully. Thirty Stukas fell before the blazing guns of the British fighters: I/St G 77 lost 12 out of 28 planes, including the Gruppenkommandeur, Hptm. Meisel. Other Stukas were so seriously damaged that they barely managed to reach the Continent. In general, Stuka losses became so enormous that the alarming shortage of crews caused the withdrawl of all Stuka units from operations in the battle. Moreover, Stuka losses were not justified by their meager accomplishments and they in fact destroyed the effectiveness of the Messerschmitt pilots, whose protection they desperately needed. The Me 109s were at their best in Freie Jagd fighter sweeps against Fighter Command.

It was on the same day that Galland's III/JG 26, while on Freie Jagd over Hornchurch and North Weald, shot down eight British fighters while losing two of their own. Oblt. Schöpfel accounted for half of the tally, while Oblt. Sprick and Lt. Ebeling downed one fighter each, and Lt. Bürschgens got the remaining two. During this action, Lt. Müller-Dühe was killed and Lt. Blume was never seen again after diving into a cloud.

At about this time, mid-August, Hermann Göring began to lose faith in his wartime buddies and other Alte Adler who were leading the Luftwaffe Jagdgeschwadern. He complained that the older but experienced fighter leaders lacked aggressiveness. The Luftwaffe Chief wanted his Jagdgeschwader Kommodores to be young, high-scoring combat aces who would personally lead the formation into battle and set an example for other pilots to follow. Göring could not be convinced that the Jagdwaffe's inability to destroy Fighter Command was not the fault of the older fighter leaders. He failed to realize that, when

opposing forces in air battles are evenly matched, the advantage is always on the side of the defenders. In a closely spaced series of transfers, he replaced the elderly Kommodores with the most promising Gruppenkommandeurs. Mölders had already replaced Osterkamp as leader of JG 51 on July 27, and now on August 22 Galland replaced Handrick in JG 26; three days later, Trautloft replaced Mettig in JG 54; on September 3, Schellmann replaced von Bülow-Bothkamp in JG 2; on October 10, von Maltzahn replaced von Cramon-Taubadel in JG 53; later, Woldenga replaced Ibel in JG 27.

Despite the infusion of young blood in Jagdgeschwader leadership, conditions could not change overnight. JG 3, JG 52, and JG 53 suffered extensive losses on August 26; on the 28th, a total of 23 Messerschmitts were lost, including 6 from JG 3. The closing days of the month witnessed the loss of 26 more Me 109s, again including 6 from JG 3, and another 6 from JG 26. Revenge for these losses was in the form of an eary morning fighter attack on the Dover barrage balloons on August 31. One after the other, the Staffels dived on the balloons until over 50 had been destroyed. It is said that the burning and smoking debris was visible across the Channel from the French coast! This was followed by raids on Biggin Hill and other airfields, resulting in a total of 1,300 fighter sorties being flown that last day of August to protect about 150 bombers. Luftwaffe lost 32 aircraft, while they destroyed 39 Fighter Command fighters. The Luftwaffe had launched 4,779 sorties against England during August.

The activities of August 31 signaled the start of a renewed effort to destroy Fighter Command, the prime objective being 11 Group. This force consisted of 22 squadrons of Hurricanes and Spitfires, responsible for the defense of southeast England and as far north as London. The area north of London was defended by 12 Group, which also served as rest area and backup for 11 Group, providing men and machines. Charged with the dual responsibility of escorting bombers and simultaneously luring Fighter Command into decisive battle, the Jagdwaffe was stretched to the limits of its capability. Yet, flying to their limit, the Jagdgeschwadern almost tipped the balance in their favor by the first week of September. The previous weeks' crippling raids on airfields and aircraft factories and the aerial onslaught, almost brought Fighter Command to their knees; but this fact was unknown to Luftwaffe intelligence. The raids had moved deeper into England and were conducted with one bomber Gruppe and an entire Jagdgeschwader to insure protection for the Heinkel and Dornier bombers. With this technique, the Messerschmitts could go on Freie Jagd while performing escort duty; but losses began to rise again. On September 2, 25 Messerschmitts were lost; 22 were lost on September 5; and 27 on the following day, including 9 planes from JG 27.

During the period of August 24 to September 6, 103 Fighter Command pilots were killed and 130 severely wounded. During the same period, Fighter Command reported 466 Hurricanes and Spitfires destroyed or seriously damaged. The ratio of aircraft losses to crew losses held steady at about two to one so that no matter how many planes the Jagdwaffe shot down, more than half the pilots survived to fight again another day!

Then the attacks were shifted to London and any hope of victory for the Jagdwaffe was removed.

Apparently in reprisal for the R.A.F. 81-bomber night raid on Berlin on August 25/26, Hitler decided on September 4 to carry out raids on the London docks. Although Hitler's intention was revenge, the Luftwaffe reasoned that an attack on the British capital would draw swarms of Fighter Command fighters into the air, where the escorting Messerschmitts could engage them. More importantly, it was hoped that the reserve 12 Group would also be forced into the air to protect London. On September 7, Hermann Göring and his World War I buddy Bruno Lörzer appeared on the Channel coast to witness the preparations for the first London air raid, scheduled for that afternoon. JG 26, JG 27 and JG 54 were assigned to escort the Heinkel He 111 bombers, which were to fly at various levels from 17,000 to 20,000 feet. Instructions were given to fly direct courses without deviation, because the Messerschmitts, flying at the limit of their range, would have even less time than usual for engaging Fighter Command aircraft. The Messerschmitt's short range was an even greater disadvantage during this period, and many pilots failed to reach the Continent before they were forced to ditch in the Channel with empty fuel tanks. On September 9, 18 Messerschmitts crashed along the French coast—some on the beaches and some in the water—because they had depleted their fuel. These were included in the loss of 28 planes reported for that day. The bombings succeeded until September 15, when a series of large, carefully planned raids with 1,790 sorties were met by 24 squadrons of Spitfires and Hurricanes, some from 12 Group. With over 300 Hurricanes and Spitfires in the air at one time, the Luftwaffe lost 60 planes, 23 of which were Me 109s from a force totalling 60 Messerschmitts. Only 26 R.A.F. fighters were destroyed. The British called it Battle of Britain Day, and it became the turning point; here-

after, the Luftwaffe was no longer able to stage such large raids. This was because the non-combatant Luftwaffe brass failed to increase Messerschmitt production to keep pace with the combat losses, thereby making the large Fighter Formation needed for bomber protection impossible to maintain. The situation worsened through September 30, when 34 Messerschmitts were destroyed: 5 from JG 2; 7 from JG 26; 8 from JG 27; and 4 each from JG 51, JG 52, and JG 53. The Luftwaffe had launched a total of 7,260 sorties during the month of September, and yet the Jagdwaffe had not achieved their objective. One could compare their frustrations, as Adolf Galland stated so well, to that of a fierce dog ordered to leap at the throat of his enemy, only to find that his chain is just short enough to keep him from reaching his victim.

The Luftwaffe was the first air force to engage in strategic bombing, although they accomplished it with tactical equipment! Their two principal bombers were the fast twin-engine Dornier Do 17 with its one-ton bomb load, and the Heinkel He III, a converted twin-engine Lufthansa transport with a two-ton bomb load. They were nothing compared to the four-engine Lancaster bomber, used a few years later in the assault on Germany, which could carry a single bomb that weighed as much as the entire Heinkel bomber! The error that was made in the 1936 decision by economy-prone and narrow-minded theoreticians had now come home to haunt the Luftwaffe, and it was too late to rectify it. The fact that the Royal Air Force could not be beaten over the British Isles with the Luftwaffe's existing equipment was still not fully realized by the Luftwaffe High Command. Henceforth, bombing would be confined to raids after dark, due to a shortage of fighter planes, which were about to assume a bombing role themselves. A total of 9,911 sorties were flown by the Luftwaffe during October, which was the most for any month during the battle. Most of the aerial combat during the attack on Britain was conducted between 15,000 and 20,000 ft., since the bombers flew at an altitude of from 16,000 to 18,000 ft. with the escorting Messerschmitts usually slightly above them.

The Luftwaffe lost about 1,750 aircraft in daylight attacks from July through October. This figure represented over half of its total strength, the greatest majority of which were bombers and Stukas. Göring decided to revive an idea that had been experimental during July: the Jabo, or Jagdbomber (fighter-bomber). The use of bombcarrying Messerschmitts for daylight raids was intended to prevent a repetition of the bomber losses of the summer. Despite the objections of the fighter leaders, who called them "light Kesselrings" instead of light bombers, orders were issued for one Staffel in each Gruppe (or about one-third of the Battle of Britain Jagdgschwadern) to be converted to a Jabo unit. Initially, level bombing was attempted with the Jabos: flying in large formations protected by unladen fighter planes. This system was later modified to intersperse the Jabos and escort fighters within the same formation. This so disgusted the Jagdfliegern that many dropped their 500-lb. bombs on the first target reached in order to eliminate the handicap of the extra load in unfriendly skies. Level bombing proved so inaccurate that the characteristic low-level dive-bombing attacks, the standard method of fighter aviation today, were developed. Obviously, small aircraft ranging over a wide area could not prove effective as bombers. This inability to perform the fighterbomber role successfully led to Göring's criticism of the Jagdwaffe's failure to simultaneously perform the impossible tactical, strategic and air defense roles—with grossly insufficient numbers of planes and pilots.

During November, the Jabo was gradually discarded and mass bombings by Luftflotten 2, 3 and 5 with fighter escorts resumed. The basic objectives were British harbors and military installations. In October, Maj. Helmut Wick had replaced Maj. Schellmann as Kommodore of JG 2 Richthofen. During an escort mission over Southampton and the Isle of Wight on November 6, the Richthofen Geschwader destroyed nine Fighter Command aircraft with Wick scoring five of the total. Oblt. Leie, Geschwaderadjutant, shot down two and Oblt. Hahn and Lt. Schnell scored one each. On the following day Wick, who at the time was Germany's leading World War II Ace, shot down another Hurricane over Portsmouth, while Oblt. Leie destroyed two Hurricanes; Oblt. Pflanz, Geschwader Technical Officer, scored two Hurricanes; Lt. Schnell got another; and Lt. Heinberg shot down the sixth over the Isle of Wight. The Jagdwaffe pilots were still unquenchably aggressive, despite the abuse heaped upon them by Luftwaffe bomber pilots, Göring, and even the German press, because they failed to perform the impossible.

Large scale raids on England diminished during the winter months: December—3,844 sorties; January—2,465 sorties; and February—only 1,400 sorties. The reason, initally, was the poor weather conditions of the English winter, and later the involvement of the Luftwaffe in the Balkan and Mediterranean campaigns. The number of sorties against England increased again in March and April, 1941,

to 4,365 and 5,448. On the first day of what became a very active April, Oberst Galland embarked on a transfer flight from Düsseldorf to Brest with his Rottenflieger, Ofw. Robert Menge. When the pair decided to take a detour over southern England, they were, not surprisingly, jumped by Fighter Command Spitfires. After each had shot down one British fighter, the Rotte sped across the Channel to France. On the 15th, Galland again taunted Fighter Command with a flight with Ofw. Hans-Jürgen Westphal over Dover. Spitfires again attacked, and Galland scored three British fighters before escaping across the Channel.

Serious attacks on Britain by the Luftwaffe ended on May 16, 1941 because, already engaged in the Balkans and Mediterranean, the Luftwaffe had to prepare for the attack on the Soviet Union. Apparently, the decision to attack Russia had already been made before the Battle of Britain began, and now the struggle in the West no longer had priority. Those who survived the Battle were too valuable to be allowed to rest, and were destined for continuous combat flying until they were either killed or exhausted from the nervous strain it inflicted upon them. The Luftwaffe might have replaced the Messerschmitt losses; however, the replacement of trained pilots was an almost impossible task.

The Fighter Command defensive strategy had been planned for the progressive withdrawal of squadrons further inland to the north in the event that south coast airfields became inoperative. This never became necessary however as the British fighters fought the Jagdwaffe to a Mexican standoff. The German figher pilots had flown themselves to physical exhaustion, and in addition were bitterly frustrated. Under adverse conditions they had shot down hundreds of Fighter Command pilots, done well in Freie Jagd and yet found large gaps in their ranks daily. This failure was attributed to the Jagdwaffe pilots by the unscrupulous Reichsmarschall Göring, who was forever looking for scapegoats to blame for his failures. He claimed the fighters had deserted the bombers over England permitting them to be shot down. However, had the Messerschmitts remained close to the bombers at all times, the primary objective of destroying Fighter Command could not have been achieved. Only through the offensive Freie Jagd fighter sweeps could success be hoped for, but there never were sufficient fighters to accomplish both tasks.

By June 4, 1941 all Jagdgeschwadern, except JG 2 Richthofen under Maj. Wilhelm Balthasar and JG 26 Schlageter under Oberst Adolf Galland, were transferred away from the Channel area. Kesselring's

Luftflotte 2 was also removed from the Channel, leaving only Sperrle's Luftflotte 3 facing west.

Staffel 10 of JG 2 was assigned as a Jabo unit, principally employed against British coastal shipping. Led by Hptm. Frank Liesendahl, the Staffel had sunk 20 ships totaling 63,000 tons, by June 26, 1941.

On the very same day that the Germans attacked Russia, Britain began its "nonstop air offensive" against Germany. JG 2 and JG 26, possessing a combined strength of from 150 to 250 aircraft, were assigned the task of defending the western European coast from the Netherlands to the Bay of Biscay. As a result, JG 2 and JG 26 flew from dawn to dusk, with each pilot assigned five or more sorties a day. On June 21, 1941 Bristol Blenheim bombers raided St. Omer with an escort of 50 Hurricanes and Spitfires. JG 26 rose to intercept and, although overwhelmed by the escort, they managed to destroy 14 British bombers. Galland scored three of the total and was, himself, shot down by the British fighters; but he survived.

THE WAR IN THE BALKANS

With the Battle of Britain finished, the next part of the world to be inflamed in war was Africa and southeastern Europe. Since June 14, 1940, the day Italy declared war on Britain and France shortly before France's fall, all had been quiet with Germany's southern partner. Without warning, on September 13, Italian colonial forces in Lybia invaded Egypt and, on October 28, Italian forces also invaded Greece. The British countered the latter move by invading the strategic Mediterranean island of Crete on the very next day, thereby endangering the southern flank of Germany's proposed eastern front via the "underbelly of Europe." Moreover, British bombers were now within range of the all-important Romanian Ploiesti oil fields. By March, 1941, the British had advanced to the Greek mainland, where the feeble resistance the Italians offered alarmed the Germans. That same month saw a military coup in Belgrade, putting Yugoslavia in a state of revolt. This gave the Germans the opportunity to invade Yugoslavia as a route to Greece, where they could assist the beleaguered Italians.

Luftwaffe operations were under the command of Gen. Alexander Lohr and his Luftflotte 4, which included aircraft from JG27, JG77 and LG 1. The Yugo-slav invasion, coded "Operation Marita," was scheduled to be carried out on April 6, 1941. Although there was little activity for the Jagdwaffe, some confusion in the fighter-to-fighter engagements did occur. Strangely, the Jugoslavenko Kraljevsko Ratno Vazduhoplovsvo (JKRV), or Yugoslav Royal Air Force, was also equipped with Messerschmitt Me 109 fighters, purchased in 1938/39. Further adding to the identity confusion was the Yugoslav aircraft insignia which included a cross. The Jagdwaffe had painted the noses of many Messerschmitts operating in the Balkans a bright yellow for identification purposes, as they had at times during the Battle of Britain. The yellow-nosed German planes gave birth to the order issued to the Yugoslav fighter pilots: "Attack all 109's with yellow noses"! The Yugoslavs also used Hawker Hurricanes, purchased from Britain before the advent of hostilities. On the first day, 10 Luftwaffe Messerschmitts were shot down, while the JKRV 6th Regiment lost 13 Me 109s and two IK-Z fighters. Precious moments were lost to the Yugoslavs because many pilots hesitated to fire on Messerschmitts without yellow noses. On April 7, the 6th Regiment was engaged heavily and lost 12 more Messerschmitts, leaving them a force of only 4 fighters with which to continue the battle. Resistance was soon quelled, and after a short Yugoslav campaign the Germans swept into Greece.

The Greek campaign was also of short duration, except on the island of Crete and the battle against British naval forces. The Cretan activity was coded "Operation Mercury," and included considerable successful Jabo activity in the surrounding waters. This became exclusively a Luftwaffe affair.

Gen. Kurt Student, an Alte Adler, directed his paratroopers in the successful aerial invasion of Crete, causing the Royal Navy to quickly seal the island off. The British cruisers and destroyers had little air cover, and the Luftwaffe ruled the skies around Crete. This condition resulted in an air/naval confrontation which built to a crescendo on May 22, 1941. In addition to escorting Stuka attacks, JG 77 under Maj. Bernhard Woldenga and I/LG 2 under Haupt. Herbert Ihlefeld, assumed the Jabo role. At 12:30 on that day, the Messerschmitts of III/JG 77 inflicted serious damage to the Royal Navy battleship Warspite. Four hours later, the cruiser Fiji was spotted by a lone Me 109 Jabo, piloted by Hptm. Wolf-Dietrich Huy. The Staffelkapitan quickly swooped down and released his 500-lb. bomb very near the ship's side, so that the explosion ripped through its hull plating. As the Fiji assumed a heavy list, Huy quickly called for assistance, forced to return to base because of a dwindling fuel supply. The summoned Messerschmitt found the crippled cruiser and scored a direct hit at 6:15 p.m. causing the Fiji to capsize. It sank one hour later. After suffering the loss of two cruisers and four destroyers due to Luftwaffe attacks, the British Mediterranean fleet set sail for Alexandria on the morning of April 23rd. Three days later, the German Navy was able to land tanks and other equipment on Crete, and by June 1, 1941 the British had completely evacuated the island. The cruiser Calcutta was sunk while covering this operation. In addition to these sinkings, the Luftwaffe had severely damaged a battleship and three cruisers.

Some of the Messerschmitt Jabo Jagdfliegern who scored decisively against the Royal Navy during the Cretan campaign were: Fw. Rudolf Schmidt of 7/JG 77, who sank two motor torpedo boats and made several direct hits on a transport in Suda Bay; Lt. Johan Pichler of the same Staffel, who sank several small ships; and Fw. Franz Schulte of 6/JG 77, who sank a transport and a motor torpedo boat (MTB).

Although fighter-to-fighter activity was very limited, Hptm. Ihlefeld and Lt. Geisshardt each scored one Hurricane near the island after flying a Jabo mission.

While the Jagdwaffe was pounding the Royal Navy near Crete, there was also considerable aerial activity over Malta, another strategic Mediterranean isle, where Joachim Müncheberg and his 7/JG 26 scored many successes. The Staffelkapitan himself shot down 19 Hurricanes over the island fortress during the spring of 1941.

THE WAR IN NORTH AFRICA

Since their attack on the British forces in Egypt, the Italians had been faring badly, especially after the December 9, 1940 surprise British offensive in Cyrenaica. Although the vaunted Italian Regia Aeronautica outnumbered the R.A.F. by a ratio of three to one, the quality of the British Gloster Gladiators and Hawker Hurricanes overcame this numerical superiority. The British drive reached Benghazi by February, 1941. This forced Mussolini to request assistance from the Germans who, realizing the strategic value of North Africa, quickly obliged by ordering Gen. Erwin Rommel to Africa. Rommel arrived on February 2, 1941.

The capture of Egypt was essential to the German war effort. With Egypt under German control, Malta would fall and the Suez Canal would be closed to

British ships, thus eliminating all British control of the Mediterranean Sea. Syria and Palestine could not hope to stand, and once in the Levant, the Germans would be in sight of precious oil wells and Turkey's strategic Dardanelles.

Rommel began his counteroffensive eastward towards Egypt on March 24, 1941. German forces soon occupied El Agheila, and by February 24th they had reached Marsa el Brega, while Benghazi was recaptured on April 4. Ten days later, No. 1 Staffel of I/JG 27 under Oblt. Karl Redlich arrived at Ain el Gazala airfield and, within a week, 2 Staffel under Hptm. Erich Gerlitz and 3 Staffel under Oblt. Gerhard Homuth relocated from the Balkan and Maltese operations with the Gruppenkommandeur, Hptm. Eduard Neumann. The Gruppe's insignia consisted of a leopard's head and a black native face superimposed on a map of Africa. Surprisingly, this insignia had been in use since early 1940 when no one ever dreamed that the unit would see service on the Dark Continent.

The pilots of I/JG 27 were veterans of the Battle of Britain, the Balkan campaign and the Mediterranean actions with a total 93 victories to their credit. Many of the men were aces by Allied standards: Oblt. Redlich, 10 victories ; Oblt. Homuth, 15; Oblt. Franzisket, 14; Lt. Kothmann; Ofw. Forster, 6; and Ofhr. Marseille, 7 victories. Hans-Joachim Marseille was destined to become a legend in the fierce aerial fighting that was about to erupt over the Western Desert.

The Gruppe first went into action on April 19, 1941, against 274 Squadron Hurricanes near Tobruk, shooting down four: one by Lt. Schrör; two by Oblt. Redlich; and the fourth by Uffz. Sippel. Later in the day when both units were in the air again, Pilot Officer Spence scored hits on Lt. Schrör's Messerschmitt, forcing him to bellyland on the desert sand. Three days later, Ofw. Kowalski and Oberfahnrich (cadet) Marseille were forced to make emergency landings because their short-range Messerschmitts ran out of fuel. The final air battle over Tobruk occurred on April 23, when the Gruppe met 55 Squadron Bristol Blenheim bombers, which lost one aircraft before Oblt. Redlich's guns. Hurricanes from 6 Squadron then engaged the Messerschmitts, and Oblt. Franzisket and Lt. von Moller each destroyed two British fighters while Hans Marseille shot down a fifth. Fw. Lange was shot down and killed over Tobruk during the melee.

Oblt. Joachim Müncheberg and his 7/JG 26 arrived at Gazala on June 1 to reinforce Neumann's I/JG 27. At this time Müncheberg was credited with over 40 victories and, although he was under Hptm.

During the British raids on the northwestern German coast in 1939, the defending German forces were under the command of Oberstlt. Carl Schumacher.

Armorers of JG 51 load the guns of an 8 Staffel Me 109E. A Jagdfleiger of 7 Staffel readies himself prior to a sortie during the Battle of France.

Neumann's command, the newcomer was treated with the great respect he deserved.

On June 14, the British mounted a new offensive known as Operation Battleaxe and the 45 Messerschmitts, assisted by 70 Italian fighters, were faced with no less than six fighter squadrons and four bomber squadrons: 1 SAAF (South African Air Force) Squadron of Hurricanes; 2 SAAF Squadron of Curtiss Tomahawks and Hurricanes; 73 Squadron of Hurricanes; 274 Squadron of Hurricanes; 250 Squadron of Tomahawks; and 6 Squadron of Hurricanes.

It was about 5:30 A.M. on the 14th when five Hurricanes of 1 SAAF Squadron escorted a 24 SAAF Squadron Maryland bomber in a raid on Gazala airfield. Oblt. Franzisket took off to intercept just as the mission was canceled because of poor visibility and began to turn back. As the Messerschmitt approached the bomber, a Hurricane piloted by Capt. K.W. Driver dived head on towards the climbing German, and both planes began firing. Capt. Driver's aim was a bit too high, but the German's cannon shells slammed into the Hurricane's auxiliary fuel tank. Both pilots continued firing until the

Much of the Jagdwaffe's success in Poland and France was due to the mobility of their ground support. Tank trucks, portable workshops, and generators traveled with the Panzers to be certain they would be available when the Messerschmitts needed them.

Air Marshal Sir Hugh Dowding, Commander in Chief of the R.A.F. Fighter Command, organized a sophisticated network of detection, fighter direction, and control from ground stations, which prevented the Luftwaffe from launching any surprise attacks.

Fighter Command 11 Group bore the brunt of the German raids during the Battle of Britain. New Zealander Vice Marshal Keith Park commanded 11 Group and directed his fighters to attack the German bombers and avoid confrontation with the Jagdwaffe whenever possible.

last possible moment, when they swerved slightly to port and collided, each plane's propeller chewing into the other's right wingtip. The Hurricane burst into flames and the pilot took to his parachute without delay. Despite his damaged wingtip, Franzisket went after the bomber and also shot it down in

flames. The South African landed near the airfield and was captured. It has often been said that the aerial combat over the Western Desert was a "gentlemen's war" and the story of K.W. Driver and Ludwig Franzisket adds credence to this belief. Victor and vanquished breakfasted in the German's

A wartime photographer caught this air action over England as a Messerschmitt approaches a Spitfire in the six o'clock high position, ready to deliver the coup de grace.

Adolf Galland (center) and Werner Mölders (right) discuss Battle of Britain fighter tactics with Ernst Udet, the highest-scoring surviving German WWI ace.

tent and later examined the Oberleutnant's Messerschmitt which was already undergoing repair. The two officers chatted amiably for a few hours, sharing photos and stories about their loved ones and Driver mentioned that his wife was in Cairo on a visit to him. Franzisket promised to drop a message on British territory so Mrs. Driver would know that her husband was alive and well. After Capt. Driver was taken away to a P.O.W. camp, Oblt. Franzisket risked his life to drop a message

container over Sidi Barrani addressed to Mrs. Driver, truly a man of chivalry, typical of the war in the desert.

During very heavy air action on June 15, I/JG 27 scored 11 victories in several encounters over Libya. On June 16, the Germans met a new adversary, the American-made Curtiss P-40 Tomahawk, which was to become a common sight in the desert skies. Two days later, seven Tomahawks were jumped by four Messerschmitts from I/JG 27, and three Tomahawks

From time to time during WWII, the Messerschmitts were fitted with bombs and proved to be successful Jagd Bombers or Jabo (fighter bombers). Observe the close-up of the bomb installation and the shallow diving angle of the Emil as it releases its lethal cargo.

were shot down by Oblt. Redlich, Lt. Remmer, and Uffz. Steinhausen. During the fighting on that day, the British lost 32 aircraft, while the Luftwaffe lost 25, and it was generally conceded that the British offensive, Operation Battleaxe, had failed. The intensity of aerial activity began to fade.

It was not until June 20, 1941 that Hptm. Müncheberg and his 7/JG 26 first met the enemy over the desert. Southeast of Buqbuq, the unit engaged Hurricanes from 1 SAAF Squadron, the Staffelkapitan scoring one and Lt. Mietusch a second fighter. Four days later, Müncheberg scored again, a 6 Squadron tactical–reconnaissance Hurricane.

Rommel, meanwhile, had captured Tobruk, and was pressing eastward toward the Nile and Cairo, but was stopped at El Alamein. This development created a demand for increased aerial activity.

Müncheberg was in action again on July 15 when he made a lone attack on a dozen Hurricanes that were annihilating a flight of Stukas and Me 100s. The Hauptmann not only broke up the British attack, but shot down a Hurricane in flames southwest of Ras Asaz for his 46th victory. On the 29th, eight

Tomahawks from 2 SAAF Squadron intercepted Stukas from I/St. G, under 7/JG 26 escort. At the onset, four Stukas and two Messerschmitts went down. Joachim Müncheberg was in the middle of the fracas and sent two Tomahawks plunging into the Mediterranean east of Bardia.

After scoring at least eight victories in Africa, five by Müncheberg, 7/JG 26 returned to Sicily on July 31. The Hauptmann constantly pressed the Luftwaffe brass to replace at once the aging Me 109E with the newer Mc 109F in order to gain aerial superiority.

The air war over the desert possessed an air of professionalism not shared by any other theater of operation in the World War II. There was no mass bombing of civilians or cities. Only military targets were attacked, and bombing was tactical rather than strategic. There appeared to be a mutual respect between enemies, because both suffered the same discomforts of oppressive heat and sand everywhere, as well as the danger to all machinery imposed by the infiltration of sand particles. Moreover, there was no place to hide during air attacks and tent-living was the rule. The only pilot with better

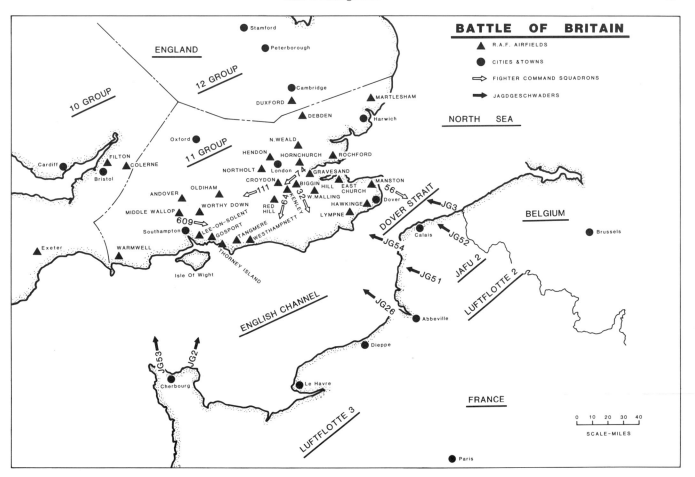

BATTLE OF BRITAIN

▲ R.A.F. AIRFIELDS
● CITIES &TOWNS
⇨ FIGHTER COMMAND SQUADRONS
→ JAGDGESCHWADERS

ENGLAND

NORTH SEA

10 GROUP

12 GROUP

11 GROUP

BELGIUM

ENGLISH CHANNEL

FRANCE

LUFTFLOTTE 2

LUFTFLOTTE 3

0 10 20 30 40
SCALE-MILES

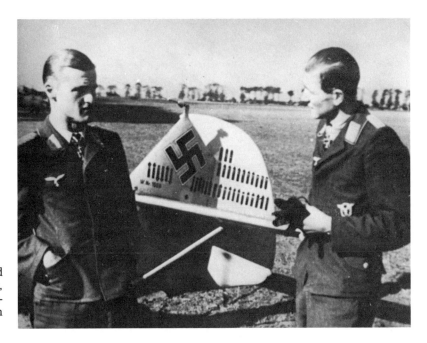

Günther Lützow, JG 3 Kommodore, and Wilhelm Balthasar, III/JG 3 Kommandeur, stand by the tail of Lützow's Me 109E discussing the Battle of Britain freie Jagd from which they have just returned.

The leading Jagdwaffe personalities are shown during a meeting at Jafu 2 headquarters to discuss Battle of Britain problems in the autumn of 1940. From left to right: Adolf Galland, Kommodore JG 26; Günther Lützow, Kommodore JG 3; Günther Freiherr von Maltzahn, Kommodore JG 53; Theodore Osterkamp, Jafu 2; and Werner Mölders, Kommodore JG 51.

The game must go on! While ground crew members roll an Me 109E-3 from their camouflage nets for an Alarmstart, two of their fellow ground crew members continue to play a game of soccer.

Hans Jeschonnek, Luftwaffe Chief of Staff; Bruno Lörzer, Kommandeur II Flieger Korps; and Hermann Göring appear concerned as they examine a battle map during a visit to Lörzer's headquarters.

quarters was Hptm. Neumann, who had been using his circus wagon in Europe and somehow managed to transport it to North Africa.

The first big aerial encounter of August was on

the 21st, when Hptm. Redlich, Oblt. Schneider, Ofw. Espenlaub, Hptm. Gerlitz, Lt. Kothman, Ofw. Forster, Oblt. Muak, and Lt. Schrör each scored one victory on assorted Tomahawks, Marylands and

As is evident in these photos, the Jagdwaffe generally operated from very primitive airfields, using pastures, hayfields, and other flat areas along the countryside. Note the splinter camouflage on the wings and tail and the gravel path used as a taxi apron and tarmac. The JG 26 Me 109E-3 was flown by Adolf Galland, who is seen emerging from his plane.

Hurricanes, with no loss to I/JG 27.

On September 14, 1941, when Rommel started his drive towards Sidi Barrani, several new British fighter squadrons appeared over that city. The most prominent of the new units was 112 RAAF (Royal Australian Air Force) Squadron, who with its "Shark-Mouthed" Tomahawks, could boast of such aces as C.R. "Killer" Caldwell and Neville Duke. I/JG scored two Tomahawks, three Hurricanes, and one Maryland bomber with no loss to themselves.

Meanwhile, Joachim Müncheberg's recommendation to his superiors did not go unheeded. The Staffels of I/JG 27 were scheduled for rotation back to Germany, to indoctrinate the pilots to the new Messerschmitt Me 109F and ferry them to the battle area. On August 16, 4/JG 27 was the first Staffel to

return to Africa with its 13 brand new Me 109F models.

Numbers 4, 5, and 6 Staffeln, led by Hptm. Rödel, Hptm. Dülling and Oblt. Strössner arrived in Africa on September 23 to assist 1, 2 and 3 Staffeln of I/JG 27. The new Staffeln formed II Gruppe of JG 27, led by Hptm. Wolfgang Lippert who was already credited with 25 victories. The II/JG 27 itself, was no stranger to combat conditions, having fought in the Battles of France, Britain, Greece, and even a fortnight on the Russian Front. The Gruppe had 141 victories to its credit when it arrived in Africa.

Despite that the majority of British squadrons in the Battle of Britain were quick to adopt the German rotte and schwarm, or double-attack, finger-four battle formation, the British and Commonwealth

One of the most successful Jagdfliegers of the Battle of Britain was the Kommodore of JG 2 Richthofen, Helmut Wick. He is shown describing a new method of attack used in a recent dogfight. The second photo shows his Me 109 E-3 ready for takeoff.

squadrons in North Africa appeared hesitant to use this tactical innovation and still flew in threes or in line abreast. Combat over the desert was generally conducted below 15,000 ft., because the attack on supply columns and military vehicles was the order of the day.

During October and November, the Messerschmitts of II/JG 27 had many encounters with the Commonwealth squadrons. The first was on October 3, when seven Messerschmitts attacked six 33 Squadron Hurricanes escorting tactical reconnaissance Hurricanes near Buqbuq, one Hurricane was shot down. Two days later, three Me 109Fs of II Gruppe jumped four Hurricanes and sent two crashing into the desert. On October 30, the Gruppe engaged 250 and 238 Squadrons Tomahawks between Bardia and Sollum. Ofw. Schulz shot down three, and Lt. Schacht scored a fourth. Otto Schulz was rapidly becoming the high scorer of the Gruppe and shot down 42 of his 51 victories in the Western Desert.

The British took the Germans by surprise on November 18, 1941 by launching another offensive, Operation Crusader. Heavy rains had fallen on the Axis fighter airfields during the previous night, turning them into a sea of mud and restricting Axis fighter operations. At this time, the opposing single-engine fighter forces were evenly matched numeri-

cally, and both sides made plans to increase fighter strength. The Luftwaffe units were reorganized about this time under a single command called Flieger-Führer Afrika. Gen. Stephen Fröhlich was selected for the post.

Lt. Remmer of I/JG 27 shot down a Blenheim bomber from the Free French Lorraine Squadron on the morning of November 28. That afternoon, Ofw. Schulz of II/JG 27 dived on a dozen Hurricanes from 94 Squadron, and shot down Pilot Officer Muhart, Flight Officer Vos and Lt. Palm in such rapid succession that the remainder of the squadron had no time to react to this audacious attack.

Important Luftwaffe reinforcements arrived in the Western Desert in December, 1941. Luftflotte 2 was transferred to the Mediterranean from the Russain front determined to reopen the North African supply route by blasting Malta, and then driving the Allies out of the Western Desert.

JG 53 Pikas and II Gruppe of JG 3 were posted to advanced airfields on Sicily while, on December 6 III/JG 53 under Hptm. Wolf-Dietrich Wilke was sent to Tmimi. The Gruppe included 7, 8 and 9 Staffels led by Oblt. Altendorf, Oblt. Heinecke, and Oblt. Götz. As with the other units sent to Africa, III/JG 53 had experienced intense combat in the Battles of France and Britain, and on the Russian front. Many of the pilots were aces, or Experten, when they arrived in

JG 26 Kommodore Adolf Galland puffs his ever-present cigar as he emerges from his Emil after a successful mission. Film from his gun camera reveals decisive hits on a Hurricane for another confirmed victory.

These Jagdwaffe pilots lounge in the French sun as they wait for the ground crews to complete the preparations of their Messerschmitts.

Africa; Hptm. Wilke, 33 victories; Oblt. Gotz, 30; Oblt. Altendorf, 15; Lt. Schramm 37; and Lt. Neuhoff, 37 victories.

The second unit to arrive in Africa was III/JG 27 on December 12, led by Hptm. Erhard Braune. The Gruppe was comprised of Nos. 7, 8 and 9 Staffels under the respective commands of Oblts. Gerlitz, Lass, and Graf von Kageneck. Many of the Gruppes members had achieved respectable scores in the Battles of France, Britain, Malta, and the Russian front: Oblt. von Kageneck, 65 victories; Oblt. Lass, 14; Hptm. Braune, 12; and Oblt. Bauler, 9 victories. Now that the entire Geschwader was brought together, the Staff Flight, led by Kommodore Bernhard Woldenga, also arrived from the Russian front at about this time.

On December 11, 1941, Germany and Italy declared war on the United States as the result of the Pearl Harbor attack and their commitment to the

JG 2 Richthofen and JG 26 Schlageter remained on the Channel coast to slow the Western Allies' nonstop bombing offensive. Shown here are Gerhard Schöpfel, Adolf Galland, and Joachim Müncheberg of JG 26; and Egon Mayer, Erich Leie, Walter Ösau, and Rudolf Pflanz of JG 2.

Joachim Müncheberg was one of the more successful Jagdwaffe pilots in the heavy fighting over the island of Malta, scoring 19 victories there in the spring of 1941. The Me 109E-7 of Müncheberg's 7/JG 26 sported the Staffel's red heart insignia. Note the long-range drop tank which proved necessary over the Mediterranean.

I/JG 27 Afrika was the first Jagdwaffe unit to arrive in North Africa to help Rommel's Afrika Korps. The Me 109E-4 escorting the Stuka dive bomber is flown by Oblt. Ludwig Franzisket, while Rainer Pötgen is caught entering his Messerschmitt for a freie Jagd against the Commonwealth forces.

This Messerschmitt was forced to land in the desert because it ran out of fuel and is being refueled so it can be flown back to its base. Short range was the Me 109's principal shortcoming.

Ludwig Franzisket guides South African Captain K.W. Driver around the JG 27 airfield after he shot him down in a dogfight. Notice the bandages around the Captain's burned neck.

The Commonwealth fighter forces in North Africa concentrated on shooting at the German airfields, while the Jagdwaffe enjoyed the freie Jagd and also escorted bombers when necessary. These Me 109Fs were damaged by a raid despite the extensively sandbagged enclosures.

Gustav Rödel, II/JG 27 Kommandeur; Eduard Neumann, JG 27 Kommodore; and Gerhard Homuth, I/JG 27 Kommandeur discuss the orders for the day under the African sun.

third member of the Tripartite Pact, Japan. This action against the United States was to seal the doom of the Axis powers, and would be felt first in Africa.

The III Gruppe of JG 53 made its first kills over the desert on December 11, when 94 Squadron sent its Hurricanes on a fighter sweep near Gazala. Three of the Hurricanes were intercepted and shot down by III Gruppe. The unit relocated to Derna on December 12 and scored seven more victories on that day. On the same day, III/JG 27 scored its initial victories in

Africa with Oblt. Erbo Graf von Kageneck's downing of two Tomahawks over Tmimi. On December 17, III/JG 53 returned to Sicily to resume operations against Malta, and three days later JG 27 was forced to evacuate their airfields at Derna and Marada because of the British advance. The Geschwader relo-

Major Eduard Neumann emerges from his Messerschmitt at the end of an exhausting patrol.

The men of JG 27 kill time between missions. The camera caught Hans-Joachim Marseille jovially threatening to stone the photographer.

cated to airfields near Magrun and Got Bersis. Fuel was in short supply and I/JG 27 barely managed to reach their new base. Before they abandoned the old airfield, they left a message for the advancing British, painted on the door of their flight shack which read: "We will be back. Happy Christmas."

On the day before Christmas, the British recaptured Benghazi. German air power at that time was reduced to only six operational Messerschmitts in the entire JG 27 due to shortage of fuel and the fact that mechanics and other ground personnel were lost during the retreat and failed to show up at the new airfields. One of the pilots who was able to take off was Oblt. von Kageneck, the high scorer of the Geschwader. The six Me 109Fs jumped ten Hurricanes of 94 Squadron near Ajedabia and, in the resulting fight, von Kageneck was shot in the stomach. He made it back to his airfield and though he was rushed to a field hospital, he died on January 12, 1942, the day the British retook Solum. By the beginning of 1942, fuel and other essential supplies began to reach the Luftwaffe units, as several supply convoys managed to cross the Mediterranean. The increased aerial activity against Malta and the British fleet facilitated these crossings. With fuel and sup-

plies, Rommel started his own offensive, now that Operation Crusader had spent itself. Intense aerial activity began on January 19, 1942 and two days later the advance started. By January 28, the Germans entered Benghazi.

The Germans found the air war in Africa a frustrating experience. Success was always dependent upon the receipt of supplies, and the logistics problem was difficult and, at times, hopeless. All war material was transported by convoy from Italian ports, but the Royal Navy invariably controlled the Mediterranean Sea! It is for this reason that Rommel's offensives eventually failed. The problem of getting supplies to North Africa and the meager German fighter-plane production prevented the Luftwaffe from building up a powerful force in the desert, without which Rommel could not succeed. Fighting against the Commonwealth forces, a first rate air arm that had no supply problem, was an almost impossible task for the Jagdwaffe in Cyrenaica.

General Hoffmann von Waldau replaced Gen. Fröhlich as Flieger-Führer Afrika in March, 1942. Also at about this time, an improved Curtiss was appearing in the desert skies in ever increasing numbers. This new six-gun fighter was the Kittyhawk.

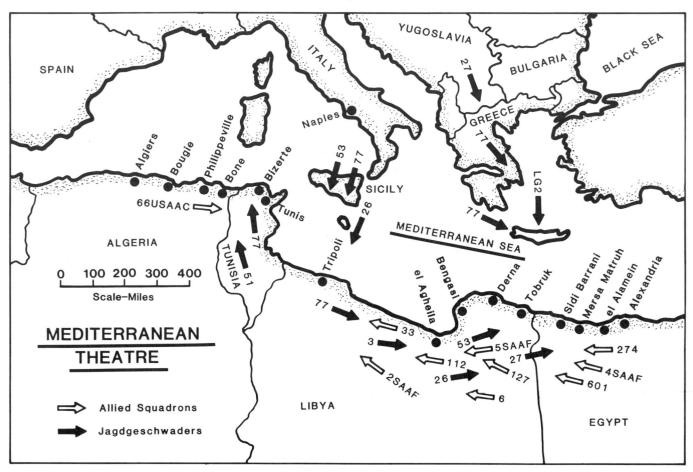

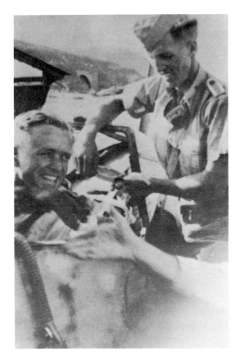

Major Günther von Maltzahn accepts congratulations as he arrives from a successful mission over the desert.

On March 24, Lt. Korner of I/JG 27 shot down a Douglas Boston, which became the 1,000th victory for JG 27.

By May, Oblt. Hans-Joachim Marseille had started to establish himself as one of the outstanding fighter pilots of the war, scoring two Kittyhawks of 3 RAAF Squadron on May 13 over Gazala. Marseille attacked 12 Kittyhawks of the same unit on May 16 and again shot down two of the Curtiss fighers. As the pilot of the second Kittyhawk, Pilot Officer F.E. Parker, took to his parachute, his uncontrolled plane became involved in one of the strangest accidents of the air war: it collided with another Kittyhawk flown by Sgt. W.J. Metherall who also crashed.

On May 20, III/JG 53 returned to the desert from Sicily and was posted to the Martuba airfield. Maj. Gerlitz was transferred from his command of II/JG 27 to become Gruppenkommandeur of the returning unit. Hptm. Rödel then took command of II/JG 27.

Friedrich Geisshardt of I JG 77; Günther von Maltzahn, Kommodore JG 53 Pikas; and Heinz Baer, also of I/JG 77, stand in front of an Me 109G being serviced in Tunisia in early 1943. JG 53 and JG 77 relieved JG 27 from their African ordeal.

The last salute is given to fallen comrades and enemy alike in this melancholy scene on the Western Desert. Notice the bent and twisted propeller in the foreground.

Messerschmitts escort a Heinkel bomber during Operation Barbarossa, one of the most successful aerial offensives ever undertaken.

On May 26, Erwin Rommel launched another offensive, which is now called the Battle of Al-Gazala, sending the Commonwealth forces into a long retreat. JG 27 and III/JG 53 experienced exhausting and violent activity with all pilots flying several sorties each day. Although sandstorms made flying dangerous, both sides flew and fought furiously.

Four Messerschmitts each from I/JG 27 and III/JG 53 were escorting a dozen Stukas over Acroma when 12 Tomahawks from 4 SAAF Squadron intercepted. In the first attack, two Stukas went down, while a Me 109 and another Stuka were damaged. The I Gruppe then slammed into the South Africans.

Marseille sent three crashing into the desert sands, while Lt. von Lieres and Ofw. Mentnich scored one each, and Fw. Steinhausen shot down two Tomahawks. Meanwhile, the III Gruppe isolated four South Africans and shot three down with no loss to themselves.

Marseille performed an outstanding feat on June 3 when he shot down six Tomahawks in only 11 minutes! Six Messerschmitts each from I/JG 27 and III/JG 53 were again escorting Stukas when 12 to 14 Tomahawks from 5 SAAF Squadron jumped the Stukas. As was customary, Marseille was the first of the Gruppe to attack, and after firing less than a

After the German attack on the Soviet Union, Finland, Hungary, Romania, and Slovakia became involved in the fighting against their common enemy, fighting alongside the Germans and using German aircraft. In the top row are a Romanian 109G and Hungarian 109G; the bottom row shows a Slovakian 109E and a Finnish 109G. Observe the cross insignia on the Romanian, Hungarian, and Slovakian aircraft, and the swastika on the Finnish plane. These had no connection with the German national or political insignia.

Werner Mölders is shown on the Russian front in early autumn of 1940, flanked by Karl-Gottfried Nordmann of JG 51 and Günther Lützow of JG 3.

Four outstanding Experten from I/JG 51 who helped it become the first Geschwader to attain 1,000 victories: Heinrich Höfmeier, 96 victories; Erwin Fleig, 66; Heinz Baer, 220; and Heinrich Krafft, 78.

Generalfeldmarschall Albert Kesselring (second from left) visited JG 53 Pikas on the Eastern front in August, 1941. He poses here with: Herbert Schramn, 42 victories; Wolf-Dietrich Wilke, 163; and Erich Schmidt, 47 victories.

dozen shots his engine cannon jammed, leaving him only two small-caliber machine guns in the cowling. Continuing the attack with his Rottenflieger, Marseille's first victory was Capt. Pare, who went down in flames at 1:22 P.M. Three minutes later, he sent Lt. Martin crashing into the desert at Bir Hacheim; at 1:27, Capt. Morrison and his Tomahawk were caught, and in less than a minute Lt. Muir and 2nd Lt. Golding became the young German's fourth and fifth victories. Marseille's sixth victim was Capt. Botha, whose Tomahawk was seriously damaged at 1:33 P.M. The South African was, however, able to nurse his plane back to base where he crash landed. Six victories in eleven minutes! There are combat pilots who flew throughout the war whose total victory score is less. Marseille's Rottenflieger, Fw. Rainer Pöttgen, stated afterward, "I was very busy counting his victories, noting the times and location, and simultaneously protecting his tail. His judgment in deflection shooting was incredible. Each time he fired, I saw his shells strike the enemy plane's nose, then travel along to the cockpit. No ammunition was wasted."

Oblt. Marseille became Staffelkapitan of 3/JG 27 on June 8, replacing Hptm. Homuth. Homuth himself was promoted to Kommandeur of I Gruppe when Maj. Neumann was elevated to Kommodore of Jagdgeschwader 27.

Although delayed by a 400-mile minefield, Rommel managed to press ahead with his Panzers, often operating behind the Allied lines. On June 14, 1942, I/JG 27 and III/JG 53 moved to an airfield near Derna to keep pace with Rommel's advance. German troops captured Tobruk on June 20, and reached Sidi Barrani on the 24th, forcing the British back to

Mersa Matrüh. Meanwhile, the Luftwaffe was flying and fighting to exhaustion, with Oblt. Marseille raising his score to a total of 95 victories. On June 17, when air operations reached a crescendo, a Schwarm of Messerschmitts engaged 20 Kittyhawks and 10 Hurricanes from 112 and 73 Squadrons near Gambut. Marseille dived to the attack at once and shot down two Kittyhawks in his first pass, killing Squadron Leader D.H. Ward and P.O. Woolley. While making evasive turns to avoid hits from Kittyhawks behind him, Marseille jumped a flight of four Curtiss fighters, and downed two more forcing P.O. Stone and Sgt. Goodwin to take to their parachutes. He then sighted a lone Hurricane, flown by Sgt. Drew of 112 Squadron about to land on Gambut airfield and quickly bounced it for his 100th victory. All five victories were scored within seven minutes! As the Schwarm reformed, two tactical reconnaissance Spitfires were observed flying high above. The young Oberleutnant climbed steeply and scored his 101st. victory by downing one of the Spitfires.

During this period, the Luftwaffe kept pace with the movement of the army, and relocated to progressively more advanced bases at Gambut and Al-Gazala. However, fuel, food, and spare parts were virtually nonexistant and the men flew their missions with empty tanks and empty stomachs! Fuel was in such short supply that, on June 27, 1942, III/JG 53 was only able to fly one Schwarm on a single mission. Conversely, the hitting power of the Commonwealth air forces increased because they were operating from well-constructed and well-supplied bases in Egypt. The farther they advanced under these adverse conditions, the greater became the Luftwaffe's losses. Then the inevitable happened; the offensive stalled west of El Alamein.

On July 1, 1942, Erwin Rommel launched his assault on the Allied line at El Alamein. The order of

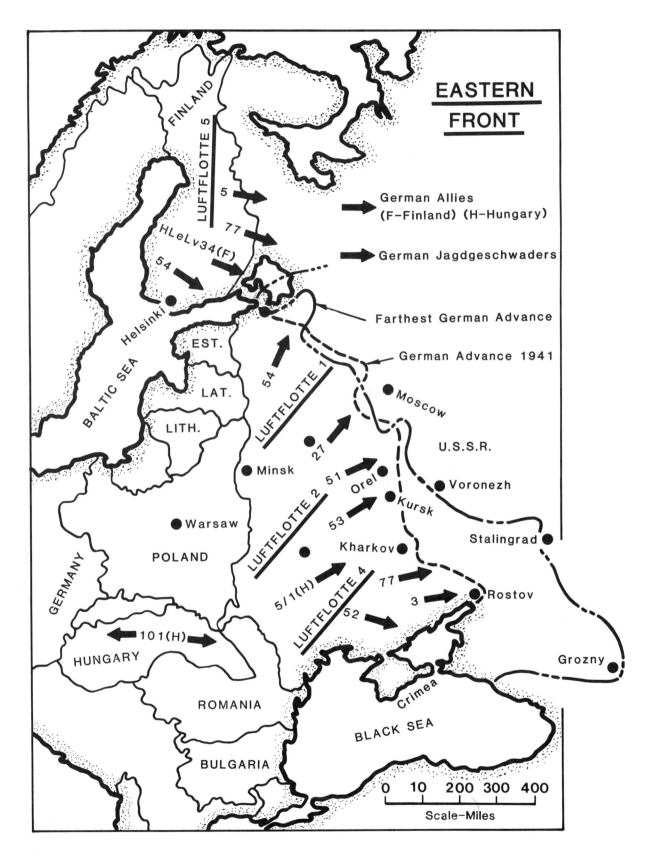

EASTERN FRONT

German Allies
(F-Finland) (H-Hungary)

German Jagdgeschwaders

Farthest German Advance

German Advance 1941

The Honor Guard of Gen. Ernst Udet's funeral cortege was composed of Jagdgeschwader Kommodores and other Jagdwaffe luminaries. In the extreme foreground is Adolf Galland followed by Walter Ösau. Fourth in the second row is Günther Lützow. Unknown to the mourners is the fact that Werner Mölders has been killed in a plane crash on his way to the funeral.

Hannes Trautloft emerges from his Messerschmitt in true Jagdwaffe style. Trautloft's JG 54 Grünherz had shot down its 2,222th victory by May 1, 1942.

The ice and snow of 1942 restricted the operation of the Jagdwaffe considerably. Here's an Emil parked on a snow-covered field, and a well-bundled member of ground crew personnel chipping away the ice and frozen snow from the tail of a Gustav.

the day for the German fighters was small flights of only one or two Schwarms at one time, whether it was a Freie Jagd or a Jabo mission. These small forces were constantly meeting Allied flights that were two to five times larger. Although the Jagdwaffe made a good accounting of themselves, this couldn't continue for very long. An example of this

situation happened on July 8 at 11:00 A.M., when 6 Me 109Fs from I/JG 27 on a Freie Jagd attacked 12 Hurricanes from 33 Squadron. Lt. Stahlschmidt scored three at once, killing P.O. Wigle and Sgt. Morris. While this was going on 12 more Hurricanes from 127 Squadron jumped the half-dozen Messerschmitts and Squadron Leader Pegge and Fl. Lt. Marples scored a 109 each. The four remaining Germans escaped these enormous odds. Even when the Jadgwaffe bettered their adversaries in spite of being overwhelmingly outnumbered, the German losses were a larger proportion of the committed aircraft and nothing could prevent attrition from taking its toll.

In an attempt at a flanking attack around El Alamein, Rommel launched a three-pronged attack on the morning of August 31, which developed into the battle of Alam el Halfa. Alam el Halfa is a ridge located midway between El Alamein and the Qat-

Two Gustavs from JG 3 Udet are shown here with various armament. The photo on the left shows a bomb installed for Jabo operations. In the photo on the right, large 210-mm. Dodel rocket tubes are fitted under the wings (between the camouflage nets) for use against vehicles and tanks.

Kommodore Wilke's JG 3 performed yeoman service at Stalingrad. Wilke is seen emerging from his Me 109G. The photo on the right shows one of JG 3's Messerschmitts up to its hubs in the Stalingrad mud.

tara Depression. As was customary, Rommel, the "Desert Fox," depended heavily on the Luftwaffe for success, because the African Campaign was ideally suited for a tactical air force. The following day hundreds of Commonwealth aircraft pounded the Afrika Korps, with enormous losses in German trucks, tanks, and other vehicles. All three Gruppen of JG 27 and III/JG 53 flew repeated sorties during the day, but failed to shoot down any Allied bombers. The heavy fighter escorts at this time invariably outnumbered the Jagdwaffe flights. Allied fighters shot down nine German aircraft, while the four Gruppen destroyed a total of 22 Allied fighters, including an American Curtiss P-40 F. Astoundingly,

17 of the 22 lost Allied aircraft were shot down by Hans-Joachim Marseille, whose meteoric rise among the German Experten made him a national hero in his homeland. More about this amazing performance appears in Part II.

Although the Luftwaffe flew with desperation, coupled with a certain amount of care to conserve their equipment, the Allied pilots apparently abused the relative abundance of their supplies, if the upswing in crash landings due to very minor damage is any indication. One example was the report from 4 SAAF Squadron stating that of 25 Kittyhawks, only five had been shot down while seventeen were crash or belly-landed with questionable necessity, leaving

This assembly of Jagdwaffe personalities was to celebrate the awarding of the Ritterkreuz to Hans Beisswenger, 152 victories (second from the left) and Horst Hannig, 98 victories (third from right), both from JG 54 Grünherz. Other celebrants and guests are JG 54 Kommodore Hannes Trautloft (extreme left); General der Flieger Helmuth Förster (third from left); Dieter Hrabak (second from right) and Josef Fözo, 27 victories (extreme right).

JG 52 Kommodore Dieter Hrabak was the dominant influence in his unit and is instructing four of his first Experten to "fly with your head and not with your muscles." The pupils are: Erich Hartmann, 352 victories; Karl Gratz, 138; Friedrich Obleser, 127; and Willi Batz, 237.

Erich Hartmann, the world's highest scoring air ace with 352 confirmed victories, double-checks his orders before starting on a mission in the Ukraine.

only three serviceable aircraft. In an attempt to halt this apparently needless destruction of good aircraft, an order was issued in early September warning pilots that those who crash-landed flyable aircraft would be forced to sit in the cockpit with full flying gear in the hot sun until the the plane was fully repaired. In cases where the craft could not be repaired locally, the pilot would be forced to walk around the plane in full flying gear in the hot sun until repairs were completed.

By the end of October 1942, the stage was set for the final act of the Western Desert war. The Allies now had 600 fighters, 250 tactical bombers, and 60 strategic four-engine bombers, compared to 350 Axis fighters, 70 dive bombers, and 170 tactical bombers. In addition, because the Western Desert air force possessed a better aircraft reclamation, salvage, and repair organization, it enjoyed a larger percentage of serviceable aircraft than the Germans. During the night of October 23, the British began an enormous offensive that opened the Battle of El Alamein. Allied fighters and bombers harassed the Afrika Corps without serious intervention from the Jagdwaffe. With one or two Schwarms attacking 12 to 30 bomber-escorting fighters, it was almost imposbile to score against the prime targets—the bombers—because they quickly demurred and allowed the escorting fighters to intervene. Even if the Messerschmitts scored one fighter with no losses before breaking off, their mission had to be regarded as a failure.

By now it was obvious to the Luftwaffe Oberkommando that the beleaguered Jadgwaffe in Africa needed help. On October 27, I/JG 77 Herzas, or Ace of Hearts, with more than 900 victories over Russia and Malta to its credit arrived from Sicily. Gruppekommandeur Hptm. Heinz Baer was one of the famous Experten, credited with over 120 victories at the time of his arrival. Other prominent members of the Gruppe included Staffelkapitans Hptm. Fritz Geisshardt, 90 victories, and Oblt. Siegfried Freytag, 70 victories. This unit was especially welcome because III/JG 53 had been recalled to Europe on the same day that I/JG 77 arrived in Africa. The III/JG 53s score in Africa was 113 victories.

Throughout the course of October 28, Rottes and

Fighting a common enemy, it was inevitable that the German and Hungarian forces would coordinate their activities at all levels of endeavor. Szazados Pottijondy (extreme left) and Ornagy Kovaks (third from right) of the Royal Hungarian Air Force 102 Fighter Group are shown meeting with Jagdfliegern from JG 52 who happen to be some of the best fighter pilots of the entire war: Erich Hartmann, 352 victories (second from left); Gerhard Barkhorn, 301 (third from left); Helmut Lipfert, 203 (second from right); and Heinrich Sturm 157 (extreme right).

Schwarms of III/JG 77 began arriving, taking their place on the same field used by I/JG 27, whose ground crew would service both. The Gruppen flew combined Freie Jagds on that morning and afternoon, with only mediocre and confusing results. Ofw. Herbert Kaiser of III/JG 77 and his Rottenflieger, on their way from Crete, spotted six British fighters strafing an Afrika Korps supply column. Kaiser quickly scored on the "tail end Charlie" with a short burst, and then after following the strafers, shot down his second victory of the day. The pair were so intent on destroying the British fighters that they neglected to scan the skies above them, from where a lone Allied fighter jumped them. The attacker sent a full burst of shells into Kaiser's engine compartment and set the oil cooler afire. The 109 went down pouring black smoke and belly-landed on the desert. His Rottenflieger reached his destination airfield at Bir el Abd and reported his leader's death. Two days later Herbert Kaiser, victor over 45 Allied aircraft at that time, walked onto the airfield from the desert, returning from the dead. The remainder of III/JG 77 arrived on the evening of the 28th with the Kommandeur, Hptm. Kurt Üben, an Expert credited with over 90 victories at that time. Some of the other Experten in III/JG 77 were: Oblt. Emil Omert, 55 victories; and Oblt. Helmut Gödert 23 victories.

The JG/77 Geschwaderstab, or wing flight staff,

arrived a short time later led by their Kommodore. This was none other than Maj. Joachim Müncheberg, who had commanded 7/JG 26 in the desert during the summer of 1941. His victories now exceeded the 100 mark.

Just after dawn on Nov. 1, 1942, while on Stuka escort, Messerschmitts from I/JG 27, II/JG 27, I/JG 77, and III/JG 77 were jumped by 40 Kittyhawks, 6 Spitfires and 20 American-made Bell Airacobras. Although the Stukas received a mauling, Hptm. Baer, Hptm. Rödel, Oblt. Unterberger, and Lt. Berres each shot down a British fighter. Two days later, JG 27 and JG 77 had a busy day, covering the beginning of the Axis forces' retreat westward from El Alamein. The units destroyed 21 Allied aircraft from 127, 335 and 450 Squadrons, among others. By early afternoon, II/JG 27 was down to only three serviceable Messerschmitts and so retreated to the Gambut airfield. On Nov. 6, II Gruppe of JG 27 was compelled to set 30 sorely needed Messerschmitts afire before fleeing the field in trucks in the face of rapidly advancing British tanks.

Adding to the retreating Afrika Corp's misery was Operation Torch, the large scale Anglo-American landings in French Algiers on Nov. 8 and in Philippeville on Nov. 9. Now the Axis forces in Africa were faced with a war on two fronts. Three days later the Germans began a drive toward Tunisia and occupied southern France to counter the Allied move. On

Hubertus von Bonin (center) succeeded Hannes Trautloft as Kommodore of JH 54 Grünherz. He is shown here with Karl Schnörrer (left) and Walter Nowotny. Nowotny led the most successful Schwarm in the Luftwaffe. During 1943, Nowotny and his three men amassed almost 500 victories. Shown below, the members of the Nowotny Schwarm are: Anton Dobele, 94 victories; Karl Schnörrer, 46; and Rudolf Rademacher, 126. The Nowotny Schwarm was part of 9/JG 54, the Teufelstaffel, or Devil's Squadron. The men slept in this converted railroad freight car. Observe the grinning Devil insignia and the victory score for the Staffel marked on the car!

this day, the British captured Bardia and the Anglo-American forces opened a new beachhead in Bougie, 120 miles east of Algiers. On Nov. 12, 1942 British paratroops landed in Böne, 150 miles closer still, and on the sixteenth captured the key airfield at Soua el Arba. The Germans in Africa were now caught in an enormous vise with no escape except across the Mediterranean Sea. At about this time

Certain Gruppen of JG 54 Grünherz operated in Finland in cooperation with the Finnish Air Force. Hans Götz of III/JG 54 and Finnish Ace Eino Luukannen discuss tactical problems alongside a Green Heart Gustav.

While two mechanics maintain a JG 54 Gustav on a snow-covered field, two other ground crew members bring tools and supplies in a horse-drawn sleigh!

General der Jagdfliegern Galland explains Operation Thunderbolt to Hermann Göring while a young orderly waits with a briefcase of maps and documents.

II/JG 27 and JG 77 retreated across the Jebel Akdar Peninsula to Magrun, leaving the Gambut airfield to South African Air Force.

The Geschwaderstab, I/JG 27, and III/JG 27 were ordered to leave Africa on November 12, 1942. I Gruppe was ordered to Germany, while III Gruppe was to report to Greece and Crete. The Messerschmitts were transferred to II/JG 27 and JG 77. During its 18 months of action in Africa, I/JG 27 scored 588 victories, while III/JG 27 scored 100 victories in its eleven-month stay.

By November 20, the Allies had taken Benghazi. German fighter force in Africa at that time numbered about 80 aircraft, only half of which were serviceable; and more and more American planes were appearing in the desert skies!

Added reinforcements arrived at Zazur, Libya, on Dec. 5, 1942, in the form of II/JG 77. This brought all of Münchberg's Geschwader together in North Africa. This Gruppe was already credited with 1,300 victories when it arrived in Africa. The

Kommandeur was Hptm. Anton Mader, with over 50 victories. The Staffelkapitans of 4/JG 77 and 6/JG 77 were Oblt. Lutz-Wilhelm Burckhardt, 53 victories, and Oblt. Joachim Deicke, 13 victories.

On December 10, 7 Messerschmitts of I/JG 77 scrambled to meet 12 601 Squadron Spitfires and 112 Squadron Kittyhawks flying cover for Curtiss P-40 Fs of 66 Squadron USAAF. Kommodore Muncheberg was flying with I Gruppe on that day. Battling just northwest of El Agheila, JG 77 scored eight Allied fighters and lost three Messerschmitts. Hptm. Heinz Baer shot down two, and Maj. Joachim Muncheberg got one American P-40 F. The last Gruppe of JG 27 were ordered from Africa on December 12, leaving the fighting in the hands of Muncheberg and his JG 77.

The German forces were retreating on the African eastern front while advancing on their new western

Oberstlt. Hans Philipp of JG 1 wears a pained expression as he conducts services for a fallen comrade. This became an increasingly common scene.

Georg-Peter Eder helped develop an effective method to use in attacking the U.S. four-engine bombers. He is shown here explaining the new tactics to fellow pilots. Of his 78 victories, 36 were four-engine bombers.

front, racing with the Anglo-American forces for the Tunisian ports of Bizerte, Bone, and Tunis. Possession of these harbors was a matter of life or death for the Afrika Korps, both as entry points for supplies and fuel and as the Germans' only means of escape should they be forced to evacuate North Africa. In one important respect, the military balance in the Tunisian Campaign had been reversed. At El Alamein, Rommel's supply lines were long while the British supply lines were short. In Tunisia, Rommel's supply lines were short while at the outset the British and American lines were long. The Germans were determined not to sell Tunisia cheaply and won the race for Tunis. The back door for the German retreat and incoming supplies remained open for the present.

The constant buildup of Allied air strength with new American squadrons made the Allies stronger and more dangerous. Constantly in action over the worst terrain imaginable, the Jagdwaffe in Africa was slowly worn down during the long retreat westward. This cost many tons of precious fuel and hard-

to-replace aircraft. Also, the Royal Air Force on Malta, reinforced by American aircraft carriers, had turned the Axis shipping lanes into a graveyard for tankers, supply ships, and transports.

A more powerful and heavily armed model of the Messerschmitt was distributed to the Luftwaffe in 1942 and was now being flown by JG 77. This was the Me 109G, and reinforcements equipped with these aircraft arrived in Tunisia in early 1943. The entire JG 53 Pikas returned to Africa with its Kommodore, Maj. Günther von Maltzahn, II/JG 51 Mölders, under Kommandeur Hptm. Hartmann Grasser, also arrived to assist JG 77. American fighters shot down and killed JG 77's Kommodore, Maj. Joachim Müncheberg after his 135th victory, and Maj. Johannes Steinhoff was selected to replace him. Despite the presence of these crack units and newer aircraft, the Luftwaffe task was an impossible one against the overwhelming odds. Allied air superiority continued to grind away at the dwindling Luftwaffe. During April and early May of 1943 as many key personnel as possible were evacuated across the Mediterranean. The Allies captured Tunis and Bizerte on May 7, signaling the end of the African campaign.

THE WAR IN ITALY

The Allies lost no time in pursuing their advantage and pressed on across the Mediterranean Sea. They landed on Sicily on July 9 and on the Italian mainland two weeks later. This forced the Luftwaffe to undergo another shift in command. Feldmarschall Kesselring was appointed Supreme Mediterranean Commander, while Gen. von Richthofen assumed command of Luftflotte 2 on the Italian peninsula. Gen. Galland, now commander of the Jagdwaffe, and Gen. Peltz, commander of the bomber arm, were ordered to personally conduct all operations in the Mediterranean and expel the Allies from Italy. The impossiblity of this task illustrates the delusion under which the Luftwaffe Oberkommando operated. The Jagdfliegern nonetheless flew and fought on with their usual vigor, despite the odds.

In the first weeks of July 1943, the Luftwaffe had less than 650 aircraft in the Mediterranean theater of operations. Adding to the dilemma were the repeated Allied raids on the Luftwaffe supply center in Bari, on Italy's Adriatic coast, resulting in the destruction of hundreds of factory-fresh aircraft. The Luftwaffe could ill afford this loss. The Jagdfliegern of Luftflotte 2 remained under severe pressure in southern Italy and Sicily. The fighter units involved in the action were Geschwaderstab, Gruppen I and III of JG 27; II/JG 51 Mölders; Geschwaderstab, Gruppen I, II, and III of JG 53 Pikas; and Geschwaderstab, Gruppen I, II, and II of JG 77 Herzas.

On July 15, 1943, 8 Staffel of JG 27—a new unit operating from Brindisi under Oblt. Wolf Ettel—attacked Allied positions near Catania. This was beyond the short range of the Me 109G, therefore long-range drop tanks were fitted to all aircraft for this mission. Just north of Sicily's Mount Etna, the Staffel was intercepted by Spitfires, one of which was downed by a burst from Ettel's Me 109G. The next day, the unit scrambled on an Alarmstart to intercept 48 British four-engined bombers with a strong Spitfire escort. During the uneven battle—12 Germans versus about 100 Allied planes—Wolf Ettel again scored, this time two bombers and a Spitfire,

giving him a total of 124 victories. The entire III Gruppe of JG 27 was assigned to attack British positions near Catania during the morning of July 17. In a low-level attack, Ettel's Me 109G received a direct anti-aircraft hit which destroyed the plane. He was killed instantly.

The Experten fought with diligence, but their efforts were in vain. Eventually many of the best pilots that Germany had to offer were vanquished in these tournaments in the sky.

THE WAR ON THE RUSSIAN FRONT

We have described the air war on the African desert as a clean war, where the adversaries respected each other's ability and demonstrated the epitome of chivalric ideals. Conversely, the air war on the German/Russian front was full of hatred. A forced landing behind Russian lines was the worst thing that could happen to a Luftwaffe pilot. If his captors shot him on sight he was considered fortunate, indeed. This was illustrated by an incident involving Soviet pilot, Lt. Vladimir Lavrinenkov, 35 victories, who shot down a Messerschmitt in Soviet territory. The German pilot belly-landed and ran to a ditch to hide from the strafing he expected from his victor. Instead, the Russian landed his plane beside the German aircraft, ran to the ditch, and choked the Jagdwaffe pilot to death. He then calmly took off and returned to his unit! This was the air war on the Russian Front.

Even before the combat pilots had recovered from the Battle of Britain, they were called upon not only to help the Italians in Africa and Greece and quench the left-wing revolt in Yugoslavia, but to undertake the biggest task of all: attack the eastern giant, Russia. Because of the enormity of aerial activity, the Russian front generated more German Experten then any other.

Called Operation Barbarossa, the attack on Russia, Germany's historic enemy, was scheduled for 3:00 A.M. of June 22, 1941. The front extended from the Arctic Ocean to the Black Sea, a distance of about 2,000 miles! Assembled for this enormous enterprise were: Luftflotte 1 under Gen. Alfred Keller covering the northern end of the front, with headquarters at Norketten/Chernya Rhovsk and including JG 54 Grunherz under Maj. Hannes Trautloft; Luftflotte 2 under Gen. Albert Kesselring covering the central area of the front, with headquarters at Warsaw/Bielany, and including II and III Gruppen of JG 27 under Maj. Wolfgang Schellmann, JG 51 under Oberst. Werner Mölders, and JG 53 under Maj. Günther von Maltzahn; Luftflotte 4 under Gen. Alexander Lohr covering the southern area of the front, with headquarters at Rzeszow, and including JG 3 under Oberst Günther Lützow, JG 52 under Maj. Hans Trubenbach, and JG 77 under Maj. Bernhard Woldenga; and Luftflotte 5 under Gen. Hans-Jürgen Stumpff covering the far north in cooperation with the Finnish air force, with headquarters in Oslo, and including 13/JG 77. The Luftwaffe committed over 1,900 aircraft to this operation of which just over 400 were single-engine fighters, mostly Messerschmitt Me 109Es with some newer Me 109Fs. This was about 60% of the total Luftwaffe air strength and yet, of the 1,900 aircraft, barely 1,300 were serviceable. This force faced a Red air force of 15,000 aircraft, of which almost one-third were fighters! Combined with the newer Russian fighters were many older types, including the Chato and Moska both of which were used in Spain.

In the darkness of the early morning, German bombers attacked the Russian airfields with 20-pound SD10 fragmentation bombs, sending shrapnel into the aircraft parked on the fields. By dawn's first light, Stukas began pinpoint bombing aircraft and fuel stores on the Soviet airfields, followed by fighters strafing the aircraft that remained on the ground, and engaging any Soviet fighters that managed to get airborne. During the first days of the drive, the Luftwaffe attacked 66 airfields along the Soviet border, concentrating on those containing the newer types of Soviet aircraft. By the end of the first full day of operation, June 22, 1941, over 1,800 Soviet aircraft had been destroyed. Most never left the ground. However, 322 of this total were shot down in aerial combat. The attacking Luftwaffe lost only 32 aircraft. Never in the history of warfare has the world witnessed such total aerial conquest of one nation by another. With the Luftwaffe's precision tactical support and total monopoly of the air, the German troops and armor hounded the retreating Red armies who now found themselves defenseless without any aerial support.

Many Messerschmitts attacked the Russian airfields with the round, SD2 fragmentation bombs. These 4½-pound, finned balls were called "Devil Eggs," because they often became stuck in the specially-constructed bomb magazines beneath the fuselage and, with fuses set, exploded at the slightest shock. A Messerschmitt could carry 96 of the missiles. It was during such a raid on the first day of hostilities that Wolfgang Schellmann, Kommodore of

JG 27, tangled with an intercepting Rata, or Soviet I-16 fighter. Schellmann soon had the Russian in his sights and fired a short burst from all guns at close range. The enemy fighter disintegrated into a thousand pieces.

The Messerschmitt had been so close, and its speed so great, that the 109 overtook the debris and was damaged by the exploding particles. Schellmann took to his 'chute, landed safely, and was captured by Soviet troops. He was never seen again, and it was learned subsequently that he was shot by the NKVD two days later. Bernhard Woldenga succeeded Schellmann to the command of JG 27.

The first months of the invasion came off better than the planners had hoped. A tremendous number of Soviet aircraft lay smashed on the airfields, and countless thousands of Soviet troops were captured. Retreat was the order of the day for the Russians; supplies, factories, and workers were all moved to the Ural mountains where they prepared to manufacture enormous quantities of war material beyond the reach of the Luftwaffe's short-range tactical bombers. Germany planned on, and needed, a victory in six to eight weeks. It turned on the full force of its Blitzkrieg to achieve this objective.

Finland, Hungary, Romania, Croatia, Slovakia and Bulgaria also became involved in the fighting against their common enemy, Russia. Gen. Francisco Franco sent the Spanish Blue Division to fight the Soviets, who had tried to thwart his revolt in Spain. Messerschmitts had already been supplied to Germany's eastern allies in the following quantities: Finland 162; Slovakia 15; Hungary 59; and Bulgaria 145. The Finnish and Hungarian pilots flew their craft with considerable success.

The Jagdwaffe continued its astounding success, shooting down 114 Soviet aircraft in a single day, June 30, 1941. Werner Mölders himself scored five Russian aircraft, his 78th to 82nd victories. Lt. Heinz Baer, who later flew in Africa, and Hptm. Hermann-Friedrich Joppien each shot down five Russian planes on that day as well, making JG 51 the first Geschwader to attain 1,000 victories. Also on June 30, Hannes Trautloft's JG 54 shot down 65 Soviet bombers which were attempting to destroy important bridges. By July 31, Günther von Maltzahn's JG 53 scored its 1,000th victory. On the very next day, Oblt. Scholtz shot down the 1,000th victory for JG 54 Grünherz, and of this total, 623 were Russian aircraft shot down in the previous ten days! Günther Lützow's JG 3 attained its 1,000th victory on August 15th, when Fw. Stechmann shot down three Soviet aircraft.

Werner Mölders had scored his 101st victory on July 15, 1941 and was the first pilot to pass the 100 mark. This remarkable man, who conceived the "finger-four" fighter formation in Spain, never lost the insight and vision required to make further comprehensive tactical innovations, many of which still are considered standard methods in virtually every major air force. Mölders flew a Fiesler Storch STOL aircraft over the front every morning, carrying his own radio. He would land at the front and hide in a foxhole. After he assessed the situation, he'd talk to his pilots in the air and direct the entire attack from his vantage point on the ground. In effect, he became a forward air controller or FAC, a position that became very important to the United States during the Viet Nam action.

Another tactical activity pioneered by Mölders was the temporary joining together, under one leader, of several independent units, including Stukas, fighters, and ground attack aircraft. Once the specific tactical objective was accomplished all would return to their original autonomy. This is similar to the air group system used by the U.S. Navy later in the war in which the temporary leader was the CAG, or Commander Air Group.

In early September, by authoritative estimates, all Soviet aircraft in service on June 22 had been completely destroyed. Yet more and more Russian planes darkened the skies as though from an inexhaustible supply. The Soviets miraculously were able to increase the number of aircraft emerging from factories in the Urals, and elsewhere in Russia, to almost 16,000 in the last six months of 1941. This was about five times the total production in the first six months of 1941; and with no interference from the Luftwaffe bombers! As in the Battle of Britain, Germany needed a long-range, four-engine bomber: the Ural Bomber of General Walther Wever. But the mistake had been made years ago and now it was too late. The Luftwaffe Oberkommando's strategic shortsightedness and false economy in weapons selection and procurement sealed the fate of Nazi Germany.

The German fighter pilots bore the consequence of this fatal error, as theirs was the responsibility of accomplishing the dual task of tactical and strategic aviation. The tactical role included the interception of enemy bombers; escorting Luftwaffe bombers to target; Freie Jagd, or fighter sweeps, to achieve aerial superiority; and strafing, or Jabo, missions to assist the ground and naval forces.

In a well-balanced air force, long range four-engine bombers range deep into enemy territory, bombing factories to halt or slow the production of war materials, thereby accomplishing the strategic role. Because the Soviet factories remained unmolested and produced aircraft by the thousands, it remained for the Jagdwaffe to destroy these aircraft after they had been constructed, armed, and manned, and in the air. In other words, the German fighter pilots were forced to execute the task of the strategic bomber, except that they had to do it the hard way: in aerial combat!

The German advance on Smolensk ground to a halt in the face of stiff Red resistance. The main thrust was therefore, diverted to Leningrad in the north. On September 5 German forces occupied Estonia. Trautloft's JG 54 was very active in the Leningrad sector during September. On September 16, Messerschmitts from this unit escorted the Stukas of St G2 Immelmann, under Oberstlt. Dinort, in an attack on Russian tanks and some ships of the Soviet Baltic fleet. Six days later, the Grünherz were at it again, escorting St G2 Immelmann a second time in bombing raids on a battleship, cruiser, and destroyer in the Baltic Sea. The raids paid off on the following day, Sept. 23, when some well-placed bombs dropped by Hans-Ulrich Rudel sent the Soviet battleship, Marat, to the bottom of the Baltic.

The Messerschmitts flown in the Russian campaign were painted in a variety of colors, reflecting the extremes in weather and terrain. Color schemes included overall white in the extreme north; a light and dark green splinter pattern; a green and brown splinter pattern; and an overall sand color for some areas of the southern and central fronts. As was customary, the entire bottom was painted a very pale sky blue.

In September of 1941, Oberst Mölders was relieved of his JG 51 command and promoted to the new position of General der Jagdfliegern, or General of the Fighter Pilots, thus becoming the youngest general in the German armed forces.

Gen. Ernst Udet, the brilliant fighter ace of the First World War who later became head of the Luftwaffe's technical department and chief of supply, began to realize the folly of the decisions to scrap the long-range bomber and the failure to place priorities on fighter production. Udet had the soul of an artist and loved flying, but was not prepared to cope with the pressures of his position or the intrigues so common to the Luftwaffe. Göring was quick to use Udet as his scapegoat for any bad decision, regardless who made it. Beset by failing health and persistent headaches, Udet began to waste away. On Nov. 17 he could take it no longer and shot himself. On the headboard of his bed was scrawled: "Reichsmarschall, why have you deserted me?" referring, of course, to Göring. Found on his office desk was a note reading: "Build fighters."

The leading Jagdwaffe pilots were summoned to Berlin to form the Honor Guard for the famous Alte Adler's funeral. Mölders, Galland, Müncheberg, Lützow, Ösau and others started for the capital to bid farewell to the departed Udet, who had been both legendary hero and comrade-in-arms to the young Jagdwaffe leaders.

Werner Mölders was directing air strikes in the Crimea when he heard the news and quickly boarded the first plane to Berlin. The Heinkel He 111 bomber crashed en route, killing the young tactician/fighter/leader. The Honor Guard was retained for Mölders' funeral and during the services, Göring selected Oberst Adolf Galland to be Mölders' successor as General of the Jagdwaffe.

Gerhard Schöpfel succeeded Galland as the Kommodore of JG 26 Schlageter. As the new General der Jagdfleiger, Galland was not only responsible for the fighters, but also for the ground-attack units. He selected Oberst Lützow for the position of Inspecteur der Jagdflieger, or Inspector of Fighters, and Oberst Weiss as Inspecteur der Schlachtflieger, or Inspector of Ground attackers. JG 51 was named "Molders" in honor of the fallen fighter leader, and JG 3 was named Udet in honor of the respected Alte Adler. Major Wolf-Dietrich Wilke was given command of JG 3 Udet.

By the end of 1941, the German Blitzkrieg had lost its momentum and the Soviet troops were ready to take the offensive. Army Group South, under von Rundstedt, suffered a serious blow in the Crimea when Soviet forces landed behind the German lines at Kerch and Feodosiya. A third landing, at Eupatoria in early January, 1942, endangered the XI German Army which counterattacked a week later. This thrust was hampered by the absence of strong Luftwaffe support. Air superiority was gradually changing in favor of the Soviet air force.

Further north, Feldmarschall von Bock's Army Group Center stalled just east of Orel and south of the targeted objective of Moscow, due to bad weather and stiff Russian resistance. In the ice and snow of January, 1942, four Soviet armies under Marshall Timoshinko advanced in the Ukraine and penetrated the boundary between Army Groups North and Center on a 60-mile front. The target was Army Group Center and already 100,000 Germans had been surrounded. By February, an airlift was organized to supply the surrounded and isolated troops. Staffels 3/JG 3 and 1/JG 51 provided escort for the Junkers Ju 52 transports as they lumbered toward the Demyansk and Kholm airfields. The Germans operated the airlift until they broke the cordon in May, keeping six divisions supplied with food, guns, and ammunition, and evacuating the wounded and flying in replacements. Soviet aircraft filled the sky all along the front, and replacements would appear as quickly as the Jagdwaffe shot them down. This could be explained by the fact that the Soviet Union produced 7,500 fighters in 1941, while Germany made only 2,300! Despite these odds and impossible objectives, the Jagdwaffe continued to run up most enviable scores. By far, the most formidable Staffel in the spring of 1942 was 9/JG 52, flying with Luftflotte 4 of Army Group South. Led by Hermann Graf, the Staffel included such Experten as Ofw. Leopold Steinbatz, Ofw. Alfred Grislawski, Ofw. Heinrich Füllgrabe, Fw. Ernst Süss as well as several others. During the day period between April 28 and May 14, Graf alone scored 47 victories! He became the seventh German pilot to score one hundred victories when he shot down seven planes on May 14 near Stalingrad. Steinbatz, who served as Graf's wingman, shot down 35 Soviet aircraft during the month of May, and became the first noncommissioned pilot to be awarded the Ritterkreutz mit Eichenlaub, or Knights Cross with Oak Leaves. On May 8, JG 52 scored its 1,500th victory and, by June 3, the score had reached 2,000.

Hannes Trautloft's JG 54 Grünherz shot down its 2,222th victory on May 14, 1942, and Oblt. Max-Helmuth Ostermann of that unit attained his 100th victory on May 12. Lt. Hans Götz of 2/JG 54 scored 25 victories during May, and Oblt. Heinrich Jung of 4/JG 54 shot down 18. Several Grünherz pilots experimented with night fighter missions. Hptm. Joachim Wandel of 5/JG 54 scored 16 victories in night actions, while Oblt. Erwin Leykauf shot down 6 Soviet planes during the night of June 22/23. JG 54 scored its 3,000th victory on Sept. 7, 1942.

Hptm. Heinz Baer, Gruppenkommandeur of IV/JG 51 Mölders, became the ninth pilot to reach 100 victories on May 19. JG 51 boasted 3,511 victories by August 4, 1942.

On May 19, JG 77 scored its 2,011th victory and on the next day the Kommodore, Maj. Gordon Gollob, became the tenth Jagdflieger to reach the 100 mark.

Wolf-Dietrich Wilkes' JG 3 Udet scored its 2,000th victory on May 28, 1942.

In early 1942, the Luftwaffe formed an entirely new Jagdgeschwader in Norway and Finland, JG 5 Eismeer, or Artic Sea. The unit was created from parts of I/JG 77 and IV/JG 1, and was placed under the command of Oberst Gotthardt Handrick.

May/June 1942 saw the German XI Army, under Gen. von Manstein, launch an offensive against the

Kerch Peninsula in the Crimea. The attack succeeded, capturing Sevastopol on July 3, and Rostov on July 23. An attempt to duplicate this success on the Leningrad front failed when the Russians began their own offensive before the Germans were ready! In August, the XI Army was transferred from Army Group South to Army Group North, where it joined the XVI Army. Manstein was to command both armies in this new assault on Leningrad, but, once again, on September 4, the Russians attacked first. The transfer of the XI Army to the north had fatal consequences for the Germans in the south because, on November 19, the Soviet forces attacked weak points left in the German line. This precipitated the Battle of Stalingrad.

By the Autumn of 1942, Gen. Wolfram von Richthofen had replaced Gen. Lohr as commander of Luftflotte 4 with Army Group South, and Feldmarschall von Manstein was appointed commander of all the Stalingrad sector forces; "Heeres-Gruppen-Kommando-Don." His objective was to halt all Soviet offensives in the area and launch attacks to recapture lost territory. This was virtually impossible, due to the immense size of the Russian forces and their complete encirclement of Gen. Paulus' VI army at Stalingrad. Reflecting on the previous spring's successful airlift to Army Group Center, it was decided to keep the VI Army supplied from the air. This required seven hundred tons to be flown every day! Remember that in 1942 the mere idea of an airlift was revolutionary, and supplying an entire army from the air was called madness. Yet, the decision held.

Poor November weather prohibited all flying and, with the Luftwaffe grounded, the Russians made the logical move; they attacked and crushed the 3rd Romanian Army guarding the VI Army's flank. This forced the airlift into action in December, 1942. The transports flew from two airfields in German-held territory outside the encirclement, Morozovsk and Tazinskaya, to two within the perimeter, Gumrak and Pitomnik. As soon as the Russians saw the airlift in progress, they made plans to capture the supplying airfields.

On November 1, JG 51 scored its 4,000 victory. During this month, Oberst Dieter Hrabak became Kommodore of JG 52. His new command reached the 4,000 victory mark on December 10, 1942.

Keeping pace with the fierce ground struggle the pilots of JG 3 and JG 52 fought against overwhelming odds, nevertheless they exacted a terrifying toll on Soviet aircraft. Wolf-Dietrich Wilke and his pilots flew several sorties each day in an attempt to stop the Soviet advance. Six volunteers from II/JG 3

formed a Pitomnik defense Staffel and based themselves within the blockaded Stalingrad perimeter. Hptm. Germeroth led the tiny unit from early December to mid-January and, due to their tireless strafing of Soviet troops and intercepting of Russian fighters and ground-attack aircraft, the intrepid band insured the inward flow of supplies and the outward flow of 43,000 wounded Germans! All this despite the fact that, very often, they had only two or three serviceable Messerschmitts, flown in a continuous rotation from dawn to dusk! In about six weeks these remarkable II/JG 3 Udet volunteers shot down 130 Soviet aircraft. The unit's high scorer was Fw. Kurt Ebener, who shot down 33 heavily-armored Shturmovik ground-attack planes, bringing his victory total to 51. But six near-exhausted pilots couldn't hold off the Russian air force and the Red Army forever.

On November 19, the Soviets mounted a massive attack against the Romanian forces north of Stalingrad, forcing them to retreat.

The Morozovsk and Tazinskaya airfields fell during the Christmas holidays. The Russians launched their major offensive on January 10, 1943, pressing inward on the perimeter toward the Pitomnik and Gumrak airfields in an attempt to seal off the VI Army. When, on January 16, Soviet troops appeared at the edge of Pitomnik airfield and began opening fire, the six Messerschmitts withdrew from the snowcovered field with six Stuka dive bombers. The Pitomnik Staffel was ordered to proceed to the other inner airfield, Gumrak, even though this field had not been resurfaced after several shellings. The first Messerschmitt overturned in a snowdrift; the second fell into a shellhole; by the time the condition of the field became evident, only one Me 109G remained airborne. The last pilot, Oblt. Lukas, gunned his engine at the final moment when he saw the wreckage-strewn field. His was the only plane of the Staffel to escape. One week later the Germans at Stalingrad surrendered.

Despite grave losses and the Soviets' five-to-one air superiority, the Jagdwaffe continued through the spring of 1943 with their astounding achievement record on the Eastern Front. Fw. Otto Kittel of JG 54 shot down a Soviet plane in flames on February 23, 1943, marking the Geschwader's 4,000th victory. On the seventh of the following month, the pilots of JG 54 scored 59 Soviet planes in the one day. On June 8, JG 51 scored 51 victories in only 20 minutes. With a strength of 4,000 aircraft in the spring of 1943 (with few, if any, reserves), the Luftwaffe even placed into action Lehrgeschwadern—advanced training units consisting mainly of instructors of advanced aerial combat concepts. The survival chances for eastern front German fighter pilots in 1943 were most unfavorable: 25% of them did not live through their first four missions. It got to the point where the poor or mediocre fighter pilot did not stand a chance against the odds he had to face several times each day and, conversely, the talented and accomplished German fighter pilot found himself in a sky full of hostile aircraft—a veritable shooting gallery. Those of indifferent talent remain unknown, their only memorial a burned-out Messerschmitt hulk, while the Experten flashed across the skies achieving never-before-imagined scores. The highest scoring aces of all time emerged from the Russian front: Erich Hartmann, 352 victories; Gerhard Barkhorn, 301; Günther Rall, 275; Otto Kittel, 267; Walter Nowotny, 258; Wilhelm Batz, 237; Hermann Graf, 212; Anton Hafner, 204 victories; and many others who hurled themselves on the enemy with amazing success.

Unlike combat against the Western Allies, the aerial fighting on the Russian front was conducted at relatively low altitudes and at slow speeds: usually under 10,000 feet, often below 5,000 feet and at speeds of 100 to 280 miles per hour. The Germans called this Kurvenkampf. At times, the aerial activity was just above tree-top level, and there is evidence of Jagdwaffe pilots crashing into trees during dogfights.

The Russian winter offensives of 1942–43 not only recaptured Stalingrad, Rostov and Kursk, but also all the territory between the Sea of Azov and the Caucasus Mountains. The resulting situation—a German bulge in the front at Orel facing eastward, and a Russian bulge in the front at Kursk facing westward—tempted the Germans to attack. Both adversaries realized the opportunity of isolating their enemy's salient with a classic pincer movement; therefore both sides prepared for a summer offensive. It was a far more important action to the Germans than to the Soviets, because to win would open the road from Orel to Moscow. It would also be a sign that the German armies were still invincible in the art of lightning war. Preparations began in May, but a continuing series of delays and postponements, such as the buildup of Gen. Model's Panzer force, gave the Russians time to prepare for the battle. They waited for the Germans to start their most important offensive of the eastern front.

Operation Zitadelle, or Citadel as it was called, was scheduled for July 5, 1943 as twin drives: one from Orel, north of Kursk, and the other from Belgorod, south of Kursk. Other fronts were drained and reserves transferred from Germany, until the Luftwaffe had available 1,700 aircraft of all types. This was to be Germany's last offensive in Russia. The Panzers lay ready to attack the waiting Russian armor, assisted by ground-attack units and supported by eight Jagdgruppen: II/JG 3, III/JG 3, I/JG 51, III/JG 51, IV/JG 51, I/JG 52, III/JG 52, and III/JG 54. The 1st, 4th, and 16th Soviet Air Armies faced the Jagdfliegern, and launched their own air attack before one German bomber had left the crowded airfields at Kharkov, just south of Belgorod. The Russian armada headed directly for Kharkov, and it appeared that the German attack would be doomed before it started! Engines idling, the Kharkov bombers' takeoff was delayed as the fighters of JG 3 taxied between them and took off to intercept the approaching Soviet Air Army. Simultaneously, the Jagdgruppen of JG 52 were taking off from their airfield at Mikoyanovka for the intercept. Within moments the first of the Jagdfliegern made contact with the Red air force, and aerial combat began. It developed into the largest and fiercest air battle of all time: four Jagdgruppen, or about 140 aircraft, against 500 Soviet bombers, ground attack planes, and fighters.

Flying the Me 109G, the Jagdfliegern shot down 432 Russian aircraft in this air battle and lost only 26. Seventy-seven victories, including 62 bombers, went to the pilots of II/JG 3. In one of the day's many air actions this Gruppe shot down 31 of a 46-plane Soviet formation. The unit's top scorer of the day was Oblt. Joachim Kirschner, who scored nine victories. II/JG 3 Gruppenkommandeur Maj. Kurt Brandle brought his victory score up to 151 by shooting down five Soviet aircraft near Belgorod. Other II/JG 3 pilots to score multiple victories on the first day of the Kursk offensive were: Hptm. Lemke, 4 victories; Oblt. Lucas, 5; and Oblt. Bitsch 6 victories. II/JG 3 under Maj. Wolfgang Ewald shot down 38 Soviet aircraft, of which 3 were scored by the Gruppen-kommandeur. Thirty-five Russian planes went down before the guns of III/JG 52, with multiple victories claimed by Hptm. Wiese, 12 victories; Oblt. Krupinski, 11; and Lt. Korts, 4. Flying up to six missions a day, the Jagdwaffe continued to the point of exhaustion.

The heavy air battles continued through the week while the world's largest tank battles raged below. It was during Operation Zitadelle that Erich Hartmann, destined to become the world's leading ace, seemed to blossom into proficiency. Flying an Me 109G with 9/JG 52, based at Ugrim in the Ukraine, he took off at dawn, which in the long north European summer is about 3:30 A.M. Hartmann was part of a four-plane Schwarm patrolling at 6,000 ft., which came upon 20 heavily-armored Shturmovik, or Stormavik, IL-2 ground-attack aircraft, flying in the opposite direction at 4,000 ft. Although almost impervious to machine-gun fire, this Russian plane did have an Achilles' heel: the underslung oil cooler in the nose. The Schwarm first overflew the Russians, and then quickly half-rolled, dived and zoomed under the Shturmoviks' tails, coming at the Russian fighters from their rear gunners blindspots. At a range of about 100 yards, Hartmann fingered the machine-gun trigger on the control stick while stroking the cannon-firing button atop the control column. When the enemy loomed large in his sight, he sent a short burst into the oil cooler. Trailing a long stream of oil black smoke, the IL-2 smashed into the ground. It was Hartmann's 22nd victory. By this time, the Shturmoviks had broken their rigid formation and divided into pairs and individual aircraft. Selecting his second victim, Hartmann dived at once. The Soviet pilot panicked and began a climbing turn, enabling Hartmann to fire a deflection burst at 150 yards, striking the Russian dead-center in the oil cooler. The Shturmovik headed groundward and Hartmann had his 23rd kill. A fast return to Ugrim, because of diminishing fuel, was in order. After a quick breakfast, a debriefing and a nap, the Schwarm was again airborne—only 45 minutes after landing! Almost immediately the four Messerschmitts encountered more Shturmoviks, and shortly after they began the attack they were jumped by LaGG-3 fighters. In the ensuing melee Hartmann downed one more IL-2, and one of the escorting fighters before returning to base for refueling and lunch. The Schwarm engaged more LaGG fighters that afternoon, three of which fell before Hartmann's guns—making his score for the day 7 victories and enlarging his total to 28. He scored 16 victories during the week of the Kursk offensive.

During the air battles of July 7, 1943, Hartmann's Geschwader, JG 52, reached the 6,000 victory mark, while the Jagdwaffe as a whole shot down 193 Soviet aircraft. JG 52 was one of the most successful fighter units, with six of the top fifteen eastern front Experten flying in this Geschwader. They shot down a total of 1,580 enemy aircraft and, despite overwhelmingly odds of 20 to 1, five of the six survived the war. Not all the members of JG 52 were German; 15/JG 52 was a special Croatian Staffel attached to the unit and led by Oberstlt. Fanjo Dzal, who scored 15 victories.

On July 11, the Russians initiated their long-dreaded counter-offensive north of Orel. This forced the German Army and Luftwaffe units to abandon the Kursk offensive to defend against this new at-tack. Russian tanks were pouring through a breach in the front north of Orel and the Luftwaffe was assigned to prevent another Stalingrad. Operating from Karachev, north of Orel, bombers, Stukas, ground-attack planes and fighters began pounding the Russian forces on July 19. Virtually every battle-worthy Gruppe on the Eastern Front had been packed into the area to concentrate on the breakthrough, and by July 21 they had rolled back the Russian thrust and saved Gen. Walter Model's two armies, the 9th and 2nd Panzer, from complete encirclement. In fact, Gen. Model officially expressed his gratitude and gave full credit to the Luftwaffe for their effort. This action proved that, when properly applied, the Luftwaffe was a most effective weapon quite capable of changing the course of battles.

Instead of returning to the Kursk effort, which had started with a measure of success, many Luftwaffe units were transferred to the Mediterranean and Italy to deal with the Allied landings on Sicily and the Italian mainland. The Kursk offensive was therefore abandoned, proving once again that the Luftwaffe was spread too thinly to be fully effective, and that too much was expected of so small a force. Although the Luftwaffe was able to destroy an entire Soviet armored brigade during one action, it could not achieve a decisive victory due to the enemy's overwhelming might. In addition to the Allied landings and the losses in Africa, the Jagdwaffe also had to worry about the ever-increasing frequency and intensity of the Anglo-American air raids on the German-held Continent. Fighter units were transferred to the west to assist JG 2 Richthofen and JG 26 Schalageter in their attempt to stem the tide of the Allied strategic bombing.

JG 51 Mölders scored its 6,000th victory late in July, 1943.

The units which remained on the eastern front fought with continued success, but were essentially engaged in a retreat action. The Luftwaffe could no longer mount huge fighter offensives because the units were so dispersed and subjected to increasingly frequent calls for assistance from the ground forces. After the nightmares of Stalingrad and Kursk, the Red air force began using newer types of fighters. These were virtually equal to the Messerschmitt, and definitely superior at the very low altitudes where they forced the Jagdwaffe to fight. Many old faces disappeared from the Staffels and the new faces were not around long enough to be remembered.

The Russians captured Kiev on November 6th.

On December 4, 1943, JG 52 scored its 8,000th victory followed by JG 54 Grünherz, which attained

Klaus Bretschneider and Konrad Bauer of Sturmgruppe II/JG 300 were among the most successful "Wild Sau" night interceptor pilots.

An Me 109G prepares to take off for a "Wild Sau" intercept.

7,000 victories on March 23, 1944, JG 51 Mölders counted its 8,000th victory on May 1, while it was not until August 15th that JG 54 scored its 8,000th. On Sept. 2, 1944, JG 52 attained the amazing score of 10,000 victories!

Based in Norway and Finland, the four Gruppen of JG 5 Eismeer, or Arctic Sea, operated with the Finnish air force at the northern extreme of the eastern front. This unit was now gradually withdrawn to northern Russia and then to the west in early 1944. Even the intrepid Finns, who scored well in the Winter War, couldn't stand for long against the Russian steamroller. Nine Finnish fighter pilots scored more than 30 victories. The top Finnish aces were: Eino Ilmari Juutilainen, 94 victories; Hasse Wind, 78; Eino Luukkanen, 54; Jatti Letovaara, 44; Puhakka, 43; Oippa Tuominen, 43; Nils Katajainen, 36; Lauri Nissinen, 32; and Joppe Karlunen, 31 victories. In addition to the Finns, two outstanding Luftwaffe Experten achieved prominence on the Finnish front: Major Heinrich Ehrler, Kommodore of JG 5 Eismeer, shot down 209 enemy aircraft while Major Theodor Weissenberger, Kommandeur of I/JG 5, scored 208 victories.

The Jagdwaffe found many of their airfields surrounded by Soviet troops in the winter of 1943/44, with no escape except to fly out. Most units caught in this predicament ordered the pilots to escape and left the ground personnel to their fate; but not JG 54 Grünherz. Seats were removed from the Messerschmitts and all extra weight was pared to the minimum, including fuel and ammunition. One mechanic crawled into the fuselage while a second perched himself where the seat had been and, in fact, became the seat for the pilot who sat on his knees. Thus JG 54 airfields were safely evacuated during this trying period for the Jagdwaffe on the eastern front.

On August 23, 1944, a coup d'etat in Romania, coupled with a surprise Russian offensive, led to the withdrawal of German forces. The fall of Bulgaria and Hungary followed as the Soviet advance remained unchecked. Gruppe I/JG 53 assisted in covering the German retreat. By Autumn, the Luftwaffe was outnumbered by about 20 to 1, and had virtually no fuel and ammunition. Retreat was the order of the day, retreat and transfer to the West to combat the thousands of strategic bombers pulverizing German cities and industry in around-the-clock raids: the Americans by day and the British by night.

THE WAR IN WESTERN EUROPE

Unlike the Luftwaffe, the Royal Air Force and the U.S. Army Air Force placed considerable faith in the four-engined, long-range strategic bomber, devoting time, talent, and money to its development. The R.A.F. Bomber Command concentrated on night bombing after the disastrous raid near Wilhelmshaven on December 18, 1939, previously described. Flying night missions over Germany during the winter of 1940/41, the R.A.F. discovered an alarming fact. After raiding two oil refineries, with about 300 bombers at night, reconnaissance revealed that the refineries were virtually intact after the raid. Bomber Command had been assuming that the night-bombing margin for error was 300 yards, which was most optimistic. The estimate was later increased to 1,000 yards, which also proved incorrect. In the Autumn of 1941, an analysis of night photographs taken by the bombers themselves, as they dropped the bombs, showed that only about 30% of the bombs fell within five miles of the target. When bombing the industrialized Ruhr Valley, only about ten percent did so.

The U.S. Army Air Force began moving aircraft, supplies and crews to Britain in preparation for the dual aerial offensive on the Continent. Unlike the R.A.F., the Americans had not experienced the dangers of daylight bombing. They decided then to conduct precision daylight bombing, and leave the night raids to the British; but it was not until mid-1942 that the U.S. launched its first raid on the Continent. Although JG1, under Oberst Erich Mix, based in northwestern Germany; JG 2 Richthofen, under Oberst Walther Ösau, based in the Netherlands; and JG 26 Schlageter, under Maj. Gerhard Schöpfel, based in France were kept busy fighting off Bomber Command's "nonstop offensive," the raids over the Continent during the 1941/42 winter were small and relatively ineffective when compared to the 1,000-bomber raids to come.

It was in January 1942 that the Jagdwaffe units in the west were called upon to perform an important task for the German navy. The 26,000-ton battleships Scharnhorst and Gneisenau, the 10,000-ton cruiser Prinz Eugen and seven destroyers were to be moved from Brest, France to safer anchorages at Kiel and Wilihelmshaven in northern Germany during early February, 1942. It was decided to make the move via the English Channel instead of circumnavigating Ireland, England and Scotland, because air cover was of prime importance and the Luftwaffe's limited range made the Channel route imperative. Luftwaffe Chief of Staff Gen. Hans Jeschonnek placed the entire operation in the hands of General der Jagdfliegern Adolf Galland, who selected Oberst Max Ibel to be the Jagdflieger-Fuhrer-Bord, or the liaison officer with the Kriegsmarine, or Navy. The name given to this operation was Thunderbolt, and it was scheduled to begin on the night of Feb. 11/12, 1942.

To cover Operation Thunderbolt, Galland was able to draw 90 Me 109Fs from Jg 26; 60 Me 109Fs from JG 1; and a dozen other Messerschmitts from the fighter school in Paris. Twin-engine Messerschmitt Me 110 night-fighters were also to be used for nocturnal operations, bringing the total number of fighters at Galland's disposal to 252. Of this number 25 to 30 were held in reserve, standing by for immediate action on various airfields along the route. The pilots sat in their Messerschmitts with belts fastened and engines warm, ready to take off at a moment's notice.

The flotilla weighed anchor on the evening of February 11, with strict secrecy and radio silence. However, by the following morning, an R.A.F. fighter had spotted the force as it approached the narrowest point in the Channel. By 1:00 P.M. Fairey Swordfish torpedo planes, escorted by Spitfires, attacked the convoy. Obserst Ibel, on board the Scharnhorst, directed the Jagdwaffe fighters to the attackers. While the Messerschmitts engaged the Spitfires, the ship's antiaircraft guns shot down six of the slow-flying Swordfish. Three hours later, the Jadgwaffe drove off five Westland Whirlwind twin-engine fighter-bombers, shot down one four-engine bomber and drove off a second. Off Cherbourg, 15 E-boats joined the convoy in order to strengthen the outer safety belt. At 3:25 P.M. two more Whirlwinds were shot down by German fighters while attacking the Gneisenau. The attacks continued throughout the day, and included raids by Bristol Blenheim bombers, Bristol Beaufort Bombers, Vickers Wellington bombers and Handley-Page Hereford bombers, plus Spitfires, Whirlwinds and Swordfish torpedo planes. Of the 250 planes that the British launched by Fleet Air Arm, Coastal Command, Strategic Bomber Command and Fighter Command, including 15 Fighter squadrons, only 39 British aircraft could get close enough to the flotilla to launch attacks!

The ships all arrived at their destination as planned. This was much to the amazement, alarm, and horror of the R.A.F., as it was the first time since 1690 that strong enemy forces had passed through the Channel successfully. Also amazing was the fact that while the bulk of the Luftwaffe was engaged in Russia and the Mediterranean, it managed to maintain a decisive superiority over the Royal Air Force. If nothing more, this proved that the Jagdwaffe could, when not saddled with an inflexible task, and even when assigned to a purely defensive role, retain its initiative and emerge victorious.

During this action, JG 26 lost four pilots and JG 2 lost three pilots. The total loss to the Jagdwaffe was 17 aircraft and 17 pilots, while they shot down a confirmed 49 British aircraft, plus 13 probables!

Feldmarschall Hugo Sperrle, commander of Luftflotte 3, issued a directive on March 10, 1942 that Jagdbomber (Jabo), or fighter-bomber, Staffeln be formed for the Richthofen and Schlageter Geschwadern, to be known as 10 Jabo/JG 2 and 10 Jabo/JG 26. The Jabo raids were aimed against factories, railyards, ships, barracks and harbor installations, with each Messerschmitt carrying one 500-kg., two 250-kg. or four 100-kg. bombs. These "hit and run" raiders ranged widely over the southeastern coast of England, seriously denting civilian morale. Even more importantly, the Jabo raids caused disruption and strain on the Fighter Command defense organization totally out of proportion to the number of Jabo aircraft involved. The Jabo was virtually impossible to counter, even by the tedious and uneconomical standing patrols introduced by R.A.F. fighters. Jabo sorties were often launched with no predetermined target. These were, in fact, searches for "targets of opportunity" and were often called "reconnaissance with bombs." Staffel 10 of the Richthofen Geschwader had been in existence since November, 1941, before Sperrle's order, and by June 26, 1942, under the leadership of Hptm. Frank Liesendahl, 10/JG 2 had sunk 20 ships totaling about 63,000 tons. The Jabo Staffels in the west were converted to interceptor duty in the summer of 1942.

Contemporary with the Jabo formation in March, 1942, the British War Cabinet decided that it was imperative to arrest German war production through the night bombing of industrial targets. The order came down that large scale raids should begin at once. Bombings began on the night of March 3/4, when 235 R.A.F. bombers attacked the Renault factory at Billancourt, France in three waves, dropping 641 tons of explosives. The first German town to suffer a mass Bomber Command night raid was the port city of Lübeck, where 191 aircraft dropped 300 tons of bombs on the night of March 28/29. Over 100 tons of the total were incendiary, and enormous fires erupted. Rostock was the next target. Four consecutive nights of bombing raids began on April 23/24, when 468 bombers dropped 750 tons of bombs, 300 tons of which were incendiary. Only 12 bombers were lost, but 70% of the city was devastated!

General der Jagdflieger Galland, Oberst Lützow and Feldmarschall Milch fully realized the impending danger of this stepped-up bombing offensive, and foresaw larger raids in the future. They argued in vain for increased fighter-plane production and additional fighter-pilot training programs. Instead of listening to his experts, Hitler embarked on a campaign of revenge, ordering more bombers and not fighters! Even the first 1,000-plane raid on Cologne, during the night of May 30/31, could not convince Germany's political leaders that more fighters were needed.

A significant event took place on Aug. 17, 1942 which cast a long shadow on the Luftwaffe defense posture in the West. On that day, 18 Boeing B-17E Flying Fortresses from the 97th Bomber Group, led by Gen. Ira Eaker, bombed Rouen–Sotteville, France without losing a single bomber. The U.S. 8th Army Air Force began their operations convinced that daylight bombing could be successful, provided the bombers were sufficiently armed. The B-17 bristled with .50 caliber machine guns and flew a formation devised for mutual defense and maximum combined fire power. They were initially escorted as far as possible by fighters. The Jagdwaffe quickly learned that individual attacks against well-armed B-17s were like flying into a hornet's nest, and only close-formation attacks were successful against these bombers. This luxury of being able to concentrate on the bombers alone didn't last long, though. Soon long-range fighters would accompany the Allied bombers all the way to their target.

A new era in the air war over Western Europe began on Jan. 27, 1943. On that day, 55 8th Air Force Flying Fortresses, escorted by P-38 Lightning fighters, bombed Wilhelmshaven harbor and only lost three bombers to the interceptors of JG 1. This was the first of many raids that the USAAF was to make on German cities. The continued success of the U.S. raids made it obvious that, although fighters were in short supply on all fronts, the defense of Germany was not receiving the attention it deserved. Finally, on March 27, III/JG 54 was transferred from the Russian Front and five days later a new Geschwader was created from I/JG 1, III/JG 1, and 2/JG 27. It was called JG 11, and placed under the command of Major Anton Mader, previously Kommandeur of II/JG 77. Also on April 1, Major Hans Philipp took over the command of JG 1 from Oberstlt. Mix, and JG 54 was transferred from Russia to Oldenburg to combat the bombers.

In addition to this minor reorganization, several experiments were conducted with new armaments with which to combat the bombers. One idea was to attach a time-fused 250-kg. bomb under the fuselage of a Messerschmitt, climb above the bombers, then drop the bomb in their midst! On March 22, Lt. Heinz Knocke of 5/JG 1 destroyed a B-17 using this method. Other tests included large-caliber cannon and 210-mm. rocket tubes under each wing. This added weight however, so reduced the Messerschmitt's performance that was no longer a match for the U.S. fighters.

The Boeing B-17 Flying Fortress bomber bristled with .50 caliber machine guns (hence the name). The volume of defensive fire from a B-17 formation was more than enough to blow an attacking fighter out of the sky. Two Jagdwaffe Experten, Georg-Peter Eder and Egon Mayer, discovered, after studying the problem, that the Fortress formation's defensive fire was weakest in its forward hemisphere. This then was the almost-impenetrable B-17 formation's

Achilles heel. Eder and Mayer's tactic of speeding head on into the bomber formation required nerves of steel and instant reflexes, because the closure rate was almost 600 miles per hour! This speed gave the bomber gunners little time to fire, and kept the tail and waist gunners from shooting because of the angle of approach and for fear of striking another bomber in the formation. Eder and Mayer proved the success of their method and a great number of Jagdwaffe pilots adopted their attack system.

German fighter production had jumped from 700 in February to 1,000 in June and, although still inadequate, the Allies across the Channel were worried by this buildup. This resulted in a plan, prepared by the chief of the 8th Air Force, Gen. Ira C. Eaker, for the total destruction of the German fighter force and its center of production. This was imperative, according to the general, because the Jagdwaffe's existence would make it impossible to carry out bombing raids on the Continent. It will be remembered that the Luftwaffe had the very same objective in the Battle of Britain, but lacked the weapons to accomplish the task. The U.S. Army Air Force however, had all the necessary weapons to achieve its objective, and this endeavor was called Operation Argument.

Meanwhile, the preoccupation of the Luftwaffe in the Mediterranean and Russia gave Britain the splendid opportunity to build a fleet of giant four-engined Short Stirling, Handley-Page Halifax and Avro Lancaster bombers. A list of prime targets on the Continent was also prepared, including Essen, Duisburg, Cologne, Düsseldorf, Bremen, Hamburg, and Schweinfurt, among others. Actually, the fate of German cities had been sealed since the Casablanca Directive, prepared at the Jan. 21, 1943 conference, gave Bomber Command the choice of bombing any German industrial city of 100,000 or more inhabitants.

On May 14, the pilots of III/JG 54 intercepted three hundred Flying Fortresses over the north German coast, losing eight Messerschmitts in the conflict. On the following day, seven more Me 109 Gs were downed by the Allies, and one of the Gruppe's leading pilots, Lt. Friedrich Rupp, 53 victories, was lost.

In July 1943, reinforcements arrived to combat the waves of bombers: JG 3 under Oberst Wolf-Dietrich Wilke returned from southern Russia; II/JG 27 under Hptm. Werner Schrör was transferred from Vibo Valentia, Italy to Weisbaden–Erbenheim, Germany; and II/JG 51 under Hptm. Karl Rommelt moved from Sardinia to an airfield near Munich. These units were to prove their worth during the Schweinfurt raid on the 17th of August when 229 Fortresses of the 1st Bomber Wing headed for a vital ball-bearing plant and were met by about 200 fighters. In furious battles, the Messerschmitts, using cannon, rockets, and bombs destroyed 39 bombers with almost 400 crew members, while another 100 Fortresses returned to base badly damaged. The Schweinfurt raid was the first serious implementation of the USAAF policy to destroy the Luftwaffe fighter force, though it proved disastrous due to the absence of escort fighters.

In addition to the unit relocations, two new specialized Gruppen were established in July: JG 25 under Maj. Herbert Ihlefeld, and JG 50 under Maj. Hermann Graf. These units were organized to combat the swift twin-engine De Havilland Mosquito intruder bombers.

As the Jagdfliegern learned more about combating the Fortresses, battle outcomes often shifted in their favor. During a July 28 attack on a B-17 formation, Fw. Fest of 5/JG 11 destroyed three bombers after a direct hit with a single 250-kg. bomb. Of the 22 Fortresses lost on this date, 11 were shot down by Hptm. Günther Specht, Kommandeur of II/JG 11. Hptm. Specht had lost his left eye in December, 1939 over the North Sea, but returned to combat to become one of Germany's outstanding pilots, and eventually became Kommodore of JG 11. On July 26, 92 B-17s bombed Hannover and 50 raided Hamburg at 24,000 ft. The Jagdwaffe shot down 16 over Hannover and 8 over Hamburg.

The Allies put Operation Gomorrah into effect late in July when, during the nights of July 25/26, July 28/29, and Aug. 2/3, 800 or more Lancaster and Halifax bombers raided Hamburg. Six thousand acres of the city were destroyed, and over 40,000 of its inhabitants perished. The R.A.F. wreaked havoc with the radar-controlled German night fighters by dropping enormous quantities of tin foil to obliterate the interceptors' radar readings. This British tactic took the Luftwaffe by surprise, and its confidence in radar-equipped night fighters was shattered. An alternate solution for nocturnal interception was desperately needed.

The best solution to this vexing problem was proposed by Maj. Hajo Herrmann, a Luftwaffe bomber pilot who was Kommandeur of III/KG 30, a group that had been especially successful in its attacks on Allied convoys. Maj. Herrmann noted that with a burning target below, his bombers were silhouetted and clearly visible from overhead. His idea was to augment this target light with flares, searchlights, and flak, and then use freelance single-engine fighters to strike at the bombers over the target area using visual sighting exclusively. The idea was approved at once and put into operation during the last days of July. The system was named Wilde Sau, or Wild Boar, and an experimental unit was organized at once, known as Kommando Herrmann. The success of this unit was such that a Wilde Sau Geschwader was established under the designation JG 300, with Maj. Herrmann in charge. This unit, in turn, proved so successful that a further two Wilde Sau Geschwadern were formed and designated JG 301 and JG 302. The three Geschwadern were united to form 30 Jagddivisionen consisting of: JG 300 under Oberstlt. Kurt Kettner, based near Bonn; JG 301 under Maj. Helmut Weinreich, based near Munich; and JG 302 under Maj. Manfred Massinger, based near Berlin.

Two outstanding Experten emerged from the Wilde Sau units: Klaus Bretschneider and Konrad Bauer of II/JG 300. The Me 109G-6 aircraft used in the Wilde Sau operations carried a radar warning and homing receiver with a thirty-mile range. This indicated direction, but not the range of an escorting Mosquito fighter, or the Messerschmitt's home airfield. In view of the shortage of fighter planes, only one Gruppe in each Wilde Sau geschwader had its own aircraft; the other Gruppen were forced to share their aircraft, and an airfield with day-fighter Gruppen. This duplication of operations meant constant action for the aircraft, and while increasing the need for maintenance it simultaneously allowed no time for it. This condition drastically reduced aircraft serviceability, and after sustaining severe losses during the winter of 1943/44, the Gruppen gradually transferred to conventional day fighter operations.

The U.S. 9th Air Force began bombing German-held territory from air bases in North Africa on Aug. 1. On this date, 178 B-24 Liberator bombers headed for the Romanian oilfields at Ploieşti. Hptm. Hans Hahn and his I/JG 4 intercepted them from their base at Mizil only twenty miles from Ploieşti. The Royal Bulgarian Fighter Regiment under Hptm. Toma assisted the Me 109 Gs of I/JG 4, and together the units shot down 50 Liberators. During the melee, a message was quickly sent to IV/JG 27 based at Kalamaki, Greece, informing them of the raid. The unit scrambled and intercepted the Liberators on their return flight to Benghazi, and Oblt. Alfred Burk's IV/JG 27 shot down four more B-24's. Fifty-five of the bombers sustained serious damage.

Another 9th Air Force raid was aimed at the Wiener-Neustadter Flugzeugwerke near Vienna, on Aug. 13. This firm produced Messerschmitts under contract license and therefore was a prime target for the U.S. Army Air Force. No fighters were available to contest the bombers and, because of this, a JafuOstmark was created for the air defense of southern Germany.

Three days later the U.S.A.A.F. inaugurated the practice of shuttle-bombing with a raid on the Regensburg Messerschmitt factory by England-based Boeing B-17's. Instead of returning to England after the bombing was complete the Fortresses turned south and continued on to U.S. bases in North Africa. This maneuver confused the Luftwaffe defense units, and before they could effectively react, the bombers were crossing the Mediterranean to Africa.

Germany's military leaders, prodded by Gen. Galland, now began to realize that fighter production must take absolute priority if the Jagdwaffe was to successfully combat the giant bombers. It was at this crucial moment that the Luftwaffe Chief of Staff Gen. Hans Jeschonnek committed suicide, realizing that many of his past decisions had been wrong and it was now too late to rectify them. Like Ernst Udet before him, Jeschonnek left a note which read: "I can no longer work with the Reichsmarschall." Göring had always denied responsibility for past mistakes and continually shifted blame to his subordinates. He could never face the true facts and, instead of solutions, he could only offer insults. General Günther Korten, deputy commander of Luftflotte 1, was appointed to succeed Jeschonnek. Despite Minister for Supply and War Production Albert Speer's efforts to boost fighter plane production, the German aircraft industry actually produced fewer fighter planes than before! This decline in production can be directly attributed to the U.S. Army Air Force's bombing program. German fighter production dropped from about 700 in July, to about 500 in September and to about 350 in December of 1943. Still, the Jagdwaffe fought well and exacted a bloody toll of bombers.

Five Flieger Divisions, or Air Divisions, were dedicated to air defense in the west. All headquarters installations were equipped with huge underground operations rooms, complete with mapping grids, charts, and communications to the various Jagdgeschwadern. Alte Adler, or former World War I pilots, were in charge of these Flieger Divisions: No. 1 Fl. Div. at Arnhem under Gen. von Döring; No.2 Fl. Div. at Stade under Gen. Schwaberdissen; No. 3 Fl. Div. at Metz under Gen. Junck; No. 4 Fl. Div. at Döberitz under Gen. Huth; and No. 5 Fl. Div. at Schleissheim under Oberst von Bülow.

Allied bombers customarily flew at altitudes over 20,000 ft., and just to reach that altitude to engage them in combat involved many hazards. The weather was often inclement at takeoff. Without adequate instrumentation and without blind-flying facilities, the pilots groped their way to the intruders. Handicapped in iced-up cockpits, the Germans often fell victim to the escorting U.S. fighter pilots.

On October 14, 1943, the USAAF launched another unescorted raid on the ball-bearing works at Schweinfurt with 291 well-armed Flying Fortresses. The operation proved a very serious defeat for the Americans, as the 300 intercepting Jagdwaffe fighters shot down 60 of the intruders, with 600 crew members, and seriously damaged 138 more bombers. The surviving bombers' return trip was lit by a trail of burning Fortresses stretching hundreds of miles across the landscape of Germany, Luxembourg, Belgium, and France. Thirty-eight German fighter planes were lost in this bloody battle. During the week ending with the second Schweinfurt raid, the 8th Air Force also raided Bremen, Danzig (Gdansk), Marienburg and Münster. They lost 148 bombers, and nearly 1,500 airmen did not return! These efforts by the Americans were part of the program to concentrate daylight attacks on factories essential to the production of fighter planes. Both sides were committed to a race: the Allied drive to eliminate the Jagdwaffe's means of production against the drive by the Jagdwaffe to destroy Allied bombers in service. The balance favored the Jagdwaffe and therefore, after the second Schweinfurt raid, the U.S. abandoned the tactic until sufficient escort fighters were available to hold off the intercepting Jagdwaffe.

The Republic P-47 Thunderbolt fighter first appeared in England in early 1943, but was not available in sufficient numbers until autumn. In the beginning of November, Thunderbolts escorted 8th Air Force bombers in a raid on Wilhelmshaven. On the 13th, more P-47s escorted 600 Fortresses as they dropped 1,600 tons of bombs on Kiel. The raid was duplicated later in November over Ludwigshaven. The P-47 was not the final answer for bomber escort, however, as its range was insufficient for penetrating deep into Germany. The P-47 was forced to turn back at the frontier and leave the bombers to their fate as they continued toward the target.

By the end of 1943, the various U.S. Air Forces were growing stronger daily and their deployment was filled with ominous forboding for Germany. The 8th Air Force in Britain had almost 1,000 operational Fortresses; the new 15th Air Force, based in Italy, was growing rapidly. These were to be supported by the 9th and 12th air forces based in North Africa.

The arrival in England of the long-range North American P-51 Mustang fighter during the end of 1943, put the 8th Air Force back in business by January, 1944. The Mustang's deployment was a turning point because of it's heretofore unequaled ability to remain with the bombers all the way to the target. This was a luxury unavailable to German fighter pilots, who continued to bail out or land wherever they could because they had fought to their very last drop of fuel! The loss of aircraft was a considerable one, and the Jagdwaffe could ill afford it.

During this period, the Messerschmitts retained the light and dark green splinter-pattern camouflage. This however was augmented by the ground crews' dabbing colors with cloths and sponges, to aid in blending the aircraft to the terrain over which it operated. This added paint could be removed with water and a special solvent when it was important to change the color.

Escorted by Thunderbolts and Mustangs, 663 8th Air Force bombers headed for German aircraft production centers on Jan. 11, 1944 in three large formations. Bad weather forced the second and third waves to drop their bombs on alternative targets and turn back, leaving only the first formation of 238 bombers and one group of 49 Mustangs to complete the mission. Over 200 Luftwaffe fighters fought their way past the Mustangs and headed directly for the bombers. Sixty American bombers and five Mustangs fell in this first escorted attempt to knock out German fighter planes production. The Americans shot down 39 Jagdwaffe fighters. This first engagement of 1944 showed that the Jagdwaffe was not yet beaten and could still make it most uncomfortable for any intruder, but any idea of ultimate victory was merely an illusion.

On February 8, 1944, the U.S. Strategic Air Forces chief, Gen. Carl Spaatz, ordered Operation Argument completed by March 1, 1944. The strength of the Jagdwaffe at this time was only about 350 single-engine fighters and 130 twin-engine fighters. The final death blow to the German fighter forces was now being prepared by the U.S. Air Force. The Americans opened their "Big Week" of planned, systematic attacks on German fighter plane factories on Feb. 19, 1944. A total of 940 four-engine bombers and over 700 fighters took off from their English airfields and headed across the Channel towards Germany. This, the most powerful strategic air attack to date, included: 16 combat wings of Fortresses and Liberators; 17 U.S. fighter groups of P-38 Lightnings, P-47 Thunderbolts, and P-51 Mustangs; and 16 R.A.F. fighter squadrons of Spitfires and Mustangs. Astonishingly, only 21 bombers were lost, as the enormous fighter escort succeeded in keeping the Jagdwaffe away.

An all-out effort to develop a weapon that would effectively knock down the Allied four-engined bombers led to the installation of various combinations of rockets on the Me 109G. The most effective was the underwing 210-mm. W Gr.21 Dodel rocket. The disadvantage was the fact that the pilot only had two shots at the bomber stream. Experiments were then conducted with a battery of four 50-mm. Rz 65 rocket tubes mounted in each wing.

Major Walther Dahl formed a new, crack bomber-interceptor Geschwader zb V; it proved successful, but was disbanded on "D-Day".

The struggling Jagdwaffe, outnumbered seven to one, was overwhelmed by the Allied fighters, and over 1,000 German fighter pilots were lost between January and April, 1944. With an average loss of 50 fighters per raid, the aerial defenders were in dire need of reinforcements. As the German Supreme Command had expressly forbidden the withdrawal of fighter units from the Russian Front, Galland could only order every Gruppe in Russia and Norway to give up one Staffel for the defense of Germany against the bombings. Apparently, this transfer went unnoticed by the Supreme Command, who still did not understand the need for more fighters and not bombers.

The raids continued to rain sledgehammer blows on the German aircraft factories throughout the week. On February 25 two bomber streams converged on the Messerschmitt factories at Augsburg and Regensburg. The southern force of 175 aircraft had no fighter escort; therefore the bulk of the German fighters was directed at this formation. Twenty percent of the bombers, 33 planes, were shot down. The larger force from the west had a Mustang escort, and lost only 31 out of 740 bombers. The raiders left the Messerschmitt works a heap of rubble; it was decided to construct a new factory instead of attempting to rebuild. Then it was discovered that the vital machine tools had emerged virtually unscathed, and in four months the factory was producing Me 109s at its former output! The day's results confirmed that unescorted bombers would always fall prey to defending fighters, and that even the most accurate precision bombing is not as effective as the attacking force anticipates.

The increase in bombing raids on southeastern Germany pointed to the need for more fighter protection in the area. On May 20, General der Jagdflieger Galland ordered Maj. Walther Dahl, Kommandeur of III/JG3, to form a new Jagdgeschwader to be based in the Nuremberg–Ansbach area. The new unit was

This Hungarian Messerschmitt Me 109G-2 was the type used by Aladar de Heppes and his wingman when they destroyed a B-24 Liberator bomber by using de Heppes' sights with the wingman's guns!

In early September, 1944, JG 52 Kommodore Dieter Hrabak reaches through an oak leaf wreath to congratulate Hptm. Adolph Borchers on his 118th victory, which became the Jagdgeschwader's 10,000th victory.

Alezredes (Lt. Col.) de Heppes, the Royal Hungarian Air Force's only wing leader, proposes solutions for the serious problems that the U.S. and Russian air forces have created for the RHAF chief of staff and other members of the High Command.

designated zbV and comprised five existing Gruppen: III/JG 3 under Hptm. Langer who succeeded Dahl; I/JG 5 under Maj. Carganico; II/JG 27 under Hptm. Franzisket; II/JG 53 under Hptm. Meimbert; and III/JG 54 under Hptm. Schrör. Flying the Me 109G, the new Geschwader proved fairly successful in its short lifetime. However, all gruppen were ordered to return to their original Geschwadern shortly after the Allied invasion of Europe. The Stab/JG zbV then became the Stab of JG 300.

By the end of May 1944, the Jagdwaffe strength had fallen drastically, totaling less than 250 single-engine fighters. The U.S. Air Forces, meanwhile, could fly up to 1,000 long-range fighters at one time, demonstrating complete air superiority over the Continent. This final victory was attained, not by the destruction of the German aviation industry on the ground, but rather in fighter-to-fighter combat in the sky. It was only because the ever-decreasing German fighter force rose to challenge the attacks on the factories that the bomber force indirectly achieved its objective, by means of the escorting fighters, of destroying the Jagdwaffe. The air war had become one of attrition, in which the Jagdwaffe could not replace their losses while U.S. industry, like the Soviet Union, was Hydra-headed and could produce two planes for every one shot down.

With the Luftwaffe fighter arm reduced to virtual impotence, the bombardment groups of the 8th and 15th Army Air Forces changed their target priorities from aircraft factories, airfields, and communications, to the basic source of German war potential: fuel. Beginning in May, they bombed oil, hydrogen, and synthetic fuel installations without respite, and production dropped alarmingly. Brand-new fighters were stranded on airfields because they lacked fuel and, in many instances, pilots as well.

THE ALLIED INVASION OF GERMANY

When the Allies invaded Normandy on D-Day, June 6, 1944, only two Jagdgeschwadern were operational in Western Europe: Jg 2 Richthofen under Oberst Büligen and JG 26 Schlageter under Oberst Priller. This was a total force of about 100 fighters. Against this meager array, the USAAF and RAF were able to concentrate over 5,400 fighters in Western Europe alone! A force of 3,500 Allied bombers was also available. By June 12, 23 Jagdgruppen were transferred into the invasion area, from either home defense or bomber interceptor units. They included: III/JG 1; II/JG 2; II/JG 3; III/JG 3; I/JG 5; II/JG 5; II/JG 11; I/JG 27; II/JG 27; II/JG 53; and I/JG 301. In only a few weeks, these units were decimated over Caen and St. Lo by the overwhelming Allied fighter forces. Yet, the remnants rose again and again to meet the U.S. and British fighters, which roamed the Continental skies almost at will. Famous Geschwadern were erased for all time, and quite often the exhausted survivors formed the nucleus for a new and inexperienced unit. Grand and glorious names were bestowed upon these new fighter units, made up of teenage boys grouped around a few hollow-eyed veterans in their midtwenties!

By June 27, the Americans had captured Cherbourg.

The many Experten lost since the winter of 1943 could never be replaced, and were sorely missed. Among them were: Egon Mayer, JG 2, 102 victories (shot down by Thunderbolts); Wolf-Dietrich Wilke, JG 3, 162 (shot down by Mustangs); Kurt Üben, JG 2, 110 (shot down by Thunderbolts); Hans Philipp, JG 1, 206 (shot down by Thunderbolts); Walter Ösau, JG 1, 123 v. (shot down by Lightnings); Josef Wurmheller, JG 2, 102 (collision); Josef Zwernemann, JG 11, 126 (shot down by Mustangs); Horst Ademeit, JG 54, 166 (infantry fire); Anton Hafner, JG 51, 204 (hit tree); Albin Wolf, JG 54, 144 (Antiaircraft fire); and Leopold Münster, JG 3, 95 victories (rammed B-17). In an attempt to produce new fighter pilots, ten new Luftwaffe training schools were opened in 1944. The amount of training time was however cut to 150 hours, about one-third the time used to train a USAAF combat pilot. With inadequate training, these young men—many were still boys—fell by the dozen before any had scored even one victory. Statistics reveal that over one-half of the new pilots were killed before they completed their tenth sortie. The Luftwaffe had been inferior in quantity for some time; then with the appearance of the new Thunderbolt and Mustang, the Messerschmitt pilots found it harder and harder to score; now, with inferior pilots added to this already serious dilemma, the situation for the Jagdwaffe had become catastrophic! By the end of 1944, 700 day-fighters and an equal number of night-fighters were operational in Germany, but it was too late. The grim reality of the situation was that the aerial juggernaut pounding the Continent could not be turned back. Yet the Jadgwaffe fought on.

During a meeting between Hugo Sperrle and Hermann Göring in the latter part of June 1944, Göring promised to make 800 fighter planes available to combat the bombers. After reflecting for a moment Sperrle told the Reichsmarschall that not more than 500 fighter pilots were available for the planes.

In addition to escorting bombers, the U.S. long-range fighters conducted intruder missions with attacks on Luftwaffe airfields. A favorite tactic was to loiter about a German airfield at high altitude, waiting for returning Jagdwaffe planes to begin landing. The Mustangs would then dive upon them, annihilating the German fighters during that moment of helplessness. The Jagdfliegern were always under close fighter surveillance, which made any surprise move on their part virtually impossible.

Meanwhile, the war on the eastern front was going badly for Germany, and especially for her smaller allies, who faced the Reds at their very borders. In addition to fighting off the Soviet air force, Hungarian, Bulgarian, Slovakian, Romanian, and Croatian airmen had to combat the ever-increasing bombing raids by the USAAF Liberators and Fortresses. Using German and Hungarian-built Messerschmitts, there pitifully small air services threw themselves at the intruders with desperation. One encounter in the skies over Hungary, on July 7, 1944, is worth recounting. Sixty B-24 Liberators, escorted by a dozen P-38 Lightning fighters, were intercepted over Hajmasker by Alezredes (Lt. Col.) Aladar de Heppes and nine Messerschmitts from his Royal Hungarian Fighter Regiment 100. Known as the Old Puma along the eastern front, de Heppes and his wingman, Fohadnagy Iranyi, were quickly boxed in by the Lightnings. Some very fancy maneuvering and shooting was required to elude their pursuers. The Hungarians then sped for a formation of unescorted Liberators, which had discharged their bombs and were returning to base in Italy. The two Messerschmitts approached the bombers from three o'clock high and, as the B-24 grew in his reflector sight, Heppes pressed the firing button at a range of 600 feet. After discharging only a few rounds his three guns fell silent. Out of ammunition! Fuel, lubricating oil, and ammunition were all in limited supply and very often, when re-arming the aircraft, the armorers only partially loaded the ammo bays so there would be enough shells for everyone! Remembering that Iranyi had fired only a few rounds, he ordered his wingman to take the bomber, but the inexperienced youngster missed the Liberator by a wide margin. The Old Puma refused to quit, and made a sweeping S turn away from the Liberator's gunners. He tucked his wingman under his right wingtip as closely as he dared, and headed for the bomber formation. Aladar's ingenious plan was to use his wingman's Messerschmitt as his weapon and lead it to the target, with last minute aiming corrections over the radio. The moment the Hungarians came within range, the B-24 waist gunners pumped a torrent of .50-caliber bullets into the leading Me 109. Heppes held his course despite the withering fire and, only when he was close enough to the target to insure a hit, did the Old Puma give the order to fire. After a small correction the shells from Iranyi's cannon found their mark. As the Liberator spiraled to the ground Lightnings appeared, forcing the Hungarians to leave the fight.

The German Supreme Commander was finally convinced, although too late, that building bombers and trying to retaliate with ineffective raids on Britain was not the way to combat the massive Allied air raids. During August 1944, virtually all bomber units in the Luftwaffe were disbanded and the pilots rushed through a fighter-pilot training course before they were posted to a fighter unit. At this time several new fighter units were established in order to accommodate this new influx of pilots. The I/JG 4 was joined by three more Gruppen: the Ramm Staffel of the Geschwader became II/JG 4; and II/JG 5 became IV/JG 4. An entirely new Geschwader, JG 6, was created with Oberst Kogler in command: I/ZG 26 became I/JG 6; II ZG 26 became II/JG 6; and I/JG 5 became III/JG 6. Finally II/ZG 1 became III/JG 76; however, after a few weeks it was changed again to IV/JG 53. Despite this increase in fighter units, the Luftwaffe was still so exhausted that no fighter operations of any worthwhile strength were possible at this time.

On Sept. 3 and 4 the Allied Army captured Brussels and Antwerp.

General Galland and his hard-working staff spent late summer and autumn of 1944 building up a reserve of fighter pilots and planes. His idea was to unleash an armada of about 2,000 fighters at the American bombers in one mighty, heavyweight punch. Evident since the Battle of Leuctra between Sparta and Thebes in 371 B.C., and later advocated by respected military scientist Karl von Clauswitz, the most important factor necessary to win battles, and eventually wars, is to be stronger than the enemy at the point of contact. An admirer of Clauswitz, Galland was planning the destruction of at least 400 of the four-engined Fortresses and Liberators with each concentrated attack. In addition, the results would destroy the confidence and morale of the Allied airmen and leaders. The Jagdwaffe boasted a total of 41 Gruppen by December, 1944. Just as Galland readied his plan, the

Supreme Commander intervened and ordered this powerful force used for ground-support missions in the Ardennes offensive, known as the Battle of the Bulge, which had started on December 16. The terrible weather reduced, however, the effectiveness of the fighters' striking power. Again, the Jagdwaffe was wasted against nondecisive ground targets. The German losses were extremely high and out of proportion with the damage inflicted; and the Allied bombers kept bringing their daily loads of ruin to the Germans.

On New Year's Day, 1945, the Luftwaffe launched its last major attack. All its remaining fighters, which numbered 750, conducted a low-level dawn surprise attack on Allied airfields in the Netherlands, Belgium, and Luxembourg. Code-named Operation Bodenplatte, the attack enabled the Jagdwaffe to destroy or severely damage about 800 British and American aircraft, many on the ground. Luftwaffe fighter losses numbered about 150, many of whom were irreplaceable experienced leaders. Oberst Günther Specht, Kommodore of JG 11, was shot down by antiaircraft fire. At this stage in the war, the Allies could easily absorb the loss; but for the Luftwaffe, it was a crippling blow.

During January, Adolf Galland engaged in a heated discussion with Hermann Göring about whether the new Me 262 jet should be used as a fighter or a bomber. In anger, the Reichsmarschall fired Galland as Chief of the Jagdwaffe and gave him a Staffel equipped with the Me 262 because of Galland's insistence that all the jets produced be used to attack the large bomber formations. Shortly after this episode, the Jagdgeschwader Kommodores selected Günther Lützow to present their grievances to Göring regarding his mismanagement of the Luftwaffe and recommendations for reform. As was customary, the Reichsmarschall exploded. He removed Lützow and Trautloft as fighter inspectors, the west and east respectively, banished Lützow to Italy, and put Trautloft in charge of a training school. Gordon M. Gollob, 150 victories, replaced Galland as General der Jagdfliegern. Göring would not admit his mistakes and continued to heap 'abuse on the Jagdwaffe in order to camouflage his own inadequacies. This episode is often called the Mutiny of the Fighters.

By Feb. 9, the Allied Army had reached the Rhine river.

The Spring of 1945 witnessed the death of more Experten, a loss the struggling Jagdwaffe could ill afford: Otto Kittel, JG 54, 267 victories (shot down by IL-2); Erich Leie, JG 77, 118 (shot down by a Yak); Rudi Linz, JG 5, 70 (shot down by a Spitfire); Wilhelm

Mink, JG 1, 72 (shot down by a Spitfire); Friedrich Haas, JG 52, 74 (shot down by a Mig); Franz Schall, JG 52, 137 (crash landing); Gerhard Hoffmann, JG 52, 125 (missing in action); and Gunther Lützow, JV 44, 108 victories, (missing in action).

The Soviet air force, like the Luftwaffe, had no strategic bombers. Therefore it requested that the Western Allies "neutralize" the city of Dresden because the Red Army was about to enter. On the night of February 13/14, RAF Lancasters dropped 2,659 tons of explosives and incendiaries in successive waves of 244 and 529 planes. In daylight, 311 Fortresses dropped 771 tons of bombs, and on the 15th, 210 Fortresses returned to unload 461 more tons of their lethal cargo on the blazing city. Dresden was defenseless, for it had no antiaircraft batteries and no fighter defense. The Germans knew Dresden was not a military objective and therefore had made no air defense preparations. Filled with refugees fleeing the Russian advance, Dresden suffered over 300,000 casualties, more than Britain suffered throughout the entire Blitz! This event is related to illustrate the enormity of the Allied bombings; the reader can sympathize with the frustrations of the Jagdwaffe when it found itself helpless to prevent this carnage and destruction.

By April 1, 1945, U.S. troops had encircled the industrial heart of Germany, the Ruhr valley.

Oberst Hajo Herrmann again came to the fore when he suggested that a special fighter unit of four Gruppen he created with student pilots. Known as Rammkommando Elbe, this Geschwader was composed of young volunteers with one or two solo flights to their credit. The only operation undertaken by these undertrained volunteers occurred on April 7, 1945, when 1,300 U.S. bombers, escorted by 850 long-range fighters, raided Dessau. At 35,000 ft., the raiders were intercepted by the 120 fighters of Rammkommando Elbe. In the ensuing air battle, the neophytes scored 50 bombers and 6 escorting fighters. Only 15 Rammkommando youngsters struggled back to their base. Enthusiasm and patriotism were not enough to make the Jagdwaffe a formidable fighting force, and the Luftwaffe's fighters never again rose in any great strength.

By May 2, the Soviet Army had captured Berlin.

There was no longer an eastern, western and Mediterranean airfront, because the sky over all of Germany was one big battlefield. The Jagdfliegern retreated from airfield to airfield across the shrinking country as the Allied armies moved in from all sides. The support organization was in chaos, fuel was virtually nonexistant, and a sky full of enemy aircraft threatened every move. The end had arrived, and there was no alternative but to surrender to the Allied armies. Silent from lack of fuel and ammunition, the Messerschmitts stood in great rows along the runways as their pilots drove off to surrender.

PART TWO

The Men:
Die Jagdfliegern

The men we are about to meet may have performed legendary feats, but they were in reality living, feeling human beings. Names like Galland, Nowotny, and Hartmann became part of postwar Western mythology, and the mere mention of their names (much like the Red Baron of World War One), draws a response not unlike that from the English-speaking people of an earlier age to the heroes and leaders of the Battle of Agincourt. They almost cease to be real. Harbor no illusions: these men were and are real!

The German fighter pilots who experienced the sweet smell of victory during the early war years, only to be crushed in the jaws of defeat a few years later proved, as a group, to be the most successful fighter pilots the world has ever seen. The intense and uninterrupted aerial fighting in which the Jagdwaffe engaged can't be compared to any other air force, nor can the toll exacted by the Jagdwaffe on its adversaries be matched: approximately 70,000 aerial victories, plus about 25,000 more on the ground! With this record of destruction, it should come as no surprise that the fighter units and individual fighter pilots accumulated scores that are enormous compared to those of the American, Soviet, and British fighters. The consequence of this excellence was a widespread reluctance to accept German claims immediately after the war. In recent years, thanks to dedicated aero-historians who have conducted painstaking research, the magnitude of the Jagdwaffe achievement has finally been accepted in Allied countries. The German penchant for precision and record-keeping has facilitated this research somewhat.

A major difference between the German and Western Allies' method of scoring victories was that the Germans were not allowed to share a victory.

Their cardinal rule was: "One pilot—one kill." In contrast, Allied pilots were allowed to share victories. If two pilots fired at an enemy aircraft and it went down, each Allied pilot received one-half of the kill. Carried to absurdity, it is conceivable that an Allied pilot could become an ace with ten or more half-victories, never scoring any victories of his own! The Luftwaffe system of awarding victories was impartial, inflexible, and far less prone to error than the American or British method.

Abschuss, or "the shooting down," was the Luftwaffe term for the destruction of an enemy plane in aerial combat. Every Abschuss had to be observed by a witness: either a ground observer of the encounter, the pilot's wingman, or a Staffel-mate. Witnesses were necessary unless the victor's aircraft had been fitted with a gun-camera and the destruction of the plane or the vanquished pilot's bail-out had been recorded on film, if the wreckage of the victory could be found on the ground, or if the downed pilot or other crew member had been captured by German forces. In effect: no witness or tangible evidence—no victory.

Every Abschuss had to be confirmed by the Oberbefehlshaber der Luftwaffe or Commander in Chief of the Air Force. Jagdwaffe pilots were at all times required to note their geographical position as well as the type and number of aircraft in enemy formations engaged. Naturally, the victor was required to log the exact time of a kill, while he maneuvered for a tactical advantage over the remaining enemy aircraft! In addition, he had to observe other actions in the air in order to be able to witness victories by his Staffelmates. Upon landing, the claimant prepared his Abschuss report for review by the immediate supervisory officer, who either endorsed or rejected the claim. If endorsed, the pilot's report

---

Abschrift

Gottlob, Oblt.   z. Zt. Gefechtsstand, den 23. 6. 1941
1./J. G. Nr. 26

G e f e c h t s b . e r i c h t

Start: 20.11 Uhr
Auftrag: Alarmstart
Landung: 21.04 Uhr

Ich flog als Deckungsrotte der Staffel, als der Staffelkapitän einen Pulk Spitfire angriff
Dabei sah ich, daß 3 andere Spitfires sich hinter die Staffel setzen wollten. Auf diese Spitfires setzte ich mit meiner Rotte einen Angriff an. Diesen Angriff erkannten die Spitfires aber
sofort und wehrten ihn ab durch sehr enges Kurven. Ich kurvte jetzt überhöhend über den
Spitfires und wollte warten bis die Spitfires die Kurve abbrachen und auf See raus flogen.
Ich mußte vorher aber nochmal nach unten weg, weil meine Rotte selbst aus Überhöhung
angegriffen wurde. Als ich diesen Angriff abgeschüttelt hatte, sah ich eine einzelne Spitfire,
die in Richtung Nordwest flog. Die Spitfire war noch über Land in 6 000 m Höhe. Ich flog
hinterher und konnte bis auf 20 m ran gehen, da mich der Pilot gar nicht bemerkte.

Ich schoß dann von hinten unten mit allen Waffen. Unter dem Rumpf der Spitfire sah ich
eine starke Rauchfahne, außerdem flogen von Rumpf und Flächen Fetzen weg. Die Maschine
zog langsam hoch und schmierte über die linke Fläche ab. Dieses Abschmieren wiederholte
sich 2—3 mal über die linke und rechte Fläche. Dann stürzte die Spitfire senkrecht nach
unten. Um sicher zu gehen setzte ich mich nochmal im Sturzflug dahinter und schoß. Ich
mußte meinen Sturzflug aber bald abbrechen, da die Geschwindigkeit zu hoch wurde. Ich
kurvte jetzt flacher werdend nach unten weiter und beobachtete die Spitfire, bis sie auf das
Wasser aufschlug.

Der Flugzeugführer ist nicht abgesprungen.
                                                                              Gottlob

---

Typical Luftwaffe combat report, victory report, and air witness report, with English translations, are reproduced here for the reader's interest and to illustrate the thoroughness with which every Jagdflieger victory claim was examined. Observe the apparently irrelevant questions asked in the victory report.

went to the Geschwaderstab, or Wing Staff, which, in turn, filed its own report and sent both to the RLM, or Air Ministry. After checking all the papers that were submitted, the official confirmation was prepared and sent to the unit. This very long bureaucratic procedure sometimes took as long as a year! During 1944, another authority was created: the Abschusskommission, which received all reports on crashed aircraft remains found by search units. This commission checked conflicting claims between antiaircraft batteries and fighter pilots, and awarded credit for the victory to one claimant or the other. This system insured that no more credits would be awarded than wrecks found.

The German system of confirming aerial victories was very effective in keeping human errors and weaknesses within limits. Despite this, the Oberkommando der Luftwaffe, or Luftwaffe High Command, considered the large victory totals during the early days of the Russian campaign as incredulous. On many occasions, they accused the Jagdgeschwader Kommodores of exaggerating the victory scores. In effect, Göring was calling the frontline pilots liars. This was one of the grievances that brought about the Mutiny of the Fighters, or the Kommodores' Revolt Conference, in Berlin during January, 1945.

When a German fighter pilot scored a victory, he would call "Horrido" on the radio. This distinctive announcement of victory alerted his fellow pilots to watch for a crash or a flamer, as well as notified ground stations, which helped to confirm many vic-

Gottlob, Oblt.
1/JG No. 26

Copy

Base of Operation, on 23.6. 1941

Combat Report

Start: 20.11 hours (8:11 PM)
Mission: Alarmstart
Landed: 21.04 hours (9:04 PM)

I flew as the protection Rotte of our Staffel, as our Staffelkapitan engaged a Spitfire. Then I saw that three other Spitfires tried to get behind the Staffel. I engaged them with my Rotte. The Spitfires went into a tight turn. I turned also and climbed above them. I saw one Spitfire flying in a north-westerly direction. The Spitfire was over land at 19,680 feet altitude. I flew behind him at a range of about 70 feet and the pilot did not take evasive action.

I fired all guns from the rear and below. I saw a lot of smoke and parts falling from his fuselage and wings. The plane climbed and slowed and rolled over the left wing. It rolled 2 or 3 times. Then the Spitfire dived down. I dived after it and fired again. I pulled out of my dive and gained altitude. I turned into a bank and saw the Spitfire hit the water.

The pilot did not emerge from his plane.

Gottlob

tories. The Jagdwaffe Experten we are about to meet cried "Horrido" many times in their military careers.

HILMER VON BÜLOW-BOTHKAMP derived his surname from his ancestral home and birthplace, Bothkamp, Holstein. Hilmer von Bülow was a Leutnant in the Luftstreitkraft, or Imperial Air Service, during the First World War. As a fighter pilot with Jasta 2 (Jagdstaffel No. 2), led by the famous Oswald Bölcke, he scored six victories. In May, 1918 Hilmer, who was sometimes called Harry, became the commander of Jasta 36, a post he held until the Armistice. Answering Göring's call to serve in the new Luftwaffe, von Bülow was posted to JG 77 under Oberst Carl Schumacher, and by mid-1939 he became Kommandeur of II Gruppe. Located in the north of Germany, the Alte Adler saw action over Helgoland as British bombers invaded German air space. In April, 1940 von Bülow succeeded Oberst von Massow as Kommodore of JG 2 Richthofen, which was the very first Luftwaffe Jagdgeschwader. He led his Jagdgeschwader in the Battle of France and the opening rounds of the Battle of Britain. After scoring eighteen victories, and becoming an ace in two world wars, his command was passed on to Wolfgang Schellmann on Sept. 3, 1940. Born on November 19, 1897, the 42-year-old von Bülow was awarded the Ritterkreuz on August 22 for his activities during the Battle of Britain. For a while, he led NJG 101, a night fighter unit, and then moved up to higher responsibilities as commander of the Fifth Fighter Division. At the war's end, he was Jafu 4 (Jagdführer 4) directing his fighters against the Allied bombers.

WOLFGANG SCHELLMANN succeeded von Bülow as Kommodore of JG 2 Richthofen. He began his scoring in the Spanish Civil War where he attained

Abschrift.
.—.—.—.—.—.—.—.—.

1. .../J. G. Nr. 26   Einsatzort, den   23. 6. 1941
(Dienstelle)

ABSCHUSSMELDUNG

1. Zeit (Tag, Stunde, Minute) und Gegend des Absturzes: 23. 6. 1941
   2050 Uhr, 5 km. nordostwärts Calais
   Höhe: 6000 m.   Meter:

2. Durch wen ist der Abschuss Zerstörung erfolgt: Oblt. Gottlob

3. Flugzeugtyp des abgeschossenen Flugzeuges: Spitfire

4. Staatsangehörigkeit des Gegners: England
   Werk-Nr. bzw. Kennzeichen: Kokarde

5. Art der Vernichtung:
   a.) Flammen mit dunkler Fahne, Flammen mit heller Fahne, (Rauchwolke)
   b.) Einzelteile weggeflogen, abmontiert (Art der Teile erläutern), Von Rumpf u. Fläche auseinandergeplatzt
   c.) zur Landung gezwungen (diesseits oder jenseits der Front, glatt bzw. mit Bruch)
   d.) jenseits der Front am Boden im Brand geschossen

6. Art des Aufschlages (nur wenn dieser beobachtet werden konnte:
   a.) diesseits oder jenseits der Front
   b.) senkrecht, flachen Winkel, Aufschlagbrand, Staubwolke (ins Wasser)
   c.) nicht beobachtet, warum nicht?

7. Schicksal der Insassen (tot, mit Fallschirm abgesprungen, nicht beobachtet

8. Gefechtsbericht des Schützen ist in der Anlage beigefügt.

9. Zeugen:
   a.) Luft:
   b.) Erde:

10. Anzahl der Angriffe, die auf das feindliche Flugzeug gemacht wurden: 1 Angriff

11. Richtung, aus der die einzelnen Angriffe erfolgten: Von hinten

12. Entfernung, aus der der Abschuss erfolgte: 20 m.

13. Takt. Position aus der der Abschuss angesetzt wurde: Von hinten unten

14. Ist einer der feindl. Bordschützen kampfunfähig gemacht worden: -/-

15. Verwandte Munitionsart: P.m.K.v., Sm.K.L Spur v.Br.Spr.Gr., M.Muni Vs.m..Muni.

16. Munitionsverbrauch: 300 Schuß M.G. und 110 Schuß Kanone.

17. Art und Anzahl der Waffen, die bei dem Abschuss gebraucht wurden: 2 M.G. u. 2 Kanone

18. Typ der eigene Maschine: Bf. 109 E 7

19. Weiteres taktisch oder technisch Bemerkenswertes: -/-

20. Treffer in der eigenen Maschine: keine.

21. Beteiligung weiterer Einheiten (auch Flak):

(Unterschrift)

Copy

1/JG No. 26   Base of Operations on 23.6. 1941

Victory Report

1. Time (day, hour, minute) and area of victory: <u>23.6. 1941</u>
    <u>8:50 P.M. Hour, 5 Km northeast of Calais</u>
2. Name of victor: <u>Oblt. Gottlob</u>
3. Type of plane shot down: <u>Spitfire</u>
4. Nationality of victim: <u>England</u>
    Serial No. or other markings: <u>Cockard</u>
5. How was it destroyed:
    a)   Flame with <u>dark</u> smoke, flame with light smoke (cloud of smoke)
    b)   <u>Single part</u> shot (which parts)   <u>Body and wings</u>
    c)   Was it forced to land (which side of the Front, good or crash landing)
    d)   If he crossed the lines did you still attack
6. How did victim crash (must be seen by victor)
    a)   <u>This side</u> or other side of <u>front</u>
    b)   Did it crash or crash-land or explode: <u>(in water)</u>
    c)   If did not see crash, why not?
7. What happened to crew <u>(dead</u>, bail out or not see.)
8. Combat Report is attached
9. Witnesses:
            a) air:
            b) ground:
10. How often attacked enemy plane; <u>1 attack</u>
11. From which direction were the attacks: <u>from rear</u>
12. Range when shooting: <u>70 ft.</u>
13. From which position was attack started: <u>from rear below</u>
14. Were the pilots wounded: -/-
15. Type of Ammunition: <u>P.m.k.v., Sm.K.L. Spur v. Br. Spr. Gr, M. Muni Va.m.Muni 06.</u>
16. Ammunition used: <u>300 shots M.G. and 110 shots cannon</u>
17. Type and number of weapons used: <u>2 MG and 2 cannon</u>
18. Type of airplane used: Me 109E7
19. Added technical remarks: -/-
20. Was your plane hit: <u>no.</u>
21. Were you assisted (including Flak)

                                                      Signed

Abschrift

Priller, Oblt.   z. Zt. Gefechtsstand, den 23. 6. 1941
1./J. G. Nr. 26

Luftzeugenbericht zu dem Abschuß von Oblt. Gottlob am 23. 6. 1941 (20.50)

Oblt. Gottlob, der als 2. Rotte in meinem Schwarm flog meldete mir, daß ich von hinten angegriffen würde. Ich zog in einer Linkskurve hoch und sah, wie meine Deckungsrotte gerade mehrere Spitfires überhöhte. Ich setzte mich oben drüber und sah Oblt. Gottlob, der jetzt allein war und auf nächste Entfernung hinter eine Spitfire zu sitzen kam und diese beschoß. Die Maschine zeigte eine starke schwarze Rauchfahne und trudelte ab. Wir gingen hinterher und ich sah die Maschine ungefähr 8 km nordwestlich Calais ins Meer stürzen.

Priller

Copy

Priller, Oblt.   Base of Operations, on 23. 6. 1941
1/JG No. 26

Air witness report of victory by Oblt. Gottlob on 23. 6. 1941 (8:50 PM)

Oblt Gottlob, flying in the 2 Rotte in my Schwarm warned me that I was being attacked from the rear. I went into a left turn while climbing and saw that my protection Rotte engaged more Spitfires at a higher altitude. I saw Oblt. Gottlob, who was alone, attacking a Spitfire from the rear and shooting at it. The plane belched black smoke and dived, and we followed behind it and watched it crash into the sea 26 miles northwest of Calais.

Oberst Hilmer von Bülow became an ace in two world wars and defeated men young enough to be his sons in aerial combat.

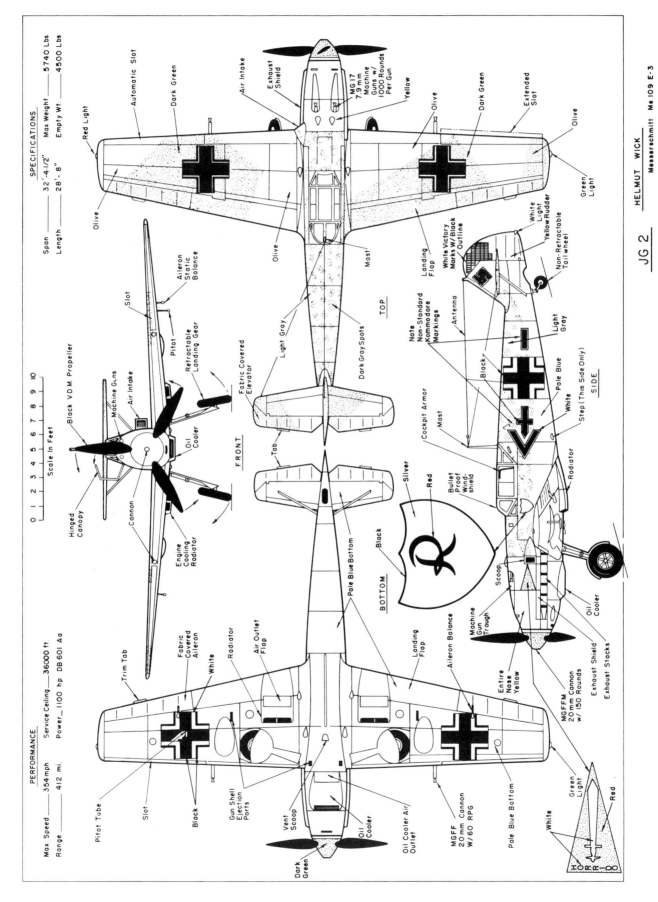

HELMUT WICK

Messerschmitt Me 109 E-3

JG 2

12 victories, second only to Werner Mölders. Born in Kassel on March 2, 1911, his first unit was I/JG 77 with which he saw action in the Polish campaign. Schellmann was then made Kommandeur of II/JG 2 and on Sept. 3, 1940, he was promoted to Kommodore of the Richthofen Jagdgeschwader. Major Schellmann was awarded the coveted Ritterkreuz on September 18 for his tenth victory and outstanding leadership. By the winter of 1940/41, Schellmann had been transferred to take over JG 27 as Kommodore. He led this Jagdgeschwader throughout the Balkan campaign, and his was one of the first units to cross into Russia during Operation Barbarossa. With 25 victories already to his credit, Oberst Schellmann led his men on a Jabo mission on the very first day of the invasion, June 22, 1941. This was his 150th sortie and, as JG 27 was in the process of releasing their Devil's Eggs, they were intercepted by Soviet I-16 Rata fighters. Schellmann quickly scored a Rata at such close range that the exploding fragments of his 26th victory damaged his Messerschmitt. Forced to bail out over Grodno, U.S.S.R., he was captured and never seen again. It is believed that he was shot by the NKVD secret police two days later.

HELMUT WICK was Schellmann's successor as Kommodore of JG 2 Richthofen, and became one of the first great German fighter aces of the Second World War. He combined all the qualities that make a successful fighter pilot: he enjoyed the excitement of combat; was a good shot; he was aggressive; and he possessed superb coolness under difficult combat conditions. He was also impetuous in many situations.

Born in Mannheim on August 5, 1915, Wick was one of three children of Carl Wick, a construction engineer. His father's vocation forced the family to move often. Helmut lived in Heidelberg, Hannover, Danzig, and Königsberg during his youth. When a young teenager, Helmut lived near an airport. He fell in love with flying, especially after his father paid a local pilot to give the boy his first ride in a plane. Although he had started his apprenticeship as a forester/game warden, Helmut leaped at the chance to join the new Luftwaffe, once it was announced in 1935. By April, 1936, he was a Fahnenjunker, in July, 1937 a Fahnrich, and by November, 1938 Wick was commissioned a Leutnant. During advanced training, his instructor had been Werner Mölders, and the two became close friends. Wick's first unit was II/JG 134, under Oberst Max Ibel, with which he flew the Arado 68 biplane. Soon transferred to I/JG 53, Wick first flew the Messerschmitt in January, 1939 and,

during the following March, Mölders became his Staffelkapitan. In September, Helmut was again transferred, this time to I/JG 2. During this month, the Polish campaign was underway, but JG 2 was assigned to protect Berlin and saw no action.

On May 10, 1940, Kommodore von Bülow led JG 2 in the attack on France. However, Helmut Wick was again deprived of action for the first several days because the engine in his Messerschmitt needed extensive repairs. Although his crew chief, Uffz. Sauerbrei, worked his mechanics day and night, it was not until the 21st that Wick could have his fighter. Flying with five others, his role was to escort a Henschel 126 on a reconnaissance mission. Despite the fact that several French Morane fighters flew close to investigate the Henschel, sorely tempting the impatient German to tangle with them, Wick remained on station because his job was to escort and protect, not to Freie Jagd. It was a bitterly disappointed Helmut Wick who landed on the I/JG 2 airfield after that mission.

On May 22, Wick's Staffel came upon 24 French bombers and fighters. The Messerschmitts bounced the unsuspecting French pilots and shot down eight, with Wick scoring two. Later in the month while separated from his Staffel over Calais, Wick spotted two British Fairey Swordfish torpedo planes. Without hesitation, the Jagdflieger made a firing pass, but noticed that the gunner in the rear cockpit was waving a white cloth. He took this as a signal of surrender. As the British pilot brought the craft down in preparation for a landing, Wick followed, but the gunner opened fire thinking Wick did not intend to accept the surrender. After a short roll, the Swordfish overturned on the rough field. Wick quickly sped after the other torpedo plane and shot it down in flames. Neither of these victories was confirmed, because there were no accountable witnesses and the wreckage fell on Allied territory. Helmut Wick, like many of the great aces, was a slow starter, but he was soon to begin his meteoric climb to fame.

Wick shot down four Bloch 152 fighters on June 5, 1940, and two more on the next day. By June 9, he had attained his 12th victory and became the most successful pilot in the Richthofen Geschwader as he destroyed a Bristol Blenheim. At this time, he was awarded the Eiserne Kreuz I or Iron Cross First Class, and was promoted to Staffelkapitan of 3/JG 2.

As the Battle of Britain entered its first stages, Wick's eagerness to conquer the enemy increased. On July 17, 1940, he went out of his way to the Isle of Wight, contrary to orders, to bag another Blenheim bomber. Instead, he found 14 Spitfires, who were surprised to find a Messerschmitt in the area. He

Helmut Wick was Kommodore of JG 2 Richthofen and Germany's leading ace when he was shot down over the English Channel. Below, Hermann Göring congratulates the young ace as Hans Jeschonnek looks on approvingly.

bounced the "tail-end Charlie," who became Wick's 14th victory, and sped away to rejoin his unit. By scoring two victories, his 20th and 21st, Wick brought the JG 2 total to 250 victories on August 27. Also on this date, the Ritterkreuz, or Knight's Cross, was presented to the intrepid pilot.

On September 9, 1940, Wick was promoted to the rank of Hauptmann and Gruppenkommandeur of I/JG 2. Shortly after his promotion, Wick's Gruppe was inspected by Feldmarschall Sperrle. Upon completion of his inspection, Sperrle complained about the general untidiness of the ground personnel. The impetuous Wick did not let this criticism go by; instead, he erupted in anger at the commander of Luftflotte 3. The Hauptmann recounted the many tasks and long hours the ground crews had to work to keep the Messerschmitts flying, and had no time to get "a damned haircut." Sperrle's monocle dropped and his mouth opened in astonishment. He knew, however, that Helmut Wick was correct and said no more.

The scoring of a double victory of Spitfires on October 2, and shooting down 5 more British fighters three days later brought Wick's score to 41. He also received the Eichenlaub, or Oak Leaves, to his Ritterkreuz on this day.

On October 19, Wick was promoted to Major, at 25 the youngest in the Luftwaffe. He was also selected to succeed Schellmann as Kommodore of the Richthofen Geschwader at this time. For his personal victory record he notched his Kommodore's Geschwaderstock, or walking cane, much like an American cowboy would notch his gun handle. His personal insignia became the word Horrido on a red pennant emblazoned with a broad sword. Wick had this insignia painted on the nose of his Messerschmitt.

Wick's victories continued to mount, scoring mostly against Spitfires and Hurricanes. He downed three on November 5, and five in 13 minutes over Southampton and the Isle of Wight on the following day.

During an early morning mission on November 28, 1940, the young Kommodore shot down his 55th victory over the Channel. This made Wick the top fighter pilot of the war at that time, surpassing Mölders' 54 and Galland's 52 victories. Late in the afternoon, the Geschwaderstab Schwarm took off on a Freie Jagd over the Channel. The flight included some of the top Experten of the Battle of Britain: Hptm. Rudolf Pflanz, Geschwader technical officer; Oblt. Erich Leie, Geschwader Adjutant; and Lt. Fiby. As the Schwarm approached the Isle of Wight, it spotted a formation of Spitfires flying towards Bournemouth. The Germans attacked at once, and it was not long before Wick scored his 56th victory, while Pflanz and Leie failed in their attack on two other Spitfires. During this fight, Wick became separated from his Schwarm, and before Leie, Fiby, and Pflanz could begin to search, they were attacked from above by another Spitfire unit. They barely escaped from this superior force. Running short of fuel, Leie and Fiby headed for the Continent. Hptm. Pflanz came out of the engagement at about 10,000 feet and, scanning the area, sighted two planes a few miles away heading towards France. Assuming they were Fiby and Leie, Pflanz started a long sweep, intending to search for his leader, when he saw the trailing aircraft fire at the leading aircraft. The Hauptmann sped to the scene where he identified the attacker as a Spitfire, and the pursued aircraft as a Messerschmitt. The Briton scored well and, as the Me 109E dived towards the foreboding waters of the Channel, the German pilot bailed out. Pflanz then recognized the markings on the plunging 109 as those of his leader, Helmut Wick. As the plane plunged into the Channel, Rudi Pflanz slammed into the Spitfire. With a single burst, he sent it crashing into the waters very close to its recent victim. Rudi circled the area several times but failed to detect any sign of life. He then called for help on his radio, cleverly announcing that a Spitfire was shot down so the British would also send out a rescue party. Pflanz continued to circle the site until his fuel tank was almost empty, and then headed across the Channel. His fuel gave out at landfall, and he forced-landed in a meadow. Major Wick was never found and the last entry by his name in the Geschwader log book read: "28.11.40, one Spitfire shot down over Bournemouth 5.13 P.M." The pilot who shot down the young Kommodore was Flight Lieutenant John "Dogs" Dundas, a Battle of Britain ace from 609 Squadron who made Wick his 13th and final victory.

Hptm. Karl-Heinz Greisert was named the acting Kommodore until February 16, 1941, when Wilhelm Balthasar was selected as Kommodore to replace Helmut Wick.

Helmut Wick's philosophy was that of a true fighter and patriot: "As long as I can shoot down the enemy, adding to the honor of the Richthofen Geschwader and the success of the Fatherland, I will be a happy man. I want to fight and die fighting, taking with me as many of the enemy as possible"; and Helmut Wick did die fighting.

RUDOLF PFLANZ throughout his combat career, flew only with JG 2 Richthofen from 1938 to 1942.

Born in Ichenheim, Baden on July 1, 1914, he was Wick's technical officer, and flew in the JG 2 Geschwaderstab with Kommodores from Wick to Ösau. He scored six British fighters on July 23, 1941, and was considered one of the most successful pilots over the English Channel. On July 31, 1942, he tangled with Spitfires while on Freie Jagd with Ösau and the JG2 Geschwader Stab. Unknown to Pflanz, his wingman had been shot down behind him during the melee. By the time Rudi discovered this fact, a Spitfire had slipped into the Rottenflieger position and was closing in on Pflanz for the kill. Still thinking it was his wingman, Rudi went about his business until he was killed by the Briton.

WILHELM BALTHASAR succeeded Helmut Wick as permanent Kommodore of JG 2 Richthofen. He was born on February 2, 1914, in Fulda and his father, a Hauptmann, was killed in action ten months later. Balthasar epitomized chivalry in battle coupled with great technical ability. He made an exceptional effort to have the RAF pilots he downed brought to the officers' mess at his airfields so he could converse with them over wine and a meal before they were taken to a POW camp. Another outstanding characteristic was his interest in instructing his young pilots in the grim business of aerial warfare.

Like many Luftwaffe Experten, Balthasar had his first taste of combat during the Spanish Civil War, where his experience was varied. He flew Jabo sorties in the Heinkel He 51, reconnaissance in the Heinkel He 70, and fighter sweeps in the Messerschmitt Me 109B. Flying with III/J88, he scored his first victory over a Russian Rata on January 20, 1938, which was the 103rd victory for J88. During a large free-for-all on February 7, Balthasar shot down four adversaries in six minutes, which became the 116th through 119th victories for J88.

Returning to Germany, the Leutnant spent some time as a Staffelkapitan in JG 131, and was then posted with JG 2 Richthofen in June, 1938. Balthasar earned international acclaim when he flew a twin-engine Siebel 104 in a 40,000-km. journey around Africa during February/March, 1939.

In December, he was promoted to Hauptmann and then transferred to JG 27 as leader of 7 Staffel, in preparation for the Battle of France.

JG 27 was very active in the spring, 1940 campaign, and Balthasar scored heavily with multiple victories. His best day was June 6, when he shot down no less than nine French planes. On June 14, Balthasar became the second member of the Luftwaffe to receive the Ritterkreuz, the same day that

Wilhelm Balthasar was the top scorer of the Battle of France and shot down four planes in six minutes in Spain. He was killed when his Messerschmitt broke up during a test flight.

the German army marched into Paris. With the Battle of France over, William Balthasar emerged as the most successful fighter pilot of the campaign, with 23 aerial victories (plus 13 enemy aircraft destroyed on the ground which, of course, could not be added to his total).

As the Jagdwaffe prepared for the Battle of Britain, Balthasar was transferred to JG 3; his responsibilities increased when he became Gruppenkommandeur of III/JG 3. On September 4 he was seriously wounded and Wilhelm never got over it: he carried the shock of this experience with him.

By February 16, 1941, he had accumulated 29 victories and was assigned to the post of Kommodore of JG 2 Richthofen. On May 5, 1941, he resumed scoring, and by June 27 Balthasar shot down his 39th and 40th enemy aircraft. The Eichenlaub, or Oak Leaves, to his Ritterkreuz was awarded on July 2.

On the following day, Wilhelm decided to take one of the unit's new Messerschmitt Me 109F4 fighters, which was to replace the older Me 109E, on a test flight. It seems that the new model had several deficiencies, including weak wings and aileron flutter. The Kommodore decided to combine his technical ability with his flying experience and check out the plane before it could cause any casualties. While he was making lazy turns and rolls near the town of Hazebrouck, Balthasar was jumped by Spitfires. The stresses caused by his evasive maneuvers were too great and the wing collapsed, sending the Kommodore crashing to his death near Aire. Inspection of the wreckage revealed no bullet holes in the plane. This tragic incident is similar to the story of German World War One Ace Heinrich Goutermann, who tested a Fokker triplane before he would allow his men to fly the questionable design, and also crashed to his death.

Balthasar's wish had always been to be buried near his father, should he die in combat. The men of JG 2 found the WWI grave of the elder Balthasar, and buried Wilhelm in the next plot. Side by side they lie near Abbeville far from their homeland in whose service they both gave their lives.

WALTER ÖSAU was selected as Kommodore of JG 2 Richthofen upon Balthasar's death. Ösau joined the army as an artilleryman but soon transferred to the Luftwaffe. Physically and mentally tough, Gulle, as he was often called, became one of the most important Experten in the Jagdwaffe. Born in Farnewinkel, Holstein on June 28, 1913, Ösau scored eight victories in Spain with the Condor Legion. When the Second World War began, Gulle was Staffelkapitan of 7/JG 51, and in August, 1940 he was elevated to Kommandeur of III/JG 51. On August 20, Hptm. Ösau was presented with the Ritterkreuz for having shot down 20 French and British aircraft, the fifth German fighter pilot to reach this score. By February 2, 1941, he had doubled this figure, the fourth German pilot to reach 40 victories.

Major Ösau was transferred to III/JG 3 Udet as Kommandeur in June, 1941, to prepare for the assault on Russia. He remained on the Eastern front until July when he was recalled to lead JG 2 Richthofen. While in Russia, Ösau shot down 44 Soviet aircraft. He had been awarded the Schwerten, or Swords, to his Ritterkreutz on July 15, 1941, for his 80th victory.

By October 26, 1941, the Oberst had shot down his 100th enemy aircraft and was the third pilot, after Mölders and Lützow, to reach the century mark. Ösau remained Kommodore of JG 2 for two years, and then was made Jafu Brittany. As the pressure of Allied bombing increased, Ösau's expertise was desperately needed at the Kommodore level: therefore,

Walter Ösau was the third pilot to reach the 100-victory mark. After he was shot down by a P-38 Lightning, JG 1 was named in his honor.

he was again transferred, in October, 1943, to lead JG 1 into battle against the waves of bombers and escorting fighters.

Caught in the remorseless grind of continuous fighting since 1939, and even before that in Spain, Ösau began showing the strain, despite his toughness.

After completing about 300 missions, his victory score had reached 123. On May 11, 1944, Ösau led his Geschwader on an intercept mission against Fortresses, escorted by Lightnings and Mustangs, over the Rhineland. Near Aachen, the Kommodore attempted to lure the American fighters away from the bombers so his men could tackle the four-engine giants unmolested. As Walter approached the nearest formation of Mustangs, he was jumped by a high-flying Lightning formation and was trapped. He couldn't make a move, nor could his men hope to intervene before it was all over, and the Kommodore was sent crashing into the Eiffel Mountains.

In tribute to Ösau's leadership ability and fighting acumen, JG 1 was given the name Ösau.

Erich Leie was Geschwader Adjutant for JG 2 with Wick, Balthasar and Ösau. After scoring 118 victories, he was killed in a freak aerial accident.

ERICH LEIE flew with the Richthofen Geschwader for about three years. He was the Geschwader Adjutant with Wick, Balthasar, and Ösau and flew with the Kommodores in their Schwarm. The Kielborn Oblt. Leie had shot down 21 planes during the Battle of Britain by the end of July, 1940, and was awarded the Ritterkreuz in early August. He became Kommandeur of I/JG 2 on May 4, 1942, and was transferred to the Eastern front in the following January, taking command of I/JG 51 Mölders. His combat successes followed him in Russia and he reached the century mark on June 11, 1943. Maj. Leie was promoted to Kommodore of JG 77 on December 29, 1944. Like Ösau, Erich Leie was bending under the strain of continuous combat without respite of any sort, although he was only 29 years old.

On March 7, 1945, a large air battle developed near Schwarzwasser, Hultschin between JG 77 and Soviet Yak fighters. As was usual for combat on the Eastern front, this battle took place below 5,000 feet. As Oberst Leie was about to score another victory, a downed Yak 9, falling out of control, smashed into his Messerschmitt. The two planes locked together

and fell toward earth. At an altitude of only 200 feet, the Kommodore bailed out, but his parachute failed to open, and the veteran of 500 missions and victor of 118 aerial encounters died instantly as his body smashed against the ground.

EGON MAYER, of all the Experten, is the most closely associated with the Richthofen Jagdgeschwader because his entire aerial combat career was spent with JG 2. Mayer was born on August 19, 1917, in Konstanz. He was a glider enthusiast and an eager participant at the Ballenberg glider field as a youngster. As with many Experten, Mayer was a slow starter, but a consistent scorer. He joined JG 2 in December, 1939 and attained his first victory during the Battle of France, but did not shoot down his 20th victory until late July, 1941. Egon received the Ritterkreuz for this scoring. During the Battle of Britain he was shot down four times and force-landed on several occasions. During one defeat, Lt. Mayer fell into the Channel and drifted for over an hour before rescuers arrived.

Egon Mayer helped develop a very successful head-on method of attacking the U.S. day bombers. His entire combat career was flown with JG 2 Richthofen.

His score mounted during the summer of 1942, when he shot down 16 British and U.S. aircraft in a 21-day period. On August 19, 1942, he scored his 50th victory. Mayer was promoted to Hauptmann in November and made Gruppenkommandeur of III/JG 2. He was awarded the Eichenlaub to his Ritterkreuz on April 16, 1943 for his 63rd victory. It was about this time that Mayer began experimenting with better methods of attacking the well-armed B-17 Fortresses. In cooperation with Georg-Peter Eder, Mayer developed the head-on attack method. This approach proved so successful that he managed to shoot down three Fortresses in 19 minutes on September 6, 1943. Promoted again on July 2, 1943, to Oberstleutnant, Mayer was advanced to Kommodore of the Richthofen Geschwader, replacing Walter Ösau. Mayer spent considerable effort indoctrinating the pilots of JG 2, as well as those from other units in the West on the fine points of the head-on attack against the bombers. It required sustained noble courage to hurl one's self at the menacing bomber streams again and again, and this took its toll on the young Kommodore.

A fighter pilot must at all times know precisely how many aircraft are in the skies around him, and whether they are friend or foe. In order to perform this task properly, he must turn his head constantly from side to side, up and down. If he does not, he will soon be jumped by an enemy fighter and become a statistic. This continuous movement forced the neck to rub against the flight-suit collar, causing severe chafing and blistering and made the skin painfully raw. The fighter pilots of the First World War, sitting in open cockpits, are always pictured with a silk scarf around their necks with the ends trailing in the slipstream. While apparently a romantic affectation, the silk scarf was necessary to form a smooth and slippery contact between the neck and collar. Sitting in covered cockpits, the usually dark-colored scarves worn by Second World War fighter pilots were not as obvious, because there was no slipstream to flutter the ends. Egon Mayer wore a white scarf, as did many other pilots, but his was more prominent, either because the scarf was larger or because of the way he wore it. The British and American pilots took notice of this and knew him as "the pilot with the white scarf." They did not know him by name, but they certainly respected his fighting ability.

On February 5, 1944, Egon Mayer became the first pilot in the West to score 100 victories. One month later, on March 2, he led his pilots against American B-17 bombers, heavily escorted by Thunderbolts. As Mayer maneuvered for his head-on at-

tack on the bombers, he was jumped by several flights of Thunderbolts. The 26-year-old ace was shot down near Montmedy, France. Egon Mayer was buried in the cemetery of Beaumont le Reger. He had shot down 102 aircraft during 353 missions. At the time of his death, Mayer was the most successful scorer against the U.S. four-engined bombers, having shot down 25 of the giants.

GEORG-PETER EDER was Egon Mayer's collaborator in the development of the head-on bomber attack. From 1941 to 1945, he was shot down 17 times, wounded on 12 occasions, and forced to bail out 9 times. Despite a body full of scars, he returned to combat each time with renewed vigor and managed to score 78 victories!

Eder was born in Oberdachstetten, Franken on March 8, 1921, and joined the Luftwaffe as a Fahnenjunker at the age of 17. His flight training at the Berlin/Gatow flying school began on April 1, 1939, and after winning his wings, the youth was assigned to Fighter School No. 1 at Werneuchen. His

One of the most chivalrous Experten in the Jagdwaffe was Georg-Peter Eder, who scored 78 victories. He was shot down 17 times and wounded 12 times.

first assignment was with I/JG 51 on the Channel coast. Like many of the Experten, he started slowly, and failed to get any victories in the Battle of Britain. The unit was moved to the East and took part in the invasion of Russia. It was there that Eder shot down his first two victories on June 22, 1941, the first day of the operation. Just after scoring his tenth victory on July 24, Eder was shot down and seriously wounded for the first time, and he spent three months in the hospital.

Upon his release, Eder was given a noncombatant job at the Zerbst Fighter School until he was considered well enough for combat again. In December, 1942 he was posted to 7/JG 2 Richthofen on the Channel coast and, by March 1943, he was placed in command of 12 Staffel. It was about this time that Hauptmann Eder began developing the head-on attack on the U.S. bombers, which proved so successful. During February, 1944, he was transferred to JG 1 as Staffelkapitan of 6 Staffel, and by June he had scored 49 victories. He was awarded the Ritterkreuz on February 22. Promoted again in September, Major Eder was made Gruppenkommandeur of II/JG 26. He ended his wartime career flying jet fighters with JG 7.

Georg-Peter Eder was renowned for his chivalry. He has often been called the most chivalrous fighter pilot in the Luftwaffe, because he never deliberately killed an enemy during his four years of combat. Eder always aimed for the engine and other vital parts of the enemy plane, rather than at the cockpit. Not only wouldn't Eder shoot at the pilot, but he also did not believe in administering the coup de grace to a crippled enemy plane. One case in point was related by Mike Gladych, a Polish pilot flying with the RAF, who met Eder after the war when the two former adversaries compared notes and verified their identities. During a dogfight over the Continent near Lille, France, Eder crippled Gladych's fighter. Instead of finishing off the defenseless enemy, which is what many fighter pilots would have done, Eder flew alongside Gladych and waggled his wings, waved a salute, and left the scene. A short time later, the two adversaries met again during another melee in the air and, once more, Eder got the upper hand. This time he decided to force his victim to land and to capture, rather than kill, him. Making his intentions known through signals, Eder followed the Thunderbolt down. Gladych, however, cleverly led the unsuspecting Eder into German antiaircraft fire, which forced him to turn away sharply. In so doing, he lost his prisoner. Gladych sped for England.

Included in his 78 victories are 36 four-engine bombers. Eder also destroyed three Sherman tanks.

Another 18 victories were not added to his score because they could not be confirmed. While flying the Me 262 jet fighter Eder once rammed an escorting Lightning so that one of his Staffel-mates could get at a Fortress!

KURT BÜHLIGEN was born in Granschütz, Thüringen on December 13, 1917. Kurt had a burning desire to fly and possessed the ability to support this ambition. He joined the Luftwaffe at its inception initially as a mechanic, soon progressing to chief mechanic. Kurt's forceful character qualified him as a fighter pilot, so the Luftwaffe accepted his application for transfer. Bühligen underwent pilot's training during 1938/39, and by July, 1940 he was assigned to JG 2 Richthofen with the rank of Unteroffizier. Kurt Bühligen is one of the lesser-known Experten, despite his superb wartime record. He rose from a noncom airplane mechanic to the rank of Oberstleutnant and Kommodore, and every one of his 112 victories was achieved against the U.S. and British. For unknown reasons, this remarkable man

Kurt Bühligen started as a mechanic and worked his way up to become Kommodore of JG 2 with the rank of Oberstleutnant.

was little publicized during the war. Bühligen scored his first victory on September 4, 1940, during the Battle of Britain. He was awarded the Ritterkreuz one year later, on September 4, 1941, after shooting down his 21st adversary. He had progressed to the rank of Oberfeldwebel by this time.

In December, 1942, Bühligen was transferred to Tunisia, along with many other Jagdwaffe pilots, in an attempt to rescue the beleaguered Afrika Korps. While in North Africa, Kurt shot down 40 enemy aircraft despite overwhelming Allied numerical superiority. He returned to the Channel coast in March, 1943, as the American daylight bombing began in earnest.

By March 2, 1944, Kurt had scored 96 kills and was awarded the Eichenlaub to his Ritterkreuz. He was a major at this time and Gruppenkommandeur of 11/JG 2. During the following May, Bühligen was promoted to the rank of Oberstleutnant and made Kommodore of JG 2. He shot down his 100th victim in June, and after scoring 12 more he was transferred to the Russian front. In early 1945, while leading his pilots in a Freie Jagd over Soviet-held territory, Kurt's engine malfunctioned and the Kommodore was forced to land. Quickly overcome by Russian troops, Bühligen was held as a POW until 1950! The war was over soon after his capture, so Bühligen had the distinction of being the last Kommodore of JG 2 Richthofen.

Hans "Assi" Hahn flew in the Battle of Britain with Wick, Balthasar, and Ösau. He later endured seven years in Soviet captivity.

HANS HAHN, another Expert closely associated with JG 2, flew in the Battle of Britain with Wick, Balthasar, and Ösau. Hans, known as Assi, was born in Gotha on April 14, 1914, and joined JG 2 in 1939 as an Oberstleutnant. Assi was a quick starter and steady scorer, attaining his first two victories, Fighter Command Hurricanes, on his very first engagement with enemy aircraft on May 14, 1940. His score reached 20 victories by September 24, 1940, for which he was awarded the Ritterkreuz and promoted from Staffelkapitan of 4/JG 2 to Gruppenkommandeur of III/JG 2. One year later, on August 14, 1941, Assi Hahn received the Eichenlaub for scoring his 41st victory, and was promoted to Hauptmann.

Throughout the Battle of Britain, Hahn was in the front rank of Jagdwaffe pilots, and his jovial personality, love of life, and self-confidence made him very popular with his fellow pilots. These factors enabled him to overcome the adversities he was to face in Russia.

After scoring 68 victories over the RAF, 62 of which were Fighter Command Spitfires and Hurricanes, Major Assi Hahn was transferred to JG 54 Grünherz on the Russian front. Hans reported to his new post on November 1, 1942, and, against the strange enemy, his score still continued to grow steadily. One of his most successful days was January 6, 1943, when he shot down eight Russian Lagg fighters over Lake Ladoga. Twenty days later, Hahn shot down his 100th victim. Assi scored his 40 Soviet victories in only seven encounters with the enemy.

During his 560th mission on February 21, 1943, while leading his Gruppe over Soviet-held terrain, Hahn's engine began to malfunction and he was compelled to negotiate a forced landing. Capture was inevitable and Hahn spent the next seven years as a prisoner in the Soviet Union.

Having scored 108 confirmed kills, plus 36 probables, by early 1943 it is impossible not to conjecture what Hans Hahn's ultimate victory count might have been had he remained in action for the remaining years of the war.

FRANK LIESENDAHL was not one of the Experten; however, his expertise in leading Jabo missions justifies his mention in this volume. Born in Wuppertal-Barman on February 23, 1915, Liesendahl joined the Luftwaffe just before the war began. After com-

Frank Liesendahl developed the technique of bombing with fighter aircraft that is still in use today by the world's major air services.

pleting his training, he was assigned to fly with JG 53 during most of 1940. In the spring of 1941 he was transferred to JG 2 Richthofen, flying with the 6 Staffel, and on November 10, 1941, he was promoted to Staffelkapitan of 10/JG 2.

The decision to employ 10/JG 2 in Jagbomber, or fighter-bomber, activities made it imperative that Liesendahl and his men attend classes on single-engine bomber techniques. Unfortunately, the only courses available were dive-bomber oriented and not suitable to the high diving speeds of contemporary fighter aircraft. It was, therefore, necessary for Oblt. Liesendahl to develop a new technique that would be successful with the Messerschmitt. After repeated tests and experiments under combat conditions, he found that a low-altitude shallow dive, with a quick zoom upon release of the bomb-load, was ideal for fighter planes. This technique was adopted by every air force in the world, and is still in use today.

Led by Hauptmann Liesendahl, 10/JG 2 pounded British coastal shipping, and by June 26, 1942, the Staffel had sent no less than 20 ships, totaling over 60,000 tons, to the bottom of the Channel. While the Experten were shooting down aircraft, Frank Liesendahl and his men were sinking supply-laden ships destined for British ports.

On July 17, 10/JG 2 was at it again off the coast of Brixham, England. Liesendahl led the attack, but somehow became separated from his Staffel as he swooped towards a cargo ship. He was never seen again nor was his plane ever located. Hptm. Frank Liesendahl was awarded the Ritterkreuz posthumously on September 4, 1942, for his outstanding success as a Jabo leader.

WERNER JUNCK was one of the Alte Adler, a former World War I pilot who had answered Göring's call to help lead the new Luftwaffe. Born in Magdeburg on December 28, 1895, Junck scored five victories in the 1914/1918 war and became the first Kommodore of JG 53 Pikas, or Ace of Spades, in April, 1938. In October of 1939, Werner was replaced by Hans Klein, another Alte Adler, who had flown with Manfred von Richthofen. In 1941, Junck led a Luftwaffe mission to Iraq and arranged to supply fighter aircraft to that country in exchange for political and military concessions. Upon his return to Germany, he was made Jafu 3. When the Anglo-American air offensive reached its peak, Gen. Maj. Werner Junck was placed in command of II Jagdkorps. His job was to blunt the sharpest thrust of the Allied air fleets. He was awarded the Ritterkreuz on June 9, 1944, for his leadership during this harrowing period.

GÜNTHER FREIHERR VON MALTZAHN succeeded Jürgen von Cramon-Taubadel (who had followed Hans Klein), as Kommodore of JG 53 Pikas on November 10, 1940. Often called Henri by his fellow officers, von Maltzahn was one of the great fighter leaders, of the caliber of Galland, Trautloft, and Lützow. Like them, he had the strength of character and sufficient interest in the welfare of his men to confront the top brass.

Born on October 20, 1910 of noble parentage (Freiherr is akin to Baron) in Wodarg, Pommern, von Maltzahn joined the Luftwaffe in the mid-thirties. By August, 1939, he was Kommandeur of II/JG 53. As Kommodore of JG 53 he led his men to battle on the Western front, Russia, the Mediterranean, and North Africa. In October, 1943, he was appointed Jafu or Jagdführer (fighter leader) of the Luftwaffe forces in Italy.

Günther flew a total of over 500 missions and scored 68 victories, 35 of which were Anglo-American.

Günther Freiherr von Maltzahn led JG 53 to battle on three fronts and took part in the Mutiny of the Fighters in an attempt to improve the condition of the Jagdwaffe.

Herbert Rollwage shot down 44 four-engined bombers and a total of over 400 crew members, more than any other Jagdwaffe pilot.

HERBERT ROLLWAGE shot down more Allied daylight four-engined bombers than any other Luftwaffe pilot: 44. He joined 5/JG 53 in early 1941 as a Feldwebel, fighting on the Eastern front, and moved with von Maltzahn's Geschwader to the Mediterranean area in January, 1942. Born in Gielde bei Goslar on September 24, 1916, the 27-year-old noncom returned to Western Europe in Autumn of 1943 to combat the waves of Allied bombers. By April of the following year, Rollwage had shot down 53 adversaries, and was awarded the Ritterkreuz on the 4th of that month. Oberfeldwebel Rollwage continued his scoring against the Western Allies and was commissioned as a Lieutenant in the field. On January 21, 1945, the Eichenlaub was added to his Ritterkreuz. Just as the war in Europe ended, Herbert Rollwage scored his 102nd victory. All but 11 victories had been Western Allied aircraft.

RUDOLF EHRENBERGER and FRANZ BARTEN were two JG 53 Experten who were shot and killed by Allied pilots as they dangled helplessly in their parachute harnesses.

Ehrenberger, an Austrian born in Erbesthal, had joined 6/JG 53 as an Oberfeldwebel in the Mediterranean area, where he remained for two years. He then fought the U.S. bombers and fighter escorts over the skies of Europe. On March 8, 1944, after scoring his 49th victory, Rudolf's plane was hit by fire from escorting U.S. fighter planes. Ehrenberger bailed out of his crippled plane near Jüterborg, and as he drifted earthward, one of the Allied fighter planes fired at the German and killed him. Rudolf Ehrenberger was awarded the Ritterkreuz posthumously on April 4, 1944.

Saarbrücken-born Barten had been posted to IV/JG 51 as a Feldwebel in 1939. He transferred to III/JG 53 in June, 1943. Oberleutnant Barten became Staffelkapitan of 9/JG 53, and had scored 52 victories by August, 1944. On August 4 Franz Barten embarked on his 895th mission to intercept U.S. bombers. He engaged in a dogfight with superior numbers of escorting fighters and received a hit, forcing him to abandon his aircraft near Soltau. While suspended from his parachute, Barten was shot by an Allied fighter and killed instantly with a

JG 53 Pikas Experten Rudolf Ehrenberger and Franz Barten reportedly were shot after they bailed out of their damaged aircraft.

bullet through his head. Franz Barten was posthumously promoted to the rank of Hauptmann and awarded the Ritterkreuz on December 6, 1944.

THEODORE OSTERKAMP was the organizer and first Kommodore of JG 51, later known as the Mölders Geschwader. Born in Düren in the Rheinland on April 15, 1892, Osterkamp commanded Marinejagdstaffel 2 in Flanders during the First World War.

He scored 32 victories in that conflict and earned the coveted Pour le Merite, or Blue Max. After the war, Osterkamp joined the anti-Communist Iron Division and fought against the Russian Bolsheviks, who were infiltrating westward from the Baltic to the Balkans.

His interest in aviation and air racing kept Osterkamp occupied until he heeded Göring's call in 1935 and joined the infant Luftwaffe. He was in command of Jagdfliegerschule No. 1 until November, 1939, when he formed JG 51.

Despite his age, which was twice that of the older members of the Geschwader, Osterkamp was no armchair commander. He led his men into battle in

Alte Adler Theodore Osterkamp became an ace in two wars and then became Jafu 2 during the Battle of Britain.

the French campaign and the Battle of Britain, inspiring them to greater achievements against the enemy. Because of this, and the fact that he assumed a paternal association with his men, he was affectionately called Onkel Theo, or Uncle Theo. After scoring six victories against the French and British, he was promoted to Jafu in the Battle of Britain during August, 1940 and directed the Jagdwaffe activity against Fighter Command. Later in the war, Generalleutnant Osterkamp was Jafu in Italy. He was awarded the Ritterkreuz on August 22, 1940, when, as a General Major, he commanded the German fighter force on the Channel coast.

WERNER MÖLDERS succeeded Osterkamp as Kommodore of JG 51 and eventually gave his name to the unit. Born on March 18, 1913, in Gelsenkirchen, he became the model for all young German fighter pilots, who discussed their idol with unbridled enthusiasm. Despite his young age, he earned the name Vati, or Daddy, from his subordinates. He became the first man to exceed Baron von Richthofen's 80 victories and the first to score 100 enemy aircraft in aerial combat.

Werner's father was a school teacher killed in the Argonne during the First World War, and Werner had been intent on a military career since boyhood. He entered the Dresden Military Academy in 1932 and graduated a Leutnant two years later. In late 1934, Mölders applied for flight training in the clandestine Luftwaffe and, although he passed all written and medical tests, he failed the centrifugal spin chair test. This test made Mölders very dizzy, and caused him to vomit, turn pale, and tremble. In effect, it made him so ill that the doctor in charge proclaimed him unfit to become a pilot and suggested that he remain in the Army with both feet on the ground. Werner was determined, however, and pursued his goal without respite. He practiced incessantly until he passed the test. This, however, did not mean that flying did not make him ill. He was often airsick as he checked out in the Heinkel He 45s and Junkers Ju 34s at the Deutsche Verkehrsfliegerschule in Brunswick, commanded by World War One bomber leader Alfred Keller. Giddiness, headaches, and vomiting continued to plague Mölders as he completed advanced training at Kampffliegerschule. After dive-bombing training at Schleissheim, he was posted to Stukageschwader Immelmann in Schwerin and slowly began to conquer his ailment.

In March, 1936, Mölders and five other pilots were ordered to Düsseldorf, where they provided air cover for the German military occupation of the Rhineland. He was then transferred to Jagdfliegerschule No. 1 under Osterkamp. Werner Mölders became the leader of Jastaschule Staffel 1 and trained many future Experten, among them Wick, Ösau, and Hahn.

As the Condor Legion was busily supporting the Nationalists in Spain, a new leader for 3 Staffel of JG 88 was needed to replace Adolf Galland. The Luftwaffe Oberkommando selected Mölders for the job, and he arrived in Spain in April, 1938. After performing for one month under the critical eye of Galland, Werner was approved for the new post. By July, the Staffel had received the Messerschmitt Me 109B, and on the 15th of the month Mölders scored his first victory. Leading his men to the attack on a formation of Polikarpov I-16 Rata fighters, Werner's first burst missed his quarry by a wide margin. Angered by his failure, he quickly closed in on another Rata and didn't fire until he was so close that the image of the enemy craft filled his windshield. This time his shells struck home and the I-16 burst into flame and smoke. He realized then that the first victory was the most difficult because, with his heart pounding and stomach turning, it was almost impossible for the novice to keep his wits about him as he closed in on his intended first victim. Hereafter, Werner Mölders devoted considerable time and effort to helping every new pilot under his command not only to score his first victory, but to overcome the shock that many pilots experience after it. This mild-mannered, sensitive, devout Catholic had experienced both previctory tension and postvictory shock, so he understood the condition and was able to help many tyro pilots overcome this serious problem.

Werner Mölders quickly realized that the aerial tactics of 1938 were geared to slow biplanes and were severely outmoded with the advent of modern monoplane fighters. It was at this time that he revolutionized fighter combat tactics with the loose two-element, finger-four formation, described in the previous chapter.

By October 31, 1938, Mölders had scored his 14th and last victory in Spain. In early November, he returned to Germany as the highest scoring pilot in the Condor Legion. Werner spent the winter months indoctrinating the Luftwaffe in his new tactics, and on March 15, 1939, he was made Staffelkapitan of I/JG 53 and promoted to the rank of Hauptmann. In August, Mölders' former pupil Helmut Wick became a member of his Staffel and, in October, 1939, Pour le Merite winner Hans Klein became Kommodore of the Geschwader. During the opening days of the Battle of France, Mölders was elevated to Gruppen-

Werner Mölders was the foremost combat tactician of WWII. Shown are the nose and tail of his Battle of Britain Emil.

kommandeur of III/JG 53.

Mölders opened his World War II scoring during the French campaign on September 20, 1939, when he shot down an American-made Curtiss Hawk 75A. On May 28, 1940, he became the first Jagdwaffe pilot to reach 20 victories and on the following day the first to be awarded the Ritterkreuz. His scoring tactic was to fire at close range, preferring the machine guns to the cannon as his principal armament.

On the morning of June 5, 1940, Mölders shot down his 24th and 25th victories over Compiegne. Later in the afternoon, he led 15 Messerschmitts on patrol over Chantilly Forest in the region of Bray-sur-Somme. The Germans encountered a triple flight patrol of Escadrille France from Groupe de Chasse 2/7, flying Dewoitine 520 and Morane fighters.

The French aircraft were led by Capitaine Hugo, who ordered Sous-Lieutenant Rene Pomier-Layrargues to take one flight up to 20,000 feet. This split patrol surprised Mölders, and he lost two Messerschmitts at the outset. While Mölders was preoccupied leading his young wingman to his first kill, Pomier-Layrargues, flying a Dewoitine, dived and raked the German's Messerschmitt with a long burst, shattering the canopy and setting the engine aflame. Mölders quickly bailed out and floated to earth near the town of Villerseau, where he was captured by French troops. The Kommandeur was taken to the Chateau de Blincourt for interrogation by Captaine Drouot and Sous-Leutnant Bassous via interpreter Zimmermann. Mölders' life as a POW ended soon afterwards because France surrendered a few weeks later. Upon his return to Germany on

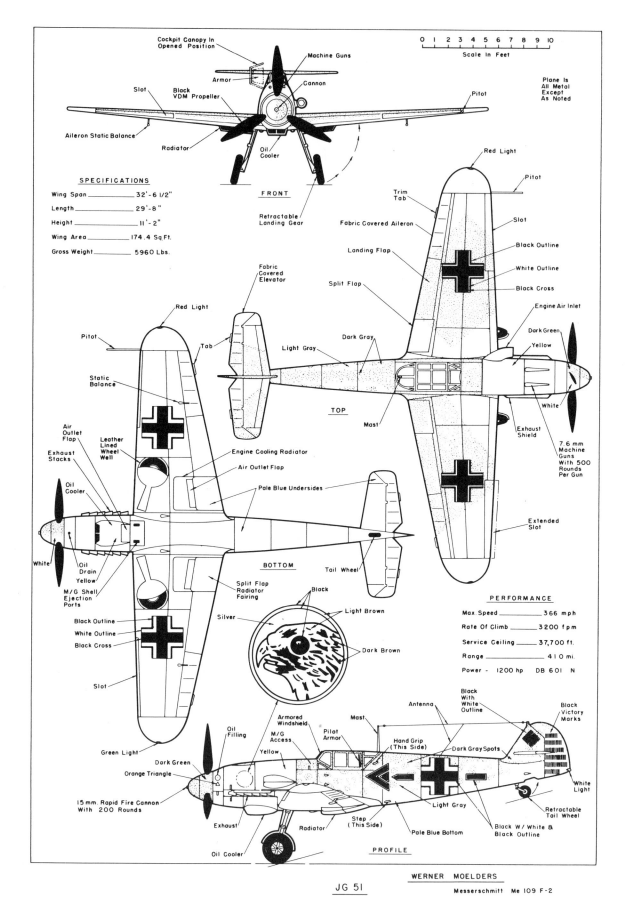

Cockpit Canopy In Opened Position

Machine Guns

Armor

Cannon

Slot

Black VDM Propeller

Pitot

Aileron Static Balance

Radiator

Oil Cooler

0 1 2 3 4 5 6 7 8 9 10
Scale In Feet

Plane Is All Metal Except As Noted

FRONT

Retractable Landing Gear

SPECIFICATIONS

Wing Span _____ 32'-6 1/2"

Length _____ 29'-8"

Height _____ 11'-2"

Wing Area _____ 174.4 Sq.Ft.

Gross Weight _____ 5960 Lbs.

Red Light

Pitot

Trim Tab

Fabric Covered Aileron

Slot

Landing Flap

Black Outline

White Outline

Split Flap

Black Cross

Fabric Covered Elevator

Dark Gray

Engine Air Inlet

Dark Green

Yellow

Light Gray

Red Light

Pitot

Tab

White

TOP

Static Balance

Mast

Exhaust Shield

7.6 mm Machine Guns With 500 Rounds Per Gun

Air Outlet Flap

Leather Lined Wheel Well

Exhaust Stacks

Engine Cooling Radiator

Oil Cooler

Air Outlet Flap

Pale Blue Undersides

White

Oil Drain

Yellow

M/G Shell Ejection Ports

Extended Slot

BOTTOM

Tail Wheel

Black Outline

White Outline

Black Cross

Split Flap Radiator Fairing

Silver

Black

Light Brown

Dark Brown

Slot

PERFORMANCE

Max. Speed _____ 366 mph

Rate Of Climb _____ 3200 fpm

Service Ceiling _____ 37,700 ft.

Range _____ 410 mi.

Power - 1200 hp   DB 601 N

Green Light

Dark Green

Orange Triangle

15 mm. Rapid Fire Cannon With 200 Rounds

Oil Filling

M/G Access

Yellow

Armored Windshield

Pilot Armor

Mast

Antenna

Hand Grip (This Side)

Black With White Outline

Dark Gray Spots

Black Victory Marks

White Light

Exhaust

Radiator

Step (This Side)

Light Gray

Pale Blue Bottom

Retractable Tail Wheel

Black W/ White & Black Outline

Oil Cooler

PROFILE

WERNER MOELDERS

Messerschmitt Me 109 F-2

July 19, 1940, he was promoted to Major.

Eight days later, Werner Mölders was selected to succeed Osterkamp as Kommodore of JG 51. On that day, during a morning Freie Jagd over England, he was jumped by famous British Ace Squadron Leader Adolf "Sailor" Malan, who riddled the Messerschmitt so badly that it barely made it back to the Continent. Mölders was wounded in the knee during the fight and crash-landed at Wissant, near Calais. Werner was ordered hospitalized, so Osterkamp was forced to remain with JG 51 for four additional weeks.

Back in action, Mölders shot down his 40th victory on September 29, 1940, again the first pilot to score this number. The Eichenlaub was added to his Ritterkreuz on this date, the second Luftwaffe officer to receive it. He was also promoted to Oberstleutnant at this time. Vati Mölders was a serious and quiet man with a strong sense of responsibility. He possessed great inner strength and directed tremendous energy into his work, combining outstanding administrative, tactical, leadership, and individual combat abilities. He believed that a soldierly, chivalrous code must be followed in war, and once, when he saw the Kommandeur of I/JG 51 strafing a train in England, he was filled with horror. Upon returning to base, Mölders summoned Hauptmann Joppien and gave him a severe lecture on the differences between military and civilian targets.

By February 26, 1941, Werner had scored his 60th victory, and was Germany's second leading ace after Hermann-Friedrich Joppien. With 68 kills to his credit, he took his Geschwader to the East, leading it in the June 22 attack on Russia. Mölders shot down four Soviet aircraft on the day of the invasion, bringing his score to 74. Later, he shot down five Reds in one day for a total of 82 victories. Mölders was awarded the Schwerten, or Swords, to the Ritterkreuz on June 22, 1941. Eight days later, JG 51 was the first Jagdgeschwader to score 1,000 victories. During this period, in a single action-packed day, JG 51 shot down no less than 96 Soviet aircraft, Mölders scoring 11 of the total! His Rottenflieger, Erwin Fleig, had a difficult time keeping up with his leader. On July 15, Werner shot down his 100th and 101st victories, the first fighter pilot to attain this score. For this achievement, he was awarded the Brillanten, or Diamonds, to his Ritterkreuz, the first member of the German armed forces to receive this award. By the end of July, Mölders' score had reached 115 victories and, realizing that Werner was too valuable to risk in combat, the Luftwaffe Oberkommando grounded him. He was given a staff position at headquarters with the rank of a full Oberst,

the youngest in the Luftwaffe.

His performance at headquarters was so outstanding that, in September, 1941, the 28-year-old Mölders was appointed Inspecteur der Jagdflieger, or Inspector of Fighters. In his new job, Mölders was seldom at his desk. He was constantly on the move, traveling along the long Russian front, wherever his expertise was required. His staff car became his office. In mid-November Mölders was in the Crimea, creating and directing battle groups of Stukas and fighters. Fighting was extremely heavy and Mölders was running into serious support problems: not enough fuel, ammunition, or spare parts, a condition which always plagued the Luftwaffe. As he was deciding to fly to Berlin to argue for support, Mölders received notice of Ernst Udet's suicide with the request that he be a member of the Honor Guard at the funeral. He lost no time in arranging for a flight to Berlin.

Despite inclement weather, Mölders took off in a Heinkel He III bomber from Kherson airport and flew to Lemberg to pick up a load of mail. The plane took off from Lemberg in a violent rainstorm, but Mölders insisted that the flight continue despite pleas from the pilot to turn back. The weather deteriorated between Lemberg and Berlin, with powerful headwinds pounding the Heinkel. As the flight neared Breslau, one of the engines stopped, and all efforts to restart it failed. Mölders then ordered the pilot to land at the nearest airfield, which was Schmiedefeld on the outskirts of Breslau. As the plane was making its final approach to the runway, the second engine failed, and the Heinkel slammed into the ground, killing Mölders, who was sitting in the copilot's seat. He died of a broken neck.

The entire nation mourned the passing of a pilot whose character and exploits had found a place in the hearts of the populace. JG 51 was awarded the name Mölders. Werner Mölders was remembered even after the war's end. In 1969, a West German missile-firing destroyer, DDG-29, was named Mölders in honor of the fallen hero.

KARL-GOTTFRIED NORDMANN was, like Mölders, one of the Jagdwaffe's leading personalities. He served as Kommodore of JG 51 about six months after Mölders' death. Nordmann was born in Giessen, Hesse on November 22, 1915, and started his combat career with I/JG 77 in Poland. In the summer of 1940, he became Staffelkapitan of 12/JG 51 on the Channel coast, and in July of the following year he was promoted to Gruppenkommandeur of IV/JG 51. On August 1, 1941, the Oberleutnant was awarded the Ritterkreuz for his 31st victory, and on

Mölders' successor to the leadership of JG 51 was Karl-Gottfried Nordmann, who scored 78 victories. He became Jafu East Prussia on the Eastern front.

Hermann-Friedrich Joppien was one of the more agressive Jagdfliegern; on more than one occasion his zeal earned a reprimand from Mölders.

September 16 he received the Eichenlaub to go with it for his 59th victory. Nordmann became JG 51 Kommodore on April 10, 1942, and two years later he was made Jafu in East Prussia on the Russian front. Having flown over 800 missions, Oberst Nordmann shot down 78 adversaries.

HERMAN-FRIEDRICH JOPPIEN served his entire combat career with JG 51. The aggressive Oberleutnant received the Ritterkreuz on September 16, 1940, for his 21st victory. Born on July 19, 1912, in Bad Hersfeld, Joppien developed into one of the most successful German fighter pilots of the early war years, shooting down 25 planes during the Battle of Britain. When he scored his 40th victory on April 21, 1941, he was the Luftwaffe's fifth-ranking Expert. Two days later, he received the Eichenlaub to his Ritterkreuz. During a very low-altitude dogfight on August 21, 1941, near Brjansk, Russia, he slipped out of a sharp turn and smashed into the ground, and his plane burst into flames. Hauptmann Joppien is officially credited with 70 victories.

HEINRICH KRAFFT also started his career with I/JG 51 in early 1940, and scored his first victory on May 21, 1940. He was awarded the Ritterkreuz on March 18, 1942 for his 46th victory and became the Kommandeur of I/JG 51 in May. The Hauptmann was born on August 13, 1914, in Bilin, Böhmen and was given the name of Gaudi. While flying over Russian-held Bjeloi on December 14, 1942, Krafft's Messerschmitt was damaged by intensive Soviet antiaircraft fire and forced to crash-land. Apparently highly decorated German officers were especially liable to brutal treatment by Soviet troops. As soon as Krafft's captors saw his Ritterkreuz, they beat the victor of 78 adversaries to death.

HANS STRELOW, born in Berlin on March 26, 1922, was a 19-year-old youth when he joined II/JG 51 Mölders in early 1941. His first victory came three days after the German attack on Russia, and by the end of the year Strelow had shot down 28 Soviet aircraft. His big month was March, 1942, when he destroyed 26 enemy aircraft in aerial combat. On March 18, Strelow was awarded the Ritterkreuz and, because of outstanding dedication to his

The victor of 78 encounters, Heinrich Krafft of JG 51 was beaten to death by Russian troops when he was forced to crash-land in Soviet-held territory.

With 189 official victories, Joachim Brendel was one of the most successful pilots in JG 51—yet he is little known for his exploits.

duties, the Eichenlaub to his Ritterkreuz only six days later, the youngest recipient of this award in the German armed forces.

With 67 victories to his credit, Strelow encountered Russian Pe-2 twin engine fighter-bombers while on a mission over Soviet territory. After shooting down one of the enemy aircraft, Strelow's Messerschmitt developed engine trouble and he was forced to land in enemy territory. As was customary, hordes of Russian infantry rushed towards the German. Having heard stories of what fate had befallen other pilots who survived emergency landings behind enemy lines, especially if the German wore medals, the 20-year-old Strelow was last seen raising his pistol to his head. Apparently, Hans Strelow preferred suicide to the indignity of being mauled, beaten, or shot by angry Soviets.

JOACHIM BRENDEL was one of the most successful pilots of JG 51, with 189 victories. Yet he is little known for his exploits. Born in Ulrichshalben bei Weimar on April 27, 1921, Brendel began his combat

Nineteen-year-old Hans Strelow preferred death to being beaten and tortured by Soviet troops; when his crash-landed Messerschmitt was surrounded by Russian troops, he shot himself.

career in June, 1941, as a Leutnant and Rottenflieger with I/JG 51 on the Russian front. He scored his first victory during his fourth mission, on June 29, but had to wait 116 missions before he scored again on March 31, 1942! By December, he had shot down only ten adversaries, a decidedly slow starter, as were many of the leading Experten.

The beginning of 1943 saw a marked change in Brendel's performance, as he progressively improved. By February 24, he had 20 kills; May 5, 30 victories; June 10, 40; and on July 9, during his 412th mission, he scored his 50th official victory. By the Oberleutnant's 551st sortie on November 22, he had almost doubled his score. His 95th official victory on that date brought him the Ritterkreuz. Brendel's score continued to climb, despite that the Jagdwaffe was becoming increasingly outnumbered by Soviet aircraft. Brendel's 150th kill came on October 16, 1944. He received the Eichenlaub to his Ritterkreuz on January 14, 1945, for his 156th victory. By this time, he had been promoted to the rank of Hauptmann and was Gruppenkommandeur of III/JG 51. Joachim Brendel's final victory was on April 25, 1945, shortly before the war's end in Europe.

ERWIN FLEIG spent his entire wartime career flying with JG 51, and became Werner Mölders' Rottenflieger. Born on December 6, 1912 in Freiburg, Breisgau, he joined JG 51 in June, 1940 as a Feldwebel, and engaged in many Jabo missions over England and in Russia. Commissioned a Leutnant in the field, Fleig was awarded the Ritterkreuz on August 12, 1941, for his 26th victory. On May 29, 1942, six months after his leader died, Erwin was shot down near Szokoloje, Russia, and forced to bail out. The winner of 66 official victories was taken prisoner by the Soviets and released in the fifties.

ANTON HAFNER was the most successful fighter pilot of JG 51, with 204 official victories. Hafner was also involved in one of the most interesting stories to emerge from the carnage of World War II. Born in Erbach bei Ulm on June 2, 1918, Hafner joined 6/JG 51 in June, 1941, as an Unteroffizier in Russia. By August, 1942, he had already scored 60 victories and was awarded the Ritterkreuz on August 23. In November, Hafner was transferred, with II/JG 51, to North Africa to combat the Americans in Tunisia.

On December 18, 1942, Feldwebel Hafner was part of an intercepting force directed against a raiding U.S. bomber formation. At about 30,000 feet, the Staffel met the escorting Lightnings near Tunis, and almost immediately one of the Americans fastened himself onto the tail of one of Hafner's buddies.

Much of an Experten's success can be attributed to the quality of his Rottenflieger. Erwin Fleig was Werner Mölders' wingman in JG 51.

Anton sped to the rescue and the three planes twisted and turned down to 15,000 feet. Hafner then scored some decisive hits on the port engine of the P-38, causing it to burst into flame. The American pilot bailed out, and as he drifted in his chute, Hafner circled several times. This made the helpless American think the German intended to machine gun him, not realizing that Anton followed the Jagdwaffe code of chivalry. The P-38 pilot landed in a swamp near the German airfield and was brought by German troops to the II Gruppe mess hall. Hafner introduced himself as the victor of the combat. The downed U.S. pilot was Lt. Norman L. Widen of Onalaska, Wisconsin, and the two men had a long talk over lunch, getting to know each other quite well. Widen gave Hafner his silver pilot's wings and the serial identification plate from his P-38. Before he was taken to a POW camp, the men agreed to meet after the war. Lt. Widen was Hafner's 82nd victory. Anton sent Widen's wings and serial nameplate to his brother Alfons, in Germany, with the request that, should he be killed in action, Alfons must find this American pilot after the war. He was to give the American one of Anton's many medals, plus an oil portrait of himself, and return the wings and nameplate as well.

Anton Hafner was the most successful Expert of JG 51, with 204 victories. He was killed when he hit a tree during a dogfight.

U.S. Lt. Norman Widen is shown in an early snapshot and, after becoming Hafner's 82nd victim, he is seen dragging his parachute, hands raised in surrender. He then jokes with his victor and other JG 51 pilots.

Alfons Hafner displays part of the legacy that his brother, Anton, bequeathed to Lt. Widen, who was his 82nd victory. The painting on the wall is also included in the legacy.

EDUARD RITTER VON SCHLEICH was the most illustrious Alte Adler to fly combat sorties in World War II. The victor of 35 aerial encounters in the 1914/1918 war, von Schleich was known as the Black Knight by friend and foe alike, due to his aircraft's jet-black fuselage. He was one of four Jagdgeschwader leaders in the entire WWI German air service, where he commanded four Jagdstaffeln. During the postwar years, von Schleich assumed an active part in stimulating interest in aviation in Germany. Employed by Lufthansa, he became one of the organizers of the Munich Sport Flyers' Club. When Hitler came to power, Ritter von Schleich joined the newly formed Luftwaffe and also became an officer in the S.S. Active in the National Socialist program, von Schleich helped organize the Hitler Youth Aviation Program, which spawned many of the Experten of the Second World War.

Ritter von Schleich led Condor Legion formations in Spain, and upon his return to Germany was promoted to Oberst and placed in command of Jagdgruppe 132 (later to evolve into the highly successful JG 26 Schlageter). He led this unit until the end of 1939, when Major Gotthard Handrick succeeded him as Kommodore. The Black Knight climb-

In the summer of 1943, Anton Hafner was back in Russia with III/JG 51 after scoring 20 kills in Tunisia. His score continued to increase rapidly, and Hafner was commissioned a Leutnant in the field during the winter. He was awarded the Eichenlaub on April 11, 1944, for his 134th victory, and elevated to Staffelkapitan of 8/JG 51 in the following month. Hafner shot down his 150th victory on June 28, and by July 17, he had vanquished 204 adversaries in aerial combat.

On July 17, while flying his 795th mission, Hafner engaged a Soviet Yak-9 in a dogfight at extremely low altitude. During an unguarded moment, his Messerschmitt skidded, lost altitude, and slammed into a tree. Hafner was killed instantly.

In 1960, Alfons Hafner sought the help of the U.S. Air Force in locating Widen, by then a Major, in order to comply with his brother's wishes. Major Widen was located and, together with his wife and their two young children, flew to Germany on a military transport plane to meet Alfons and collect this most unusual legacy. It has been said that war brings out either the best or the worst in human behavior; in this story the heat of battle transformed adversaries into friends!

The Black Knight of World War I, Eduard Ritter von Schleich, flew combat missions in Spain as well as France. He is shown here in 1937, wearing the WWI Blue Max at his throat.

Adolf Galland is one of the most widely known of the Experten. He is shown here in an official portrait, and with his mechanic near his Emil.

ed the ladder to greater responsibilities and, with the rank of Major General, was placed in command of all Luftwaffe units based in Denmark. He soon retired from this post due to failing health. Eduard Ritter von Schleich died in 1947.

ADOLF GALLAND, who greatly admired von Schleich, can be said to have succeeded his hero to the leadership of JG 26, as Handrick had led the unit for only seven months before Galland became Kommodore on August 22, 1940. Galland, with Helmut Wick, and Werner Mölders, did much to attract attention to the Jagdwaffe during the Battle of Britain. Today, he is the informal representative of the Jagdwaffe on the international scene, and is to be found wherever fighter pilots congregate.

Born on March 19, 1912 in Westerholt, Westfalen, Adolf was descended from a family of Huguenots who emigrated to Germany from France to escape persecution. His father was bailiff to the Graf von Westerholt, a position of honor held by all Galland family heads. Adolf was an air-minded youngster, and was gliding by the time he was 19. Upon graduation from the Gymnasium at Buer, Westfalen, Galland enlisted in the Deutches Fliegerschule in Bruns-

wick in 1932. Managed by Alte Adler Alfred Keller, the school was, of course, a subterfuge to train future pilots of the yet-unborn Luftwaffe.

Adolf crashed once during basic training, injuring his eye and smashing his nose. The eye injury impaired his vision to the point where he couldn't read the eye chart. This was important because, although he passed his initial exam, the students were given physicals periodically throughout the training period. So strong was Galland's desire to fly that he managed to memorize the standard eye chart and passed all subsequent physicals. He still carries a scarred eyebrow as a reminder of his training crash. Upon completion of advanced training in Grotaglia, Italy, he became an instructor at the clandestine Jagdfliegerschule at Schleissheim near Munich. When the Luftwaffe was announced to the world in 1935, Galland was posted with JG 2 Richthofen.

He was promoted to the rank of Oberleutnant on August 1, 1937, and, shortly thereafter, volunteered for action in Spain with the Condor Legion. As Staffelkapitan of 3/J 88, Galland flew 300 ground-support sorties in Heinkel He 51 biplanes. His plane's obsolescence and the nature of his missions prevented Galland from scoring any victories. He

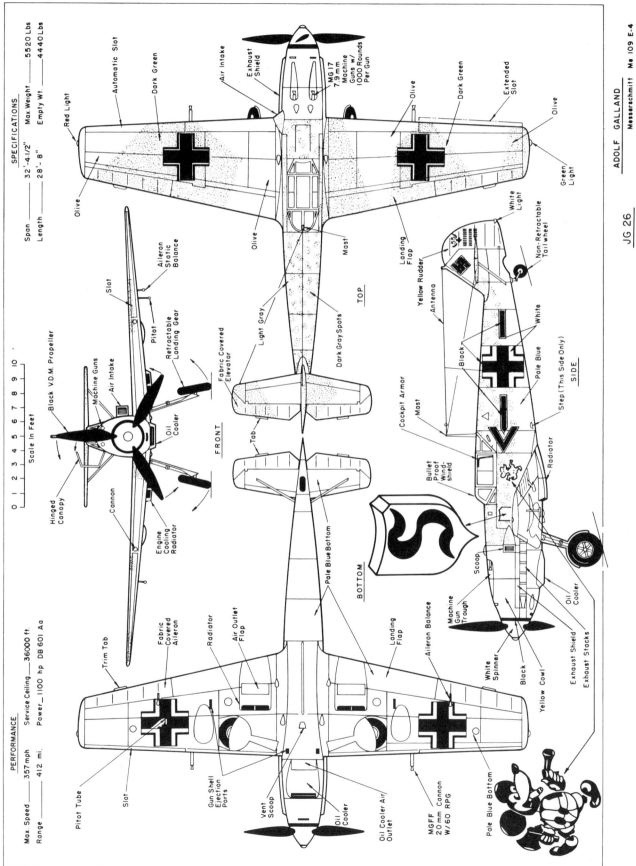

ADOLF GALLAND   Messerschmitt   Me 109 E-4

JG 26

SPECIFICATIONS

Span	32'-4-1/2"	Max Weight ___ 5520 Lbs
Length	28'- 8"	Empty Wt. ___ 4440 Lbs

PERFORMANCE

Max. Speed ___ 357 mph	Service Ceiling ___ 36000 ft.
Range ___ 412 mi.	Power ___ 1100 hp DB 601 Aa

Scale In Feet

0 1 2 3 4 5 6 7 8 9 10

TOP

FRONT

BOTTOM

SIDE

The fuselage and rudder markings of Galland's Emil clearly show the JG 26 Schlageter Shield, the cigar-smoking Mickey Maus, and the victory marks on the rudder (58 victories).

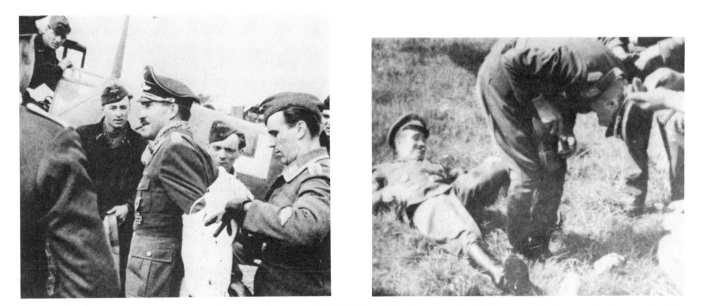

Renowned for his cigar smoking and sense of humor, Adolf Galland is shown on the left preparing for a mission during the Battle of Britain. Observe the many attendants—almost the equivalent of outfitting a medieval knight for battle. On the right, Galland reclines on the grass while a fellow officer repairs the heel of his boot.

was replaced by Mölders and returned to Germany in May, 1938. In appreciation for his ground-support achievements, Francisco Franco presented the Spanish Cross in Gold and Diamonds to Galland on June 7, 1939.

Upon his return to Germany, Galland was assigned to prepare reports and recommendations on ground-support tactics, in view of his experience gained in Spain. Although the pilot found the desk job abhorrent, he completed his paperwork and set the pattern for Luftwaffe ground-support tactics used throughout the war. After equipping and training two new ground-support Geschwadern for the 1938 Sudentenland occupation, Galland became Staffelkapitan in II (s) LG 2 Lehrgeschwader in the spring of 1939. By September, he was involved in the invasion of Poland, flying the Henschel Hs 123 ground-attack biplane up to four times a day in the first real test of the effectiveness of his ground-support theories in conjunction with quick-moving tank warfare. The test was a success, and Galland was promoted to Hauptmann on October 1, 1939, and awarded the Eiserne Kreuz, or Iron Cross.

Galland's hunter instinct impelled him to apply for transfer to the Jagdwaffe, and in April, 1940, he was assigned to JG 27 as Geschwader Adjutant for Alte Adler Oberst Max Ibel. Adolf was assigned this post because of his desk experience in Berlin. During the opening days of the French campaign, JG 27 was very active but, as Adjutant, Galland was included in very few sorties. Sorely disappointed, he stole away on individual combat sorties. These unofficial flights did not go unnoticed by Oberst Ibel, who chose to ignore rather than dampen Galland's enthusiasm for combat.

Adolf Galland shot down the first of his many victories on May 12, 1940, when he and Lt. Gustav Rödel attacked eight RAF Hawker Hurricanes west of Lüttich. Galland scored two that morning. Later that day he shot down another Hurricane out of a five-plane flight. Additional victories in the French campaign included two Curtiss Hawks, three Potez 163s, one Morane fighter, and several Bristol Blenheim bombers.

After the fall of France, Galland was transferred to JG 26 Schlageter, the unit with which he has always been associated, as Gruppenkommandeur of III Gruppe. Galland scored two victories on his first mission with the new unit, as the Battle of Britain erupted in the summer of 1940. Promoted to Major on July 18, he was awarded the Ritterkreuz on August 1 for his 17th victory. On August 22, Galland was made the Kommodore of JG 26, succeeding Gotthard Handrick, and led this Geschwader during

the difficult months of the Battle of Britain. The new Kommodore was awarded the Eichenlaub on September 25 for his 40th victory. Galland was at this time one of the leading aces of the Luftwaffe. On November 1, Galland shot down his 50th kill and was promoted to Oberstleutnant; by December 8, he had become a full Oberst.

Adolf was a constant cigar smoker. In fact, the insignia on his Messerschmitt depicted a Mickey Maus brandishing a pistol and a hatchet, as well as smoking a big cigar! The Kommodore consumed up to 20 cigars a day and, according to famous British Ace James E. Johnson, Galland actually wrote orders giving himself permission to smoke while flying on a mission! His was the only Messerschmitt in existence with a cigar lighter, and a cigar holder for when he was on oxygen!

On May 1, 1941, the Schlageter Geschwader scored its 500th victory. On June 22, many Luftwaffe units were involved in the attack on the Soviet Union; however, JG 26 remained in France facing the British nonstop bombing offensive. Galland openly envied his friend, Werner Mölders, who was leading his unit against the Russians. JG 26 was based at the Pas de Calais, in a position to intercept the British attacks on German ships both underway and in port. On June 22, British Blenheims, escorted by Spitfires and Hurricanes, attacked German airfields and ships in port. JG 26 intercepted a British contingent raiding St. Omer just after noon. Galland was one of the first to score, and shot down a Blenheim in flames for his 68th victory. Four minutes later, another bomber fell before his guns, but, before he could recover from the attack, two Spitfires were on his tail. Decisive hits were made on his wing radiators, and the loss of coolant made the Daimler-Benz engine overheat and seize within a few moments. Galland made a successful belly landing and was picked up by a liaison plane which returned him to the JG 26 airfield. After a hurried lunch, the Oberst was off again to intercept another raid southeast of Boulogne. Again, Galland was quick to score, flaming a Spitfire for his 70th victory. In the heat of battle and flushed with victory, Galland was guilty of the most serious mistake that can be made by a fighter pilot: he followed the flaming Spitfire down so he could register the kill. As he did so, he was bounced by another Spitfire and riddled with bullets from stem to stern. The wings were perforated; the right side of the fuselage blown away, the pilot wounded in head and arm and the fuel tank and radiators were leaking. Adolf was considering a belly landing when his fuel tank erupted into a ball of flame. Bail out was the only viable alternative, but the canopy was jammed! The Oberst slammed his body against the hatch again and again as the Messerschmitt hurtled earthward. Finally, the canopy opened and the determined pilot leaped for freedom. However, his parachute harness caught on the radio antenna mast, and Galland found himself being dragged to earth by his flaming plane! After several agonizing moments he broke loose, and his 'chute opened only a few seconds before the plane smashed into the ground. Settling to the earth beside the Forest of Boulogne, Galland found he couldn't walk because of a painfully swollen ankle and collapsed from exhaustion. French peasants carried him into a farmhouse until German troops arrived. Shot down twice in one day and survived—the story of the Jagdfleiger!

Shortly after this episode, German and British pilots engaged in a wide free-for-all over the Pas de Calais. The leader of the Fighter Command forces was Group Captain Douglas Bader, the legless wonder of the RAF. As a member of the prewar RAF aerobatic team, Bader had suffered a terrible crash in which he had lost both his legs. With superhuman determination, he learned to fly with two artificial limbs and became one of the most famous aces of the Battle of Britain. Bader had the misfortune of having his Spitfire crippled by one of the JG 26 pilots. As he prepared to bail out, one of Bader's artificial limbs caught between the seat and the aircraft structure in the cramped Spitfire cockpit. Bader tugged and yanked in desperation and finally unfastened the leg, leaving it wedged in the aircraft as he took to his parachute. Upon landing, Bader's remaining leg couldn't withstand the impact and broke. Galland entertained his famous guest and forwarded a request via the International Red Cross for another set of artificial legs to be flown from England with guarantees of safe passage. Contrary to Galland's suggestion, the RAF dropped the replacement legs during a bombing raid. German doctors fitted the legs and Bader walked again. Chivalry in an age of cynics!

As previously recounted, Ernst Udet's suicide and Werner Mölder's accidental death catapulted Galland into the position of General der Jagdwaffe, or General of the Fighter Arm, and he became the youngest general in the German armed forces. Gerhard Schöpfel succeeded Galland as Kommodore of JG 26. Galland became the second member of the German armed forces to be awarded the Brillanten, or Diamonds, to his Ritterkreuz on January 28, 1942.

Adolf Galland successfully executed Operation Thunderbolt, otherwise known as the Channel Dash of the Scharnhorst and Greisennau, during February, 1942.

In his new post, Galland found himself constantly at odds with Hermann Göring who, after making poor decisions, blamed their failure on the Jagdwaffe. One of his worst decisions was the concept of a peripheral aerial defense, instituted over Galland's objection. Galland insisted on an aerial defense in depth, where the invader would meet successive waves of interceptors all along the flight patch to his objective, instead of only at the territorial borders. Their differences reached a climax in January, 1945, when a hysterical Göring dismissed Galland as General der Jagdflieger, and replaced him with Gordon Gollob.

Galland returned to combat service in January, 1945, organizing and leading an elite group of pilots to fly the Messerschmitt Me 262 jet fighter. This unit was the renowned JV 44, Jägerverband 44, and included some of the finest fighter pilots in the world. On April 24, 1945, Galland scored his 104th and final victory, a U.S. Marauder bomber.

After Germany surrendered, Galland was taken to England for interrogation by officers of the Royal Air Force. At Tangemere Aerodrome, he again met Group Leader Bader, who had since been repatriated to his homeland. The story goes that Galland had twenty boxes of cigars among his personal possessions in England.

General Galland was held as a POW until 1947, when Juan Peron offered him a contract to help organize an Argentine air force. He returned to Germany from Argentina in 1955 and started his own aerospace consultant business in Bonn. Galland married his secretary and fathered a son in 1966. A virtual living legend, Adolf Galland still contributes his talents to solve the problems plaguing the free world's air forces.

GERHARD SCHÖPFEL was born in Erfurt, Thüringen on December 19, 1912. Schöpfel transferred to the Luftwaffe from the infantry in 1935, and was Staffelkapitan of 9/JG 26 at the beginning of hostilities. He shot down his first victory, a Spitfire, during the Dunkirk evacuation. Schöpfel succeeded Galland as Kommandeur of III/JG 26 when the latter was promoted to Kommodore. The Hauptmann received the Ritterkreutz on September 9, 1940, for his 20th victory and was considered one of the most successful Jagdwaffe pilots in 1940. He served as Kommodore of JG 26 for just over one year, and in January, 1943 became Fighter Operations Officer for southern Italy. Schöpfel then became Jafu Norway, and in June, 1944, Kommodore of JG 4. That November, he became Jafu Hungary and, in April, 1945, Kommodore of JG 6 in northern Czechoslovakia. He was captured there by the advancing Russians, and remained a POW in Russia until 1949.

Upon his release, Schöpfel worked as a chauffeur and in other jobs until he secured an executive position with Air Lloyd at Cologne/Bonn airport.

Gerhard Schöpfel flew 700 missions and scored 40 victories during his career with the Jagdwaffe.

GORDON M. GOLLOB succeeded Adolf Galland as General der Jagdflieger. Born in Vienna on June 16, 1912, Gordon was a fighter pilot in 1936, and later a fighter instructor in the Austrian air arm with the rank of Leutnant. At that time his name was Gordon McGollob; definitely not of Teutonic origin. This obviously Scottish name was changed to Gordon M. Gollob by order of the Oberkommando der Luftwaffe. Originally a zerstorer (destroyer) pilot with I/ZG 76, Gordon flew extensively in the Polish campaign, where he scored the first of his 150 victories. In April, 1940, he participated in the Norweigian campaign as Staffelkapitan of 3/ZG 76. In the following October, he transferred to the fighters and was assigned to II/JG 3 on the Channel coast. By the summer of 1941, he was involved in Operation Barbarossa.

On July 1, 1941, Gollob was promoted to Gruppenkommandeur, and, by September 18, he had scored 42 victories and earned the Ritterkreuz. Gollob's victory score mounted rapidly, and on October 18, 1941 alone, he shot down nine enemy aircraft. Six weeks later, on October 26, he received the Eichenlaub for his 85th victory. In December he was recalled from the front and assigned to the aircraft test center at Rechlin, where he remained until May, 1942. He returned to the front as Kommodore of JG 77 Herzas, or Ace of Hearts, Jagdgeschwader, where he became the tenth Jagdwaffe pilot to reach the 100-victory mark. He was awarded the Schwerten to his Ritterkreuz on June 24, 1942.

Under his leadership, JG 77 performed with great success on the southern Russian front, and on August 29, 1942 the Kommodore became the Luftwaffe's leading ace with 150 victories. He became, on the following day, the third Luftwaffe officer to receive the Brillanten to his Ritterkreuz.

From October, 1942, until April, 1944, he was Jafu 5 on the Channel, and again became involved in new fighter projects, such as jet and rocket-propelled aircraft. In December, 1944 he headed a special fighter staff for the Battle of the Bulge, and became General der Jagdflieger on January 31, 1945.

In only 350 missions, Gollob scored 150 official victories; however, his greatness cannot be measured by his successes as a fighter pilot alone. His

Austrian-born Gordon Gollob succeeded Galland as General der Jagdflieger after he served as Gruppenkommandeur, Kommodore, and Jafu 5.

work at the test center and with the Ministry of Armament revealed his technical ability in the development of revolutionary new aircraft designs.

JOACHIM MÜNCHEBERG became the Kommodore of JG 77 Herzas when Gollob assumed the position of Jafu 5. Müncheberg was born in Friedrichshof, Pomerania on December 31, 1918. Since his boyhood, Joachim, or Jochen as he was called, was a firm believer in physical fitness; he exercised whenever he had the opportunity. He was a well-known athlete in his youth. His interests, however, were not confined to the physical. Müncheberg also had a taste for philosophy; his favorite motto can be translated as "Take care that life teaches you that the honors are not the honor."

Müncheberg joined the Luftwaffe on December 4, 1936, and entered the Luftkriegsschule in Dresden as a Fahnenjunker. He completed his flight training one year later, and by September, 1938, he was assigned, as an Oberfahnrich, to I/JG 234 based in Cologne. On November 8, he received his commission as Leutnant, and in September, 1939 Müncheberg was assigned as Gruppe Adjutant with III/JG 26. He scored his initial victory, an RAF Blenheim

Joachim Müncheberg fought on every front in the European and Mediterranean theaters of the war. His 7/26 typified the nomadic existence of many Jagdwaffe units, transferring from airfield to airfield as their presence was needed.

bomber, on November 7, 1939; he got eight more during the drive through the Low Countries; and he totaled 17 by September 7, 1940. Jochen had, meanwhile, been promoted to Oberleutnant and Staffelkapitan of 7/JG 26. By September 14, his score reached 20 kills and he was awarded the Ritterkreuz.

On February 9, 1941, Müncheberg and his 7 Staffel entered into a nomadic existence in the Mediterranean area unequaled by any other unit. The odyssey began by moving to Gela, Sicily. On April 6, 7, and 8th, the Staffel operated against the Yugoslavians, and then returned to its Sicilian base for action over the bastion island of Malta. On May 1, Müncheberg shot down three Hurricanes, bringing his score to 41. Six days later, Jochen was awarded the Eichenlaub to his Ritterkreuz. Later in the month, he took his unit to Catania, and then to Molaoi in the Peloponnesus, Greece. After another move in May, the Me 109Es of the Staffel operated from Salonika, and on June 1 Müncheberg flew to Ain el Gazala, Libya, to help stem the Allied advance in North Africa. The Staffel cooperated closely with I/JG 27 under Hptm. Eduard Neumann. By July 29, Jochen had 48 victories to his credit, and three days

later he was ordered to take his unit back to northern France. During its service in the Mediterranean area, 7/JG 26 shot down 52 adversaries, 25 of which were scored by Müncheberg!

On September 19, 1941, Müncheberg was promoted to Hauptmann and assigned to II/JG 26 as Gruppenkommandeur. Jochen's score continued to mount reaching 62 by the end of 1941, and on June 2, 1942, he shot down his 80th kill. It was at this time that Müncheberg was awarded the coveted Italian Medal for Bravery in Gold for his outstanding performance in North Africa. On July 21, Müncheberg left the Schlageter Geschwader, with 83 victories, and toured the Eastern front in preparation for promotion to Kommodore. After the Kommodore of JG 51 Mölders, Karl-Gottfried Nordmann suffered a fractured skull on the Russian front, Joachim was pressed into service as the Geschwader's temporary Kommodore. On September 5, he reached the 100-victory mark and four days later was awarded the Schwerten or Swords to his Ritterkreuz for 103 kills. In the eight weeks he spent in Russia, Müncheberg shot down 33 adversaries.

Joachim Müncheberg replaced Major Gollob as Kommodore of JG 77 on October 1, 1942. The unit was in the process of relocating to Africa from southern Russia. Promoted to Major in December, 1942, Müncheberg shot down his 133rd adversary on March 13, 1943, operating against the U.S. forces over Tunisia. Ten days later, with two more recorded victories, the Kommodore led his men on his 500th mission. Vastly outnumbered, JG 77 engaged U.S. fighters over Tunisia and, at the onset, Müncheberg found himself surrounded. Maneuvering skillfully, he was about to elude his pursuers when his wings sheared off and the Messerschmitt plummeted to earth. Killed instantly, Müncheberg was buried at El Aounia, and later reinterred in Tunis Cemetery, where over 500 Luftwaffe personnel are buried.

Had he not met death so early in the war, in all probability Müncheberg would have become one of the highest scorers of the war. Even more important than his outstanding individual combat record was his ability to approach the center of problems and disregard the irrelevancies. His men followed this youthful, intelligent leader without hesitation. While a strong self-disciplinarian, he realized the failings of others and never asked of his men what he would not do himself.

JOHANNES STEINHOFF succeeded Joachim Müncheberg as Kommodore of JG 77. The victor of 176 aerial encounters, Steinhoff was born in Bottendorf, Saxony on September 15, 1913. He scored

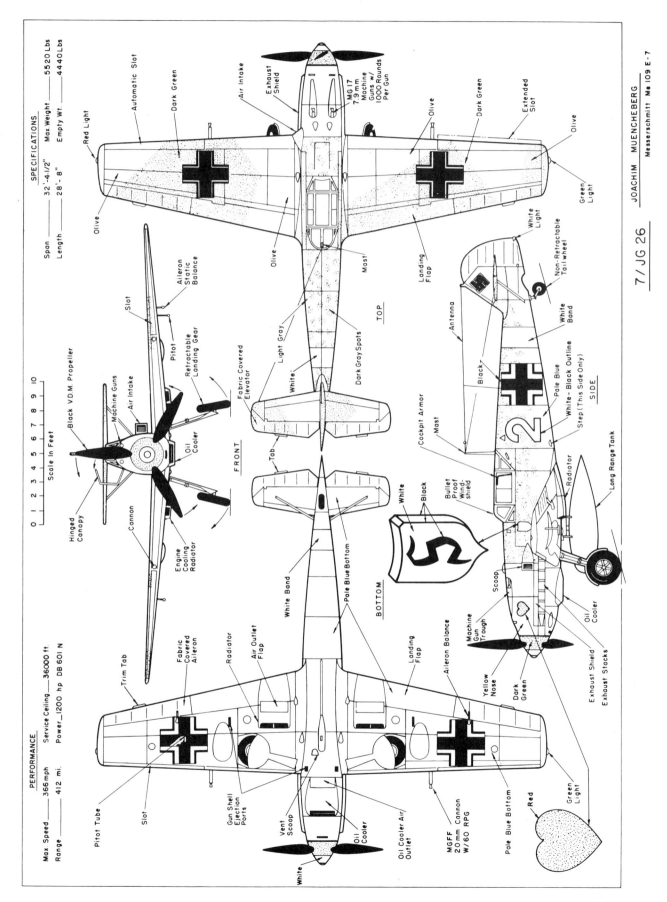

SPECIFICATIONS

Span	32' - 4-1/2"	Max Weight ____ 5520 Lbs
Length	28' - 8"	Empty Wt. ____ 4440 Lbs

PERFORMANCE

Max Speed ____ 366 mph   Service Ceiling ____ 36000 ft.
Range ____ 412 mi.   Power ____ 1200 hp DB 601 N

Scale In Feet
0 1 2 3 4 5 6 7 8 9 10

TOP

FRONT

SIDE

BOTTOM

Labels (top view): Automatic Slot, Dark Green, Air Intake, Exhaust Shield, MG 17 7.9 mm Machine Guns w/ 1000 Rounds Per Gun, Olive, Dark Green, Extended Slot, Olive, Green Light, Red Light, Olive, Olive, Light Gray, White, Dark Gray Spots, Mast, Landing Flap

Labels (front view): Black V.D.M. Propeller, Machine Guns, Air Intake, Pitot, Slot, Aileron Static Balance, Retractable Landing Gear, Fabric Covered Elevator, Tab, Oil Cooler, Hinged Canopy, Cannon, Engine Cooling Radiator

Labels (side view): Antenna, Cockpit Armor, Mast, Black, White Light, Non-Retractable Tail wheel, White Band, Pale Blue, White - Black Outline, Step (This Side Only), Long Range Tank, Radiator, Scoop, Machine Gun Trough, Yellow Nose, Dark Green, Exhaust Shield, Exhaust Stacks, Oil Cooler, Bullet Proof Wind-shield, White, Black

Labels (bottom view): Trim Tab, Fabric Covered Aileron, Radiator, Air Outlet Flap, White Band, Pale Blue Bottom, Landing Flap, Aileron Balance, Pitot Tube, Slot, Gun Shell Ejection Ports, Vent Scoop, Oil Cooler, Oil Cooler Air Outlet, MGFF 20 mm Cannon W/60 RPG, Pale Blue Bottom, Red, Green Light, White

Johannes Steinhoff scored some of the first victories of the war in 1939 and fought until he was horribly burned in a jet accident late in the war.

some of the first victories of the war when he shot down two Wellington bombers near Wilhelmshaven. Called Macki by his friends, Steinhoff was Stafflkapitan of 10/JG 26 by late 1939, and in February, 1940 transferred to the leadership of 4/JG 52. His score reached 35 by August 1941, and the Oberleutnant was awarded the Rittenkreuz on August 8. Promotion to Hauptmann and Kommandeur of II/JG 52 came in February, 1942, and on August 31 he shot down his 100th adversary. The Eichenlaub was awarded three days later. Steinhoff's 150th victory came on February 2, 1943, just before he assumed the leadership of JG 77, where he stayed until December, 1944. He was awarded the Schwerten, or Swords, to his Ritterkreuz on July 28, 1944, after his 167th victory. From December, 1944, to the following December he led JG 7 flying jet-powered fighters.

In January, 1945 Galland selected Oberstleutnant Steinhoff as one of the founding members of the general's JV 44 Expertenstaffel, equipped with jet-powered fighters. Macki Steinhoff was placed in charge of pilot-recruiting for the unit. After scoring six victories with his twin-jet fighter, Steinhoff began his 900th mission on April 8, 1945. Taking off from a hastily-repaired runway at 125 mph., one of the wheels of Steinhoff's speeding plane dug into a partially filled crater causing it to veer and lose its landing gear. Momentum carried the craft up an in-

cline and into the air at the end of the runway. Fifty yards away, it smashed into the ground and burst into flame. Horribly burned, Steinhoff fought his way out of the flaming wreckage as the plane's rockets exploded from the intense heat.

Oberst Johannes Steinhoff proved to be the model of human endurance and determination. His face was terribly seared about the cheeks and ears, and his eyelids were burned away! Macki Steinhoff did not close his eyes from 1945 until 1969 when an RAF surgeon made new eyelids from skin taken from Steinhoff's arm.

Always an enthusiastic pilot, General Johannes Steinhoff became the commanding officer of the West German air force in the seventies and is instrumental in the selection of the equipment for that service.

JOHANNES WIESE is a little-publicized, high-scoring Jagdwaffe pilot, known as the Kubanski Lion to the Soviet pilots along the central Russian front. He succeeded Steinhoff as Kommodore of JG 77. Born in Brelau, Schleisen on May 7, 1915, Wiese joined the Luftwaffe in 1936 and was an instructor for three years. When the war began, Wiese was a reconnaissance pilot and did not become a Jagdflieger until he joined JG 52 in the summer of 1941. He became Staffelkapitan of 2/JG 52 on June 25, 1942.

By January, 1943, he was a Hauptmann and had 51 victories to his credit. Johannes was awarded the Ritterkreuz on January 5. He was in continuous combat during the Kursk offensive, flying several missions every day. On July 5, 1943, he shot down 12 Soviet fighters and ground-attack aircraft, while experiencing five emergency landings, a hectic pace for anyone who did not have a cast-iron constitution. He was awarded the Eichenlaub on March 3, 1944 for his 125th victory.

It was during the heavy fighting over the Kuban Bridgehead that Wiese scored phenomenally, especially against the heavily armored IL-2 Shturmovik. The Soviet pilots would radio to each other: "Vniemanie Torretchi?" or, "Kubanski Lion in the Air?"

Taking command of JG 77 in the West in December 1944, he was patrolling high over Essen with his Rottenflieger on Christmas Eve when the pair was attacked by a formation of Spitfires. Losing his wingman almost immediately, Wiese fought desperately for several minutes, eventually sustaining a number of serious hits. He was forced to abandon his Messerschmitt at 27,000 feet! After drifting earthward to an altitude of about 200 feet, the Major's chute, apparently damaged, collapsed and dropped him to

The Kubanski Lion, Johannes Weise, was feared by the Soviet pilots on the Eastern front. After the war, he was turned over to the Soviets by Germans.

Heinz Baer scored 220 victories in an action-packed career on every front; he finally became the world's leading jet ace.

the ground! His injuries were so serious that Wiese spent the winter hospitalized. Oberstlt. Erich Leie succeeded Wiese as Kommodore of JG 77.

At war's end, the Kommodore surrendered to the U.S. forces and was soon released. In September, 1945, German Communists recognized Wiese and had him arrested by the Russian occupation forces. He was held prisoner for four and one-half years. Upon his release he lived in Breslau, East Germany, until 1965, when he moved to West Germany. Wiese joined the German Federal air force the following year as a Gruppenkommandeur, and later was placed in charge of ground organization of the air base at Ahlhorn.

HEINZ BAER was one of the most personable and popular German pilots in the Luftwaffe. Pritzl Baer epitomized the fighter-pilot image, and fought in first-line operations throughout the conflict. He flew 1,000 missions, covered every German front of the war, and is credited with 220 victories. Baer was shot down 18 times sustaining wounds on many occasions, and emerged from the war as the Luftwaffe's eighth-ranking ace.

Born on March 25, 1913, in Sommerfeld bei Leipzig, Heinz joined a glider club in 1928 at the age

of 15. He wanted to be a Lufthansa pilot and, in order to do so, he entered the clandestine German training program in the early thirties. As the skies of Europe darkened with the impending war, Heinz found himself a member of 1/JG 51. Baer scored his first victory on September 25 by destroying a French Curtiss Hawk 75A fighter over Weissenberg. By July 2, 1941, he had 27 victories to his credit and was awarded the Ritterkreuz. Lt. Baer was transferred to the Eastern front as part of IV/JG 51 on July 27 to participate in the Russian invasion.

His performance was so outstanding that Oblt. Baer was awarded the Eichenlaub on August 14 for his 16th conquest. The Schwerten followed on February 16, 1942, for his 90th victory. He was also promoted to Hauptmann at that time.

After spending ten months fighting the Russians with JG 51, Baer was transferred to I/JG 77 on May 1, 1942. The 18 months that Baer served with JG 77 were filled with fighting over Italy, Sicily, and North Africa, as well as Malta. Heinz Baer reached the 100-victory mark on May 19, 1942.

He was moved again on December 28, 1943, joining II/JG 1 to aid in the defense of the Reich against the Allied bombers. By April 28, 1944, he had reached the 200-victory mark. In June he was pro-

Wolf-Dietrich Huy of JG 77 not only scored 40 victories but caused considerable damage to the British fleet in the Mediterranean with his Jabo attacks. His bombing helped secure the island of Crete for the Germans.

Another JG 77 Jabo expert was Emil Omert, who sank naval craft on two fronts and attained 70 victories. He was killed during the Ploesti oil-field raid.

moted to Major and transferred to the Geschwaderstab of JG 3. Heinz Baer spent the last months of the war flying jet fighters, in which he scored 16 victories. His victories included 21 four-engined bombers. He finished the war with the rank of Oberstlt.

Heinz Baer became an aviation consultant after the war. On the 30th anniversary of his 200th victory, he was demonstrating a light plane near Brunswick, when it suddenly spun in from an altitude of 150 feet, killing the pilot instantly.

WOLF-DIETRICH HUY was a native of Frieburg, Breisgan, born on August 2, 1917. He started his military service as a naval officer and joined III/JG 77 on July 1, 1939 as an Oberleutnant. Huy scored his first two victories during the Dunkirk evacuation and was especially effective in Jabo operations against naval targets.

During the assault on Crete, he damaged and sank several ships, including the British cruiser Fiji and the battleship Warspite. He was awarded the Ritterkreuz on July 5, 1941, for his 22nd victory. Wolf was shot down by Spitfires over North Africa on October 29, 1942, and survived the crash behind Allied lines. He became a prisoner of war at the age of 25. In over

500 missions, he scored 40 aerial victories and considerable naval damage in his Jabo operations.

EMIL OMERT was another Jabo and low-level strafing expert of JG 77. Born in Ginolfs/Rhoen on January 1, 1918, he served with II/JG 3 and II/JG 2 before joining III/JG 77 in early 1941. Omert distinguished himself in the Balkans and Russia, scoring his first victory over Yugoslavia. He was awarded the Ritterkreuz on March 19, 1942, for his 40th victory. Emil was promoted to Hauptmann and made Gruppenkommandeur of III/JG 77 in March, 1944. During the Ploesti oil field raid by U.S. bombers on April 24, 1944, Omert's plane received some decisive hits, forcing him to take to his parachute. As he floated earthward, the gunners finished the job, killing Omert in his parachute harness.

The Hauptmann is credited with 70 official aerial victories out of 675 missions. He is also credited with 25 aircraft destroyed on the ground during 125 support missions. He also destroyed a Soviet torpedo boat.

RUDOLF SCHMIDT AND FRANZ SCHULTE were two more JG 77 members adept at Jabo attacks on naval targets (especially during the attack on the

British fleet near Crete). Oberfeldwebel Schmidt sank two British motor torpedo boats in Suda Bay and severely damaged a large troop transport ship. Feldwebel Schulte sank a large cargo ship and an MTB. Each man shot down close to 50 aircraft—and both were missing in action in Russia in 1942. Rudolf Schmidt received the Ritterkreuz on August 30, 1941, for 27 victories, while Franz Schulte was awarded the Ritterkreuz posthumously on September 24, 1942.

GÜNTHER LÜTZOW was the model German officer: a man of breeding and character, dedicated, articulate, and descended from a family with a long military tradition. Franzl, as he was called by close associates, was born on September 4, 1912 in Kiel and received his education in a cloister school with emphasis on religion. It was the custom in Central Europe for members of the leading families to enter one of three vocations: religion, law, or the military. Günther first chose religion, and then changed to a military career.

Lützow joined the Luftwaffe in the mid-thirties and served in Spain, where he scored five victories. Upon his return to Germany, he became a training leader at Jagdschule No. 1. At the outbreak of the Battle of France, he became Gruppenkommandeur of I/JG 3, with the rank of Hauptmann. In August, 1940, he was promoted to Kommodore of the Geschwader, and on September 19 Franzl was awarded the Ritterkreuz for his 15th victory.

He led his Geschwader in the Battle of Britain, where one of his Gruppenkommandeurs was Wilhelm Balthasar. Lützow took his unit across the Soviet border in the summer of 1941. Major Lützow received the Eichenlaub on July 7, 1941 for his 42nd kill. The Schwerten followed on October 11 (for his 92nd victory), and two weeks later he became the second fighter pilot to reach the century mark.

Günther Lützow's combat career was interrupted on May 17, 1942, when Gen. Galland appointed him Inspecteur der Jagdflieger, or Inspector of Fighter Pilots. Wolf-Dietrich Wilke, who was a member of the Geschwaderstab, succeeded Lützow as permanent Kommodore.

Oberst Lützow was heavily involved in the Kommodore's Conference, also called the Mutiny of the Fighters. General Galland, dismissed in January, 1945, was organizing his JV 44 Jet Fighter Unit when Lützow was chosen as the Jagdwaffe's spokesman. His dignity, courage, breeding, and debating ability made him the ideal choice to confront Hermann Göring with the complaints of the Jagdwaffe. As soon as the Oberst began describing Göring's misapplica-

Günther Lützow was the second pilot to reach the 100-victory mark and became Inspeckteur der Jagdflieger under Galland. He was heavily involved in the Mutiny of the Fighters.

tion, distrust, and abuse of the Jagdwaffe, and enumerating the Kommodore's grievances, Göring exploded into a rage and threatened to have Lützow court-martialed. Instead, Lützow was sent to Italy in a sort of exile, as Jafu Italy, at a time when his expertise was sorely needed to fight the Allied bombers.

A few months later, he volunteered for Galland's JV 44 and was happily welcomed. Lützow scored two victories with his jet fighter and during an April 24, 1945 intercept over Donauwörth, the Oberst was reported missing after making an attack on a formation of Fortresses.

Günther Lützow scored 108 official victories during 300 combat missions.

WOLF-DIETRICH WILKE succeeded Lützow as the Kommodore of JG 3. He possessed an aristocratic air, was poised and had a passion for well-tailored clothes. Wilke became a superb combat leader, greatly admired by his fellow officers, not only for his fighting ability, but also for his talent to set an example and direct others.

He was born in Schrimm/Proving Posen on March

The victor of 161 adversaries, Wolf-Dietrich Wilke led JG 3 Udet into the Stalingrad pocket in an effort to save the surrounded German Army.

11, 1913. He joined the Army in the spring of 1935, serving in a cavalry regiment until October when he decided to join the Luftwaffe. During the trip to Perleburg for flight training, Wilke shared his train compartment with a fellow volunteer. He offered his companion a cigarette from his silver cigarette case in his customary aristocratic gesture. In the barracks, he was assigned to share his quarters with the same officer and, again, offered a cigarette in the same manner. This gave birth to the nickname given to Wilke by his fellow officers: Fürst, which is an aristocratic nickname describing princely behavior; and he carried the name until his death.

Having completed basic flight training, Fürst applied for fighter training in the spring of 1936, but was sent to Fassberg for observation training, instead. He eventually transferred to fighters and, upon completion of gunnery training at Schlichting, he was assigned to Döberitz-based JG 1, flying the old Heinkel 51 biplanes.

It was during the fall of 1937 that the clothes-conscious Wilke had a nonregulation, long, dark leather coat made to his order. The other pilots at Döberitz liked the appearance and soon the entire Ge-schwader sported the smart leather coats. The idea spread like wildfire, until the leather coat became the mark of the Jagdwaffe pilots! Even Feld-marschall von Blomberg couldn't resist having a coat made once he saw the pilots wearing them.

In early 1939, Wilke was sent to Spain, where he served for only a few months, returning to Germany in the spring. He was assigned to III/JG 53 under Mölders, and by September was leading 7/JG 53 in the Battle of France. Wilke's first victory came on November 7, 1939, when he shot down a Potez 63 twin-engine fighter. His first defeat came on May 18, 1940, when he was separated from his Staffel and jumped by eight French Curtiss 75A fighters. Fürst bailed out and was captured but, like Mölders, his captivity was short-lived and he was repatriated to Germany during the following month.

When Mölders left III/JG 53 to become Kommodore of JG 51, he was replaced by Hptm. Harro Harder. Harder was shot down, however, during the early days of the Battle of Britain, and Wilke was selected as Gruppenkommandeur on August 13, 1940. As with many other Experten, Wilke was a slow starter and by the end of the Battle of Britain in late spring of 1941 his official score stood at a modest 13 victories. During the Battle he narrowly escaped death when either engine trouble or an empty fuel tank forced him to ditch into the Channel. He was rescued by moonlight.

Wilke's score began to climb with the attack on the Soviet Union. He shot down five Red aircraft on June 22, 1941, the first day of the invasion. On August 6, Wilke received the Ritterkreuz for his 25th victory, and by December the Gruppe was transferred to Sicily. In the air battles over Malta, Major Wilke scored his 36th victory by downing four Spitfires.

On May 18, 1942, Wilke became Kommodore of JG 3 Udet, operating on the southern Russian front. By September 6, he reached the century mark and three days later was awarded the Eichenlaub. That December, JG 3 was fighting from dawn to dusk, escorting Stukas from StG 2 and Heinkel bombers from KG 27 and KG 55, in an attempt to save the German troops in the Stalingrad pocket. The Geschwader succeeded in penetrating the Soviet fighter screen and actually landing and operating within the Communist cordon. One Staffel was assigned the task of protecting these small airfields against the Russian fighters and Shturmoviks. The advancing Russian infantry overran the fields so rapidly that JG 3's ground-support organization could not keep up with the pilots and aircraft as they rushed from field to field. The protection Staffel was eventually

Kurt Ebener was the real hero of the Stalin-grad pocket. A member of the JG 3 Airfield-protection Staffel, he scored 33 victories during this very dangerous assignment.

Alte Adler Max Ibel helped in the creation of the Luftwaffe and played an important part in the Channel dash of the German naval ships.

reduced to three Messerschmitts, due to the absence of spare parts and repair and maintenance facilities. The entire Staffel shared the three Messerschmitts and the planes were in combat around the clock. The three remaining planes are credited with the destruction of 130 Soviet aircraft during this trying and hectic period!

Wilke, now an Oberst, scored his 150th victory on December 17, and was awarded the Schwerten to his Ritterkreuz six days later. The Geschwaderstab was relocated to Germany on January 16, 1943, to battle the U.S. Fortresses, while the remainder of JG 3 continued to fight on the Eastern front. Orders from the Luftwaffe Oberkommando grounded Oberst Wilke, because he was considered too valuable to risk in combat. However, realizing that the shortage of fighter pilots was endangering the lives of thousands of innocent civilians, Fürst begged permission to fly on intercept missions. This was granted on some occasions, and Wilke scored four B-17s and a Mustang on these isolated sorties.

By March 23, 1944, Wilke had scored 161 victories. On this day, he led the Geschwaderstab against raiding U.S. Fortresses and their Mustang escort, between Magdeburg and Brunswick. A melee ensued, in which Wilke and his Rottenflieger, Lt. von Kapherr, became separated from the others. During

a pass at the bombers, the Mustangs interfered and split up the Rotte. At that moment, Fürst saw a Mustang closing in on von Kapherr and sped to the rescue, disregarding the U.S. fighters on his own tail. His aim was true and the Mustang became victory Number 162. By this time it was too late to execute any evasive maneuvers and the chasing Mustangs raked his Messerschmitt with .50-caliber bullets, sending Oberst Wilke crashing to the ground near the town of Schöppenstadt, killing him instantly. He was succeeded by Oberstlt. F. K. Müller who was, himself, shot down two months later.

GEORG SCHENTKE and KURT EBENER were two members of the JG 3 Airfield Protection Staffel, which was deeply involved in the attempt to break the Stalingrad cordon. Schentke entered the war as an Oberfeldwebel and scored his first victory with 9/JG 3 on June 8, 1940. He was awarded the Ritterkreuz in September of the following year when his score reached 30 and, after a short time as a fighter instructor, he returned to action as a Leutnant. After scoring 87 victories, he was forced to bail out over Soviet-held territory while protecting Stalingrad's Pitomnik Airfield on Christmas Day of 1942. Oblt. Schentke was never seen again. Kurt Ebener joined II/JG 3 in December, 1941 as a Feldwebel and

Eduard Neumann only scored 13 victories but left his mark by leading JG 27 over the African desert. He is often credited with developing and encouraging superior combat flyers such as Hans Marseille.

flew with the Airfield Protection Staffel for a month in the 1942/43 winter. During this harrowing period and under the most adverse conditions, Ebener scored 33 victories. He was awarded the Ritterkreuz on April 7, 1943, for his 52nd victory. With a final score of 57 kills he was seriously wounded on August 23, 1944, and captured by U.S. forces.

JOACHIM KIRSCHNER, DETLER ROHWER, and FRANZ SCHWAIGER were three members of JG 3

Udet who met undeserved fates contrary to noble military tradition. Hptm. Kirschner entered the conflict with II/JG 3 Udet in late 1941 and was soon leading 5/JG 3. He received the Ritterkreuz on December 23, 1942, for his 51st kill, and scored his 150th victory on July 5, 1943, when he shot down nine adversaries. Upon transfer to IV/JG 27 he fought in Greece and the Balkans, where on December 17, 1943, during a dogfight with Spitfires, he bailed out near Metkovic, Croatia. He was captured by partisans of the 29th Communist Brigade and shot to death. Kirshner is credited with 188 victories. Hptm. Rohwer fought in I/JG 3 during the Battle of Britain, and was awarded the Ritterkreuz on October 5, 1941, for his 28th victory. By October, 1942, he was Staffelkapitan of 2/JG 3 on the Russian front, and one year later he was leading II/JG 3 fighting the U.S. bombers over Germany. On March 29, 1944, Rohwer forced-landed near Ibbenburen while attacking U.S. Fortresses, and was strafed to death by overzealous P-38 Lightning pilots. A similar fate was shared by Ltn. Schwaiger who flew with 6/JG 3 at the onset, and then became Staffelkapitan of 1/JG 3. After scoring a Mustang for his 67th victory on April 24, 1944, his Messerschmitt ran out of fuel and he negotiated a forced landing on a pasture near Rain am Lech. Again, overzealous pilots in the remaining Mustangs strafed the stranded German to death.

The African Eagle poses proudly with a Bristol Blenheim bomber he shot down, then wears a big smile as he waits for his mechanic to paint yet another victory mark on the rudder of his Messerschmitt.

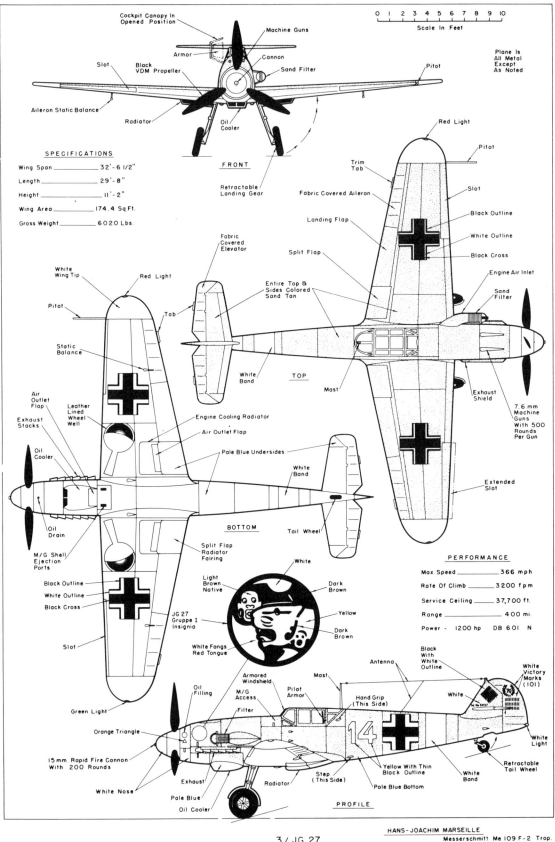

Cockpit Canopy In Opened Position
Machine Guns
Armor
Cannon
Sand Filter
Pitot
Slot
Black VDM Propeller
Aileron Static Balance
Radiator
Oil Cooler
FRONT
Retractable Landing Gear

0 1 2 3 4 5 6 7 8 9 10
Scale In Feet

Plane Is All Metal Except As Noted

SPECIFICATIONS

Wing Span _____ 32'-6 1/2"
Length _____ 29'-8"
Height _____ 11'-2"
Wing Area _____ 174.4 Sq.Ft.
Gross Weight _____ 6020 Lbs.

Red Light
Pitot
Trim Tab
Fabric Covered Aileron
Slot
Landing Flap
Black Outline
White Outline
Split Flap
Black Cross
Entire Top & Sides Colored Sand Tan
Engine Air Inlet
Sand Filter
Fabric Covered Elevator
White Wing Tip
Red Light
Pitot
Tab
Static Balance
Air Outlet Flap
Leather Lined Wheel Well
Exhaust Stacks
Engine Cooling Radiator
Air Outlet Flap
Pale Blue Undersides
White Band
TOP
Mast
Exhaust Shield
7.6 mm Machine Guns With 500 Rounds Per Gun
Oil Cooler
Oil Drain
M/G Shell Ejection Ports
Split Flap Radiator Fairing
White Band
Tail Wheel
Extended Slot
BOTTOM
Black Outline
White Outline
Black Cross
White
Light Brown Native
Dark Brown
Yellow
Dark Brown
Slot
JG 27 Gruppe I Insignia
White Fangs Red Tongue
Green Light

PERFORMANCE

Max. Speed _____ 366 mph
Rate Of Climb _____ 3200 fpm
Service Ceiling _____ 37,700 ft.
Range _____ 400 mi.
Power - 1200 hp   DB 601 N

Armored Windshield
Pilot Armor
Mast
Antenna
Black With White Outline
White
White Victory Marks (101)
Oil Filling
M/G Access
Hand Grip (This Side)
White Light
Orange Triangle
Filter
14
Retractable Tail Wheel
15 mm Rapid Fire Cannon With 200 Rounds
Exhaust
Radiator
Step (This Side)
Yellow With Thin Black Outline
White Band
White Nose
Pale Blue
Oil Cooler
Pale Blue Bottom
PROFILE

HANS-JOACHIM MARSEILLE
Messerschmitt Me 109 F-2 Trop.

Hans-Joachim Marseille shot down more British aircraft than any other Jagdflieger for a total of 158. He is shown on the left in an official portrait, and on the right, playing the piano for his mother while on an enforced leave in Germany.

Marseille's batman (or servant) was a native of the Transvaal named Mathias; the two became very good friends. Mathias placed a necklace of 158 seashells on Marseille's coffin, one for each victory.

MAX IBEL was another Alte Adler who assisted in the creation of the Luftwaffe and was among the pioneers who trained in Lipetsk, Russia. In 1939, Ibel organized JG 27 and led it successfully during the Battle of France. He received the Ritterkreuz on August 22, 1940, and was given a staff position three months later. In June, 1941, Bernhardt Woldenga succeeded Ibel as Kommodore of JG 27, and he in turn was replaced by Wolfgang Schellmann two months later. In June, 1941, Max became Jafu 3 and six months later he was Jafu West. During the last two years of the war General Major Ibel was Kommandeur of 2 Jagd Division and at the very end he became Inspector of Jet Operations.

EDUARD NEUMANN succeeded Schellmann as Kommodore of JG 27, and led the unit during its struggle against superior forces over the North African desert. While fighting in Spain he acquired a colorful abandoned circus wagon and used it as his living quarters. Neumann had been Gruppenkommandeur of I/JG 27. He then became Kommodore of the Geschwader during the meteoric combat career of Hans-Joachim Marseille, and did much to develop the young Eagle's talent. Neumann's official score is 13 victories. Oberstlt. Edu Neumann became Jafu Italy when the Luftwaffe abandoned North Africa, and later filled several staff positions.

HANS-JOACHIM MARSEILLE was known variously as the Star of Africa, Young Eagle, Yellow 14, African Eagle, and Star of the Desert. In just one year, he became the highest scorer against the Royal Air Force, flashing across the North African sky in a blaze of glory. Marseille enlisted at 18 and was dead four years later, a legend.

Born in Charlottenburg, Berlin, on December 13, 1919, Hans was the son of Sigfried Marseille, a World War I pilot and later a General Major in the 1939–1945 conflict. The general was killed on the Eastern front in 1943. Jochen, as he was called by his friends, loved airplanes as a youngster and, at the earliest opportunity, he enlisted in the Luftwaffe. Marseille began his flight training on November 7, 1938, and, although he showed superb flying ability, he did not take well to military discipline. He was too casual, informal, and individualistic, and was often reprimanded for such breaches of discipline as stunt flying the training planes!

By August 1940, he was flying in 4/JG 52 under Staffelkapitan Johannes Steinhoff, assigned to Channel duty during the Battle of Britain. Jochen scored his first victory on his third sortie, downing a Spitfire. During his service with JG 52, Hans shot down seven Spitfires, but was himself shot down four times! On each occasion he belly-landed on the French shore near Cape Griz Nez. His rank at this time was Oberfahnrich, and he served as a Rotten-flieger.

Early in 1941, Marseille was sent to Döberitz air base to join I/JG 27. On April 22, the Gruppe arrived in North Africa to bolster the sagging Regia Aeronautica against the British Commonwealth forces. Hans was assigned to 3/JG 27 under the command of Oblt. Gerhard Homuth, a strict disciplinarian, who was quite tough with Marseille. On the day after arrival in Africa, 3 Staffel completed three missions over the desert. Marseille scored the Staffel's first victory, a Hurricane, during the first mission, but was himself shot down by Free French Sous Lt. James Denis. He belly-landed without personal injury, although the ground crew discovered over thirty bullet holes in his Messerschmitt's fuselage!

Five days later, while on patrol with the Staffel near Tobruk, Marseille spotted a line Bristol Blenheim bombers flying low on the deck. Before any of his Staffel-mates had even sighted the quarry, Hans dived upon it and began pumping shells into the engines! The bomber crashed into the sea before the victor had even returned to his formation! Needless to say, the young Bohemian was severely reprimanded for not announcing his initial sighting of the enemy, and for breaking formation without permission! Marseille's problem was that he was an individualist who found it very difficult to fight in a concerted attack with his Staffel-mates. He was impetuous and raced headlong through enemy formations, thereby returning to base with his Messerschmitt riddled with enemy bullets. His Gruppenkommandeur was perceptive enough to recognize Marseille's tremendous potential as a fighter pilot, and began to educate rather than discourage the young lion, and so Eduard Neumann let Hans play it by ear realizing that Marseille had a "hang-up" when it came to teamwork.

Marseille was promoted to Leutnant in May, 1941 with 14 victories to his credit. As an officer, he was now entitled to a batman, or servant, and he selected a black native of the Transvaal named Mathias. The two became very close, and their relationship was that of friends rather than that of master and servant.

The first of his many multiple-victory dogfights came on November 22, 1941, when 3 Staffel engaged 16 Hawker Hurricanes. Although the British outnumbered the Germans, they were flying lower and expected the Messerschmitts to attack from the superior position of greater altitude. As a protective measure, the Hurricanes formed a Lufberry circle, whereby each plane protects the other's tail. Still no attack was made and the "waiting game" continued. Suddenly, Marseille bolted from the formation so quickly that his wingman could not follow! Pulling the control stick into his belly, Marseille climbed into the sun with his eyes closed. He turned quickly and, with the glaring disk behind him, Marseille tore at the Lufberry circle. Firing at long range with his engine cannon, Hans sent the nearest Hurricane crashing into the desert. Then, with flight pressure on the rudder pedals, he fired at the second Hurricane which burst into flames. Again, he climbed for the sun. The Lufberry Circle remained intact and 3 Staffel was still hesitant to attack. As Marseille dived out of the sun for a second time, the circle broke, and 14 eight-gunned Hurricanes turned to face the young daredevil. Hans scored again as the Staffel finally attacked. During the melee that followed, Marseille destroyed two more of the British fighters, while his Staffel-mates shot down three, with no loss to themselves. The eight remaining Hurricanes sped for their home base.

By December 2, Hans Marseille was credited with 33 victories and was awarded the German Cross in Gold from Feldmarschall Kesselring.

Marseille's score increased phenomenally now that he had found his combat style and was encouraged to apply it. Two weeks later he scored his 48th victory! He then contracted a local fever and was out of action for a month. Upon his return to action, he flew five or six patrols each day. He was in the air virtually every waking hour. Flying and fighting rejuvenated him, and Marseille only became tired when on the ground! He was like a human computer in the air: sharp eyesight, three-dimensional thinking, and an uncanny shooting eye of deadly precision. This, coupled with fearlessness and agressiveness, made him an adversary hard to beat. He used very little ammunition, averaging 15 shells per victory, and once used only ten cannon shells and 180 rounds from his machine guns to shoot down six Hawker Hurricanes! Often Marseille scored his second victory before the first had even hit the ground! Rainer Pöttgen, his Rottenflieger, had a difficult time following his leader, as he darted from victim to victim. Because Pöttgen kept track of Marseille's scoring, the men of the Staffel called him the "adding machine."

On February 22, 1942, Marseille was awarded the Ritterkreuz on the occasion of his 50th kill, and in April he was promoted to Oberleutnant. At this time, Edu Neumann was made Kommodore of JG 27 and Homuth took over I Gruppe. Marseille was then given command of 3 Staffel.

Tragedy struck during this period when Jochen's sister, Inge, died. Marseille was shattered. He spoke to no one, became morose, and lived only to fly and fight. He had been extremely devoted to her and lost all contact with reality in his bereavement. On June 3, 1942, he shot down six Curtiss Kittyhawks of South African No. 5 Squadron in only 11 minutes. Three days later he received the Eichenlaub for his 75th victory. He attained the century mark on June 17 when he shot down ten adversaries, six of which were dispatched in seven minutes!! He was then promoted to Hauptmann and received the Schwerten to his Ritterkreuz on June 18. Hans-Joachim was by now a national hero, especially among the young women of Germany.

During a visit to Germany in the summer of 1942, Marseille met Haneliese Bahar, fell in love, and became engaged, setting the wedding date for Christmas. In Rome, he received the Italian Medal for Bravery in Gold. Only two other men received this award during the Second World War: Joachim Müncheberg and the Duke of Aosta. Even Erwin Rommel only received it in Silver!

Marseille's men called him Chief to his face, but referred to him as Jochen among themselves. Feldmarschall Rommel refused to call him Marseille because it was "too French sounding," and chose to call Hans "Seille" (say) instead. Marseille's radio call was Elbe One.

The Luftwaffe was outnumbered six to one when Marseille returned to Africa, but he nonetheless scored ten victories on the first day of action, August 31. At dawn on the following day, 3 Staffel escorted Stuka dive bombers on a ground-attack mission just south of Imaid. Flying at 10,000 feet, ten Kittyhawks attacked just as the Stukas began their dives. Marseille lost no time in slamming into the interceptors, flaming one at 8:28 A.M. with a quick burst at 30-yards range. Two minutes later a second was sent crashing into the desert sands. Then six other British fighters turned on Yellow 14 in an attempt to eliminate their nemesis. Marseille allowed the six fighters to close in and then made a quick turn, scoring on the last plane of the British formation at 8:39 A.M. Later that day, at 10:20 A.M. Marseille was escorting Stukas again with two companions, bound for Alam el Halfa. His keen eyes suddenly sighted a formation of Allied bombers escorted by Kittyhawks in the distance. Three of the Kittyhawks turned to attack, and Marseille shot them all down at about 10:55 A.M.! At 11:02 A.M. he led his men to the attack, and destroyed two more Kittyhawks. Hans then turned to another Curtiss formation and scored two more! 3 Staffel was in the air again at five that afternoon, escorting Junkers 88 bombers from LG 1, when 15 Kittyhawks attacked them. Between 5:47 and 5:53 Marseille shot down five Kittyhawks, making a total of 17 kills for the day on September 1, 1942! He was awarded the Brillanten (Diamonds) to his Ritterkreuz on the next day.

One of his most difficult victories was his last. On September 28, 1942, Marseille faced five Spitfires high over the desert. As he was dispatching two of the British fighters, two more Spitfires dived from above and joined the fray. Running low on fuel, the German tried to lure the Spitfires over German-held territory, but only one aggressive Englishman dared follow and he began peppering the Me 109 with shells. Marseille performed every evasive maneuver in the book, but his adversary hung on. With fuel dangerously low, Marseille climed steeply into the sun with his eyes closed; however, in order to follow the German, the Spitfire pilot had to keep his eyes open! Hans turned abruptly, diving and turning, and soon closed in behind the bewildered Spitfire pilot. A well-placed burst sent the British fighter down in flames for Marseille's 157th victory. The Messerschmitt barely made it back to base on the remaining fuel.

Marseille was finally beginning to show signs of the strain created by never-ending aerial combat.

Hundreds of German and Italian military personnel traveled long distances to the cemetery at Derna to pay their respects to the fallen hero. The Italians erected a pyramid over the gravesite with a bronze plaque that read: "Here lies undefeated Hptm. Hans Marseille."

On September 30, 1942, Hans-Joachim Marseille climbed into his Messerschmitt emblazoned with the yellow "14" and took off with his Staffel to intercept a British formation in the Cairo sector. However, no Allied aircraft were found, so Marseille led 3 Staffel back towards their base. Near El Alamein, at about 11:20 A.M., members of the Staffel noticed wisps of blue-black smoke trailing from Marseille's engine compartment, and heard him shouting over the radio. He reported smoke entering his cockpit, that he was choking and couldn't see, and even opening the cockpit vents didn't help. His Rottenfleiger, Rainer Pöttgen, directed Marseille's flying via the radio and, once over German-held territory, Jochen decided to bail out. Following the prescribed procedure, he inverted the Messerschmitt and dropped out of the cockpit. However, the pilotless plane dropped slightly before Marseille could clear the tail and he was struck by the fin. No parachute opened, and Marseille fell to earth four miles south of Sidi el Aman at 11:26 A.M. on September 30, 1942.

The victor over 157 British aircraft was buried in the military cemetery at Derna. Germans and Italians traveled long distances to pay their respects at the burial. Mathias placed a necklace of 157 sea shells on the coffin as a parting gift to his friend. The Italians erected a stone pyramid over the gravesite with a bronze plaque reading: "Here lies undefeated Hptm. Hans Marseille."

In just over one year, Marseille flew 388 sorties. General Galland extolled him as the "Virtuoso of the Fighter Pilots."

WERNER SCHRÖR was the most successful Jagdflieger in North Africa after Marseille, having scored 61 victories in this combat theater. Born in Mülheim, Ruhr on August 12, 1918, Schrör joined I/JG 27 in August, 1940, and fought in the Battle of Britain until transferred to North Africa. He became Staffelkapitan of 8/JG 27 on July 1, 1942, and on October 20, the Leutnant was awarded the Ritterkreuz for his 49th victory. By August 2, 1943, Schrör was a Hauptmann and Gruppenkommandeur of II/JG 27, and owner of the Eichenlaub for his 84th kill. He transferred to Kommandeur of III/JG 54 on the Eastern front, and was again promoted to Major and Kommodore of JG 3 Udet by February, 1945. The Schwerten were presented two months later. Major

Gerhard Homuth was Marseille's Staffelkapitan and then his Gruppenkommandeur.

After Marseille's death the most successful Jagdflieger in
North Africa was Werner Schrör, who scored 61 victories
in this theater.

Ludwig Franzisket was one of Marseille's
closest friends and a firm believer in chivalry.

Schrör flew a total of 197 missions and scored 114
official victories.

GERHARD HOMUTH was Marseille's Staffelkapitan and later, his Gruppenkommandeur. He
was a strict disciplinarian and disapproved of the
liberties given to Marseille by Eduard Neumann.
Born in Kiel on September 20, 1914, Homuth scored
15 victories in the battles of France and Britain and
46 more in North Africa. After serving as assistant
to the Luftwaffe representative in Bulgaria, he returned to action on the Eastern front as Kommandeur of I/JG 54 in July of 1943. Major Homuth
was declared missing in action when he failed to return on a mission near Orel.

LUDWIG FRANZISKET was one of Hans Marseille's
closest friends and once saved Jochen's life during a
dogfight over the desert. Born in Düsseldorf on June
26, 1917, he entered the war as a Leutnant with I/JG
1 and fought in the Polish campaign. During the
Battle of Britain, he joined I/JG 27 and worked his
way up through Staffelkapitan and Gruppenkommandeur to Kommodore of JG 27 in December, 1944.
Major Franzisket was a soldier of the old school. He
believed in chivalry, and this attitude could have
contributed to his rather modest score of 43 victories.

HANNES TRAUTLOFT belongs to aerial history as a leader and educator as well as for his strong sense of responsibility to the Jagdwaffe, rather than as one of the Experten, which he was. He shares the spotlight with Mölders and Galland. He was worshiped by his men, but feared and banished by the Oberkommando der Luftwaffe.

Born in Grossobringen, Thüringen on March 3, 1912, Hannes joined the army after graduating from high school and technical school. By 1935, he had transferred to the new Luftwaffe and during the following year he was among the first six German pilots to arrive in Spain. After scoring four victories with the antiquated Heinkel biplane, he received the first Messerschmitt for combat evaluation and, with calm judgment and perseverance, Trautloft paved the way for the final refinements of the design.

Returning to Germany, Hannes Trautloft was a member of the three-man team that won the Alpine Circuit Race for formation flying at the 1937 Zurich International Air Competition. His next assignment was as Staffelkapitan of 2/JG 77, plus a promotion to Hauptmann. On September 19, 1939, he was placed in command of III Gruppe of JG 51 under Osterkamp. This unit experienced plenty of action in the Battle of France and the opening days of the Battle of Britain. His leadership of the Gruppe was so outstanding during this period that Trautloft was advanced to the command of his own Geschwader and took over as Kommodore of newly created JG 54 from Maj. Mettig on August 25, 1940. JG 54 had been formed from 76 Gruppe with two new Gruppen added. Trautloft will be forever associated with JG 54, because it was he who inspired it to win immortal fame on the Russian front. One of Hannes' first decisions was the selection of a Geschwader insignia, or identifying badge. Because he came from Thüringen, a verdant forest region called "the Green Heart of Germany," he chose a green heart with a narrow white outline. Thereafter, JG 54 was known as Grünherz, or Green Heart. Because of the added responsibility of Kommodore, Trautloft was promoted to the rank of Major.

At 3:00 A.M. on June 22, 1941, the Grünherz were the first to cross the Soviet border in Operation Barbarossa. By late afternoon the unit had flown many missions, with the Kommodore shooting down his first Russian bomber. During the first four days of the battle, JG 54 shot down 500 Soviet aircraft! On June 27, Trautloft was awarded the Ritterkreuz, after his 20th victory, for his excellent leadership of JG 54. By September 17, the Grünherz had destroyed 1,300 Russian planes in aerial combat and by April, 1942, they increased their score to 2,000 victories!

Hannes Trautloft was a leader and educator as well as a superb pilot. He fought in Spain, participated in the Zurich Air Meet in 1937, and was also involved in the Mutiny of the Fighters.

Under Trautloft's expert leadership, JG 54 continued its phenomenal scoring, reaching 3,500 by February, 1943. Many of the Green Hearts became unbelievably successful: Otto Kittel, 267 victories; Walter Nowotny, 258; Hans Philipp, 206; Erich Rudorffer, 222 victories; plus many others. Leading and inspiring men such as these proved a moving experience for Trautloft, and he will always be remembered for putting the Geschwader before his personal requirements.

Leading JG 54 Grünherz was the high point of Trautloft's military career. In July, 1943, General Galland appointed him Inspector of Day Fighters, East, a higher position than Kommodore but not as satisfying an assignment to Trautloft. Hubertus von Bonin succeeded him as JG 54 Kommodore. Together with Galland and Lützow, Oberst Trautloft tried to stem the side of destructive Allied bombings in the West and the Russian steamroller in the East. Deeply involved in the Mutiny of the Fighters in early 1945, Trautloft was removed from his post as were the others, and placed in charge of 4 Fliegerschule Division, a post he retained until war's end.

Hannes Trautloft emerged from the war with 57 victories, including four in Spain. He helped create the present West German air force, and became its Inspector General during the 1960s.

WALTER NOWOTNY was a young, impulsive, and individualistic Jagdflieger, cut from the same cloth as Marseille. The Luftwaffe's fifth-ranking Expert was born in Gmünd, Austria on December 7, 1920, and joined the Luftwaffe at the outbreak of the war. On December 1, 1940, he was assigned to the Ersatzstaffel of JG 54, a training unit at the fighter school at Schwechat near Vienna. Upon completion of the course, he was assigned to 9/JG 54, the Teufelstaffel, or Devil's Squadron, whose insignia was a grinning red Satan head.

Nowotny entered the war as a Rottenflieger, or wingman, but seldom remained in his proper position in the Rotte or Schwarm. His impetuous spirit couldn't resist attacking the enemy before the order was given, and for this he received many reprimands.

The young Leutnant scored his first victories on July 19, 1941, when he shot down three Soviet I-15 biplanes over Ösel Island, Estonia. Flak was exceptionally heavy, and his engine received a critical hit, causing him to lose altitude deep over Soviet territory. Nowotny quickly turned toward the Baltic, and chose to ditch in the water rather than be captured by the Russians. He radioed for help and then pancaked his Messerschmitt on the cold water. After paddling for three days and nights in his inflated raft, he reached friendly shores, suffering from exposure. As Nowotny was being driven to the hospital, he insisted on driving the car himself. The noncom at the wheel protested, but the young Leutnant pulled rank and took control of the vehicle. Nowotny was so exhausted from his three-day ordeal that he

Walter Nowotny was the Luftwaffe's fifth-ranking Experten, with 258 victories. He flew with 9/JG 54 Teufelstaffel for most of his career.

fainted, which caused the car to leave the road and smash into a tree, giving him a brain concussion! This episode proved a sobering experience for the young pilot.

Nowotny scored 7 victories on August 4, 1942, bringing his total to 54, and one month later was awared the Ritterkreuz. On October 25, he was given command of the Teufelstaffel and chose his close friend Karl Schnörrer as his Rottenflieger. The pair called each other by nicknames they had chosen for each other, Nowi and Quax, and soon the entire staffel used these for Walter and Karl.

Nowotny was promoted to Oberleutnant on February 1, 1943, and began to assemble the members of his Schwarm, a unit that was to become the most famous and successful of its kind. He achieved 66 victories by March 7, and 82 by May 20, but his combat career really took off in June, 1943. In this month he shot down 41 adversaries, scoring 10 on June 24 alone, and he reached the century mark on June 15. Another spurt of 49 victories came in August, with his 150th victory confirmed on August 18. He scored his 200th kill on September 4, and was awarded the Eichenlaub on the following day. The Schwerten were presented on September 22. Between October

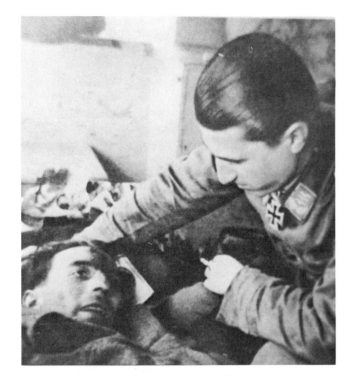

Nowotny comforts the wounded Schnörrer, his buddy and Rottenflieger. Shown is a note that Walter sent to Karl at this time. It reads: "My Dear Quax—In memory of the many critical and chancy situations which we managed together in this enormous war and those which we will still have to manage. I don't want to mention gratitude. Remain a good guy, Yours, Nowi."

Walter Nowotny shows Kommodore von Bonin a bullet hole in his flight suit upon his return from a mission. Everyone smiled at this very close brush with death; however, the end finally came, and Nowi received a full military funeral with honors.

5 and October 15, 1943, Nowotny shot down 32 Soviet aircraft which brought his official score to 250 victories, making him the top-scoring Jagdflieger at that time. Hauptmann Nowotny was awarded the Brillanten to his Ritterkreuz on October 19, 1943, the eighth member of the Luftwaffe to receive this award. Nowi also claimed about 50 additional victories which could not be confirmed during this period.

During 1943, Nowotny's Schwarm of four pilots amassed almost 500 victories! Nowotny, Karl Schnörrer, Anton Döbele, and Rudolf Rademacher operated together with great precision, like a well-oiled machine, and filled the Soviet pilots with fear when the Schwarm was in action.

The strain of continuous combat was beginning to affect Nowi, evidenced by the terrible recurring nightmare that plagued him: While in the process of attacking a large airplane, a hand stops him and indicates that 281 victories is enough—he must die now. His fellow pilots made great sport of these nightmares, except for Schnörrer, who understood what his friend appeared to be suffering. Kommodore von Bonin, recognizing the symptoms of combat fatigue, ordered Nowotny on leave for rest and recuperation in November, 1943.

When he was again ready for action, Walter was given the post of Kommodore of Schulgeschwader 101, a training unit located in France, in an effort to produce more trained pilots for the Fatherland.

In July, 1944, Major Nowotny was placed in charge of an Me 262 jet-fighter–equipped unit based at Achmer and named Kommando Nowotny. Although no longer with the Grünherz Geschwader, Walter had a green heart painted on the side of his jet because of the fond memories he had of serving under Trautloft in JG 54. Kommando Nowotny was formed to test the suitability of jet aircraft for fighter activities.

On November 8, 1944, Nowi took off from Achmer on an intercept mission. After scoring three B-17 Flying Fortresses, he tangled with the escorting P-51 Mustang fighters and experienced a flameout in one of his engines. This greatly reduced his battle ability so Nowotny dived into the clouds and worked his way back to Achmer preparing to land. It was standard operating procedure for U.S. fighters to wait above the German jet-fighter airfields for the jets to return and begin to land. When the Jagdwaffe jets were in this helpless position, the Americans attacked and invariably scored. As Nowotny made his approach to Achmer, waiting Mustangs jumped him and sent the German plunging to earth. Plane, pilot, and Ritterkreuz were a tangled mass. Walter

Nowotny was credited with 258 official victories. If we add his 23 unverified kills to this figure, the result is 281 victories, the same as in his recurring nightmare!

Kommando Nowotny became the nucleus of a new jet Jagdgeschwader, JG 7, led by Johannes Steinhoff.

KARL SCHNÖRRER was Nowotny's Rottenflieger during most of the latter's combat career and was a member of the famous Nowotny Schwarm. Considerable credit must be given to Schnörrer for protecting his leader during Nowotny's amazing string of victories in 1943. Born in Nuremberg, Bavaria on March 3, 1919, he joined 1/JG 54 in the summer of 1941 as an Unteroffizier and scored the first of 46 victories on the last day of the year. He earned the nickname "Quax" because of the trouble he had landing the Messerschmitt 109, crashing three of the narrow and weak landing-geared fighters. Quax was an accident-prone cartoon character, so the name was well chosen for Karl.

Schnörrer was seriously wounded on November 12, 1943, as the Nowotny Schwarm broke up. Upon his return to active duty several months later, Quax was assigned to E-Gruppe Lechfeld, the test unit that became Kommando Nowotny, flying the Me 262 jet fighter. He later became Staffelkapitan of 2/JG 7. On March 22, 1945, Schnörrer was awarded the Ritterkreuz, and eight days later he bailed out of his crippled jet during an intercept mission over Hamburg. Although he survived, Karl's wounds were so severe that it was necessary to amputate his left leg.

ANTON DÖBELE and RUDOLF RADEMACHER were the third and fourth members of the Nowotny Schwarm. They scored most of their combined 220 victories during 1943 while with this famous formation. Döbele joined JG 54 as a Feldwebel in mid-1941, and after a year of combat had only four victories to his credit. His scoring increased rapidly in early 1943 after joining the Schwarm, reaching a total of 94 by the end of the year. Leutnant Döbele was killed in action on November 11, 1943 over his airfield near Smolensk, when he collided with another German fighter. The Leutnant was awarded the Ritterkreuz posthumously on March 26, 1944. Rudolf Rademacher joined JG 54 in late 1941 as an Unteroffizier and scored his first victory on January 9, 1942. He was transferred to the Nowotny Schwarm in March of the following year, and, as with Nowotny, Schnörrer, and Döbele, he scored with amazing regularity during 1943. He was seriously wounded on September 9, 1944, during an intercept mission against U.S. Fortresses. Returning to action

Karl Schnörrer was called Quax because he cracked up so many Messerschmitts in takeoffs and landings. Quax was an accident-prone cartoon character. In the air, however, it was a different matter.

The Nowotny Schwarm was the most successful in the Jagdwaffe, and Anton Döbele and Rudolf Rademacher complemented Nowi and Quax in the four-plane fight.

Erich Rudorffer was one of the deadliest marksmen in the Jagdwaffe and scored more multiple kills than any other fighter pilot. He was known by the Soviets as the "Fighter of Libau." The rudder of his Messerschmitt with victory bars is from his early days with JG 2 Richthofen.

in January, 1945 he was assigned to 11/JG 7 where he flew jets for one month, scoring eight victories. Rademacher survived the war, with 126 victories to his credit. He retained his interest in flying, especially gliding, during the postwar years and was killed in a gliding accident on June 13, 1953, over his hometown of Lüneburg.

ERICH RUDORFFER was the master of multiple scoring, having achieved more multiple kills than any other fighter pilot. He fought from the snow-covered airfields of Finland to the hot sands of the African desert, scoring his 222 official victories along every part of this vast combat arena. Saxon-born in Zwickau on November 1, 1917, Rudorffer became one of the deadliest marksmen in the Jagdwaffe. This, combined with his superb piloting and quick thinking in the midst of battle made him a hard-to-beat adversary.

Erich began his wartime career in January, 1940, when he joined I Gruppe of JG 2 Richthofen in Frankfort-am-Main as in Oberfeldwebel. He scored his first victory over a French Curtiss 75A near Sedan on May 14, and had a total of nine by the time of France's capitulation. With his score climbing slowly during the Channel fighting, Rudorffer was promoted to Leutnant on October 2, and awarded the

Ritterkreuz on May 1, 1941, for his 19th victory. Promotion to Adjutant of I/JG 2 and then Staffelkapitan of 6/JG 2 came in June. His 25th victory was not scored until August 6, 1941, because Rudorffer was a slow beginner, as were many of the high-scoring Experten.

In November, 1942, Rudorffer was transferred to Tunisia, North Africa, with II/JG 2 and made Kommandeur of the Gruppe in the following month. His first multiple kills didn't come until February, 1943, when he shot down eight British aircraft in 32 minutes on the 9th and seven more in 20 minutes on the 15th. In April, 1943, Rudorffer was back on the Channel coast after scoring 26 victories in Tunisia.

After destroying 74 adversaries with JG 2 Richthofen in the West, Rudorffer was transferred to the Russian front in June, 1943, as Gruppenkommandeur of II/JG 54 Grunherz in the Leningrad area. On August 24, he shot down five Soviet aircraft in four minutes on the day's first mission, and scored three more in seven minutes during the second. On October 11, Rudorffer scored seven victories in seven minutes, from 12:20 to 12:27! His outstanding feat of aerial combat came on November 6 when, in the 17 minutes between 1:00 P.M. and 1:17 P.M., Erich Rudorffer shot down no less than 13 enemy aircraft!

After spending the 1943/44 winter fighting in Finland, Major Rudorffer was awarded the Finnish Cross of Liberty, as well as Honorary Pilot's Wings of the Finnish Air Force. The Eichenlaub was awarded on April 11, 1944, for the Experten's 113th victory.

Rudorffer was known to Soviet pilots as the "fighter of Libau" and an incident on October 28, 1944, illustrates the reason. One of the last to land at the Libau base after a morning mission, Rudorffer spotted an armada of sixty Shturmoviks heading for the airfield. He slammed the throttle of his Daimler-Benz engine, retracted the Messerschmitt undercarriage and zoomed up to meet the heavily armored attack planes. Between 11:46 and 11:56, Rudorffer threw the attackers into a panic-filled retreat, shooting down nine of their number in just ten minutes! During an afternoon mission, Rudorffer shot down two more Russian planes in just two minutes, making it eleven for the day.

Major Rudorffer was awarded the Schwerten to his Ritterkreuz on January 26, 1945, for this 210th victory. Shortly afterward he was recalled from the Eastern front to assist in the defense of the Reich. In February he was placed in command of II/JG 7, flying jet fighters, and became one of the first jet aces in the world, scoring a total of 12 in these new aircraft.

In his action-packed career, Erich Rudorffer never went on leave; he was shot down 16 times; he bailed out 9 times; he flew over 1,000 missions; and he became the seventh-ranking Expert of the Luftwaffe.

When last heard from, Erich Rudorffer was serving with the West German equivalent of the U.S. Federal Aviation Agency (F.A.A.).

OTTO KITTEL was the most successful pilot of JG 54 Grunherz, with 267 official victories. This little-known fourth-ranking Luftwaffe ace was born in Kronsdorf, Sudetenland on February 21, 1917, and joined 2/JG 54 as an Oberfeldwebel in late 1941. He suffered through a long adjustment period before finding his shooting eye, and consequently it was not until May, 1942, that he scored his 15th victory. He registered his 39th in February, 1943.

Like Nowotny and others, Kittel's score began to rise in 1943, a time when German forces were beset by reverses. He was awarded the Ritterkreuz on October 29, 1943, for his 123rd victory. Promoted in the field to Leutnant, he received the Eichenlaub on April 14, 1944, for his 152nd kill, and the Schwerten on November 25 for his 230th victory. By this time he had been elevated to the rank of Oberleutnant.

While on his 583rd mission, attacking a formation of low-flying Shturmoviks, Otto Kittel's plane

Otto Kittel was the highest-scoring pilot of JG 54, with 267 victories. He was the Luftwaffe's fourth-ranking Experten.

Hans Philipp was an outstanding dogfighter and was the second pilot to attain 200 victories. He is shown here with Hannes Trautloft in Russia.

smashed into the ground. Some say he was hit by Russian flak, while others insist it was the Shturmovik gunners who killed Otto Kittel.

HANS PHILIPP, a talented dogfighter with 206 victories, preferred combat with enemy fighters rather than bombers because, like a fencer, he enjoyed the parry and thrust. He was the fourth pilot to reach 100 victories and the second to attain 200 kills. The son of a doctor, Hans was born in Meissen in Saxony on March 17, 1917, and first saw action in the Polish campaign. He scored his first victory there with Jagdgruppe 76. Philipp joined 4/JG 54 Grünherz in late 1940 as Staffelkapitan, fighting over the Channel and received the Ritterkreuz on October 22 for his 20th victory. His rank at this time was Oberleutnant.

He participated in the attack on Russia under Trautloft, and was awarded the Eichenlaub on August 24, 1941, for his 62nd kill. Fips, as he was often called, became Gruppenkommandeur of I/JG 54 in February, 1942, and was in command of Walter Nowotny and other outstanding Grünherz Experten during this time. He joined the century club during the following month.

On April 1, 1943, Philipp was transferred to the West to combat the U.S. bombers. Promoted to Oberstleutnant and Kommodore of JG 1, he fought the giants for six months until October 10, when he led his men in an intercept over Nordhorn. Escorting Thunderbolts quickly surrounded the Kommodore as he pressed his attack on the bombers. They shot him out of the sky before he could defend himself like the duelist he was and as he would have wanted.

Emil Lang shot down 18 planes in one day and 72 in three weeks. He was shot down when his landing gear dropped off and cut his speed and maneuverability.

EMIL LANG shot down 72 adversaries in three weeks, and holds the single-day record of 18 victories. Bully Lang was born in Thalheim, Oberbayern on January 14, 1909, and was a well-known track and field athlete in his youth. He joined Lufthansa as a pilot before the war and transferred into the Luftwaffe at the outbreak of hostilities. He entered the Jagdwaffe in 1942, posted to 9/JG 54 on the Russian front.

Already an accomplished pilot, Lang needed no breaking-in period. He had scored 119 victories by November, 1943, for which he was awarded the Ritterkreuz. In the following April, Lang received the Eichenlaub to his Ritterkreuz for his 144th victory. Although considered old for a fighter pilot, Bully Lang exhibited unsurpassed dash and daring in combat, cutting a swath across the skies of the Eastern front.

On June 29, 1944, Hptm. Lang was transferred to the West as Gruppenkommandeur of II/JG 26 Schlageter. After scoring 25 victories against the U.S. forces, for a total of 173 kills, he engaged in combat with U.S. Thunderbolts near St. Trond. During the battle, Lang's hydraulic system was hit, causing his landing gear to drop away. This cut into his speed and maneuverability such that he was easy prey for the pursuing Thunderbolts, who quickly shot him down.

HERBERT IHLEFELD was one of the old fighter leaders who helped form the Jagdwaffe. Born in Pinnow, Pommerania on June 1, 1914, he saw action in Spain as an Oberfeldwebel, where he scored seven victories. In 1938, he joined I/JG 77 and became its Kommandeur in August, 1940. Oblt. Ihlefeld received the Ritterkreuz on September 13, 1940 for his 21st victory, and by the end of the Battle of Britain, he had scored 25. On April 22, 1942, he became the fifth fighter pilot to score 100 victories. In the following month, he was promoted to Kommodore of JG 52, a post he held until November, when he became, consecutively, Kommodore of JGs 103, 25, 11, and 1. Decidedly one of the leading Jagdwaffe personalities, Oberst Ihlefeld scored 130 victories, 15 of which were four-engine bombers.

DIETRICH HRABAK succeeded Ihlefeld as Kommodore of JG 52 and is also considered a leading Jagdwaffe personality. Born in Gros-Deuben bei Leipzig on December 19, 1914, Dieter was the son of an architect. His interests turned to the air at an early age, and he became enthralled with the ex-

Herbert Ihlefeld helped to create the Luftwaffe and is considered to be one of the leading Jagdwaffe personalities.

Dietrich Hrabak was truly the dominating influence in JG 52 and helped mold it into the
unit of Experten.

ploits of the day's famous aviators. Upon graduation
from Gymnasium, Dieter joined the German navy in
1934 and transferred to the Luftwaffe when he
qualified as a pilot, two years later. Like many
famous aces, Hrabak was not a natural pilot and
cracked up several planes during his training
period.

In February, 1938, he was posted to the Vienna
Jagdgruppe, which was the nucleus of the yet-to-be-
formed JG 54. One year later, he was the Gruppenkommandeur and assigned to the Polish campaign,
where he became one of the first Jagdwaffe pilots to
be shot down! He managed a belly landing on his
very first mission on September 1, 1939. The Vienna
Jagdgruppe became Jagdgruppe 76 early in the
Polish campaign and continued to see action in the
Battle of France. Here, Hrabak scored his first victory, a Potez 63, on May 13, 1940. By the summer, JG
54 had been formed, and Dieter was a founding
member. He fought in the Battle of Britain under
Trautloft and was awarded the Ritterkreuz on
October 21 for his 16th victory. Hptm. Hrabak
fought with JG 54 in the Balkans, Greece, and Russia
until November 1, 1942, when he was promoted to
Kommodore of JG 52 in the southern sector of the
Russian front.

Oberst Hrabak became the dominant influence in
JG 52, molding it into one of the most successful fighter units, home of the highest-scoring aces in combat
aviation. His interest in his men shaped the careers
of many of the successful pilots who flew with the
Geschwader. He had two basic rules, which he
never failed to impress upon his young pilots: "Fly
with your head and not with your muscles," and "If
you return from a mission with a victory, but without
your Rottenflieger, you have lost your battle."

He was awarded the Eichenlaub on November 25,
1943, for his 118th victory and then transferred to
the leadership of JG 54 Grünherz on October 1, 1944.
Dieter Hrabak flew a total of 820 missions and
scored 125 victories. After the war, he was sales
manager for a machinery manufacturer, and later
worked for Chancellor Adenauer in the formation of
the new West German air force. He was one of the
first German pilots to travel to the U.S. in 1955 for
jet fighter training. General Major Hrabak married
the former Marrianne Röver in 1970 in Cologne.

HERMANN GRAF succeeded Hrabak as Kommodore of JG 52, and was one of only nine Luftwaffe
members to receive the coveted Brillanten to his
Ritterkreuz. Graf was born the youngest son of a

Hermann Graf beat the Soviet pilots at their own game by learning how to enter combat at a low altitude. He was called "King of the hedge-hopping attack" and was one of the most highly publicized German aces. Shown here are an official portrait and the cover of an aviation magazine, *Der Adler* or "The Eagle."

blacksmith in Engen, Baden on October 24, 1912. His humble birth forced him to miss a secondary school education, which was an essential prerequisite to a professional officer's career. Despite this initial disadvantage, he worked himself up through the ranks to Kommodore of a most successful Jagdgeschwader, and became one of the most publicized Experten of the war.

After working as an apprentice blacksmith, factory worker, and clerk, he took seriously to the sport of gliding in 1933, and by 1936 was flying powered craft. Hermann first caught public attention as an outstanding amateur soccer player, for which he was remembered throughout his career. As a member of the Luftwaffe reserve pilots, Graf was called up at the outbreak of hostilities and made an instructor in a Jagdfliegerschule, due to his status as an accomplished pilot.

In July, 1941, the Feldwebel was posted to 9/JG 52, and began one of the most fantastic combat careers

ever recorded. After scoring his first victory on August 3, Graf quickly learned to beat the Russian pilots at their own game. He became adept at low-altitude fighting, which was difficult for many Jagdwaffe pilots to master. Graf's score rose rapidly, and he was commissioned a Leutnant in the field before the year was out. Within eight months Graf had received the four highest German decorations!

On January 24, 1942, Leutnant Graf was awarded the Ritterkreuz for his 42nd victory; on May 17 the Eichenlaub for his 104th kill; two days later the Schwerten; and on September 9, 1942, he became the fifth Luftwaffe member to be awarded the Brillanten for his 172nd victory!

During this meteoric climb to fame, he shot down seven adversaries each on May 2 and May 14, and scored 47 victories during the 17-day period ending on May 14. During the bloody air battles around Stalingrad and the Crimea, Graf flew up to five missions a day and became known as the King of the hedge-hopping attack and as the Hero of Stalingrad. Oberleutnant Graf continued his phenomenal scoring in 1942 by shooting down 52 adversaries during the three weeks ending September 27, and became the first pilot to reach 200 victories, five days later. By this time he had been promoted to Hauptmann and leader of his Staffel.

In early 1943, Graf sustained an arm wound and after a stay in the hospital, he traveled on lecture tours in Germany, often appearing at soccer matches for propaganda purposes. He found himself a hero virtually overnight, his picture appearing on front pages of newspapers and magazines. Progaganda Minister Göbbels called Hermann Graf the finest example of Nazi manhood and wrung every drop of propaganda benefit from the naive Graf.

Fully recovered by the spring, Graf was promoted to Major and assigned to lead the newly-formed Jagderganzungsgruppe Ost (Fighter Supplementary Group East) and JG 50 to combat the U.S. bombers. Although he did very little flying during this period, Graf managed to shoot down two B-17F Fortresses on September 6. Two months later he became Kommodore of JG 11, assigned to the Reich home defense. Graf scored two more Fortresses on March 3, 1944, and then rammed one of the escorting Mustang fighters! After a year of occasional flying, during which he shot down ten U.S. Fortresses, Graf returned to JG 52, this time as Kommodore to succeed Hrabak, in October, 1944.

Germany's collapse found the JG 52 airfields surrounded by Russian troops. Graf, however, was determined to surrender his men only to American forces. The Oberst ordered all planes burned and other equipment destroyed. The entire Geschwader, ground personnel and pilots alike, then retreated on foot from Bohemia to Bavaria. Mostly unarmed, the Graf Storm Regiment, as it became known, lived off the land and fought off pockets of armed Czechoslovakian partisans until finally meeting U.S. Forces. The Germans were well treated for ten days by the Americans and then handed back to the Russians!

Once the Soviets identified Graf as the famous German hero, they treated him poorly and kept him in solitary confinement for long periods. In order to reassure himself of his identity, the Oberst kept his last order hidden in the heel of his shoe and read it periodically. Even this was not enough, and Graf finally succumbed to Communist pressure in much the way many U.S. pilots reacted to Red torture when captive in Korea. Released from prison in 1950, Hermann Graf now lives in East Germany, condemned by many of his peers, but understood and forgiven by many more.

Gerhard Barkhorn is the world's Number Two ace with 301 victories. As with most Jagdwaffe pilots, he was shot down many times but preferred to ride his plane to a crash landing rather than bail out.

GERHARD BARKHORN is the world's second-highest-scoring ace, with 301 official victories, who flew with JG 52 for over four years. Born in Königsberg, East Prussia, on March 20, 1919, he began his military flying career in 1938. He first saw action during the opening phase of the Battle of Britain with JG 2, and not only failed to score, but was shot down twice within a few days. In one incident over England, a Spitfire hit his oil cooler, and as he nursed the crippled Messerschmitt past the Dover Cliffs and over the Channel, he was again attacked, sending his craft downward. Barkhorn elected to bail out. Luckily, a Staffelmate saw him hit the water and directed a nearby German patrol boat to the rescue. They picked up the downed flier just moments before a British rescue boat arrived at the scene! After this close call, Barkhorn never again took to his parachute, preferring to remain with his crippled plane right down to the crash landing. This he was forced to do eight times during his combat career.

Barkhorn joined II/JG 52 in August, 1940, but failed to score a victory until his 120th mission on July 2, 1941, truly a slow starter! By August 23,

1942, the Oberleutnant had been awarded the Ritterkreuz for his 59th kill, and scored his 100th victory five months later. He received the Eichenlaub on January 11, 1943, for his 120th victory; and by November 30, his score stood at 200, the fifth pilot to reach the double-century mark. Hptm. Barkhorn became the third fighter pilot to reach the 250-victory mark on February 13, 1944, and was awarded the Schwerten on March 2.

Gerhard Barkhorn was now Gruppenkommandeur and the Luftwaffe's leading scorer, with Erich Hartmann a close second. In the summer of 1944, as Gerhard was returning from his sixth mission of the day, his flight made contact with a large formation of Russian bombers. Barkhorn turned to engage the enemy, but fatigue had made him careless and he violated one of the basic fighter pilot rules: Always look behind you. Cannon shells and machine gun bullets tore into his Messerschmitt from behind, as an American-made Airacobra fighter closed in at six o'clock high. Wounds in the right leg and arm required a four-month stay in the hospital, during which time Hartmann took the scoring lead and kept it. It has been speculated that Soviet Ace Alexander Pokryshkin was the pilot of that Airacobra, and that Barkhorn is one of his 59 victories.

During his hospital stay, Barkhorn's unit relocated to Hungary, where he joined it in the fall. In January, 1945 he was elevated to Kommodore of JG 6 Horst Wessel. He joined Galland's JV 44 flying jet fighters late in the war. Barkhorn flew a total of 1,104 missions and logged over 2,000 hours of flying time in the Messerschmitt Me 109.

Today Gerhard Barkhorn flies jet fighters in the West German air force, which he joined in 1956.

HEINZ EWALD was Barkhorn's Rottenflieger and scored 84 victories with JG 52 on the Eastern front. Danzig-born Lt. Ewald received the Ritterkreuz on April 20, 1945, for his 82nd victory. The Rotte or two-plane element depended upon close teamwork for success and Barkhorn and Ewald fulfilled that requirement.

HELMUT LIPFERT is the world's 13th-ranking fighter ace. Although shot down 13 times by antiaircraft batteries and twice by Russian fighters, he was never injured. Born in Lippelsdorf, Thüringen on August 6, 1916, he joined II/JG 52 on December 16, 1942, and within a month scored his first victory, a Soviet fighter plane. Lt. Lipfert received the Ritterkreuz on April 5, 1944, for his 90th kill, and joined the century club six days later. Promoted to Hauptmann and Gruppenkommandeur in the summer of

Heinz Ewald was Barkhorn's Rottenflieger. He proved to be a good teamworker and, besides protecting his leader, he scored 85 victories of his own.

Helmut Lipfert was shot down 15 times but never wounded. He scored 203 victories in 700 missions.

1944, he scored his 200th victory on April 8, 1945. Lipfert shot down 203 adversaries, including two U.S. four-engine bombers over Romania, in 700 missions. Today Helmut Lipfert is a quiet, dignified schoolteacher in West Germany who refrains from association with his former comrades in an effort to build a new life.

WALTER KRUPINSKI, known as Graf Punski or Count Punski in the Jagdwaffe, was a swashbuckling fly-boy, who not only never lost a wingman, but also had the ability to help beginners develop to their fullest capacity. One of these latter was Erich Hartmann. Born in Donnau, East Prussia, on November 11, 1920, he joined JG 52 in January, 1942, and by the end of the year had scored 66 victories (earning the Ritterkreuz in late October). He was promoted to Hauptmann and 7/JG 52 Staffelkapitan in the spring of 1943, and on July 5 he scored victories 80 to 90 (11 in one day). After yeoman service on the Russian front, he was transferred to combat the U.S. bombings with I/JG 5 in the spring of 1944. He became Kommandeur of II/JG 11 and finally Kommandeur of III/JG 26 Schlageter. In March, 1945, he joined

Walter Krupinski flew 1,100 missions and scored 197 victories. "Count Punski" never lost a Rottenflieger, and taught many beginners the art of aerial combat.

Galland's JV 44 and flew jet fighters until the war's end. After flying 1,100 missions, Major Krupinski was officially credited with 197 victories.

ERICH HARTMANN, the world's top-scoring fighter pilot, shot down the equivalent of almost 15 Allied squadrons in aerial combat! The Russian pilots both feared and hated him, calling him the "Black Devil of the Ukraine." Flying 1,425 missions over the Caucasus, southern Russia, Romania, Hungary, and Czechoslovakia, Hartmann engaged in over 800 dogfights and suffered 13 accidents or equipment failures. Preferring to ride his damaged plane to 12 crash landings, Hartmann bailed out only once, over Romania. His score of 352 victories will probably never be equaled in the history of combat aviation.

Hartmann was only 17 when the war began. He was born in Weissach, Würtemberg on April 19, 1922. He was the only son of a physician and his wife, a brilliant sportswoman. An aviation enthusiast, Erich's mother taught him how to fly a glider by age 14 and a powered plane two years later. Upon graduating from college in late 1940, he joined the army, transferring to the Luftwaffe six months later. An adept pupil, he soloed in less than one month, but experienced three crash landings during the training course. By October, 1942, he was assigned to 7/JG 52 based at Soldatskaya in the Caucasus. His first assignment was as Rottenfleiger for Fw. Edmund Rossmann but, overly enthusiastic, Hartmann fouled up his first few attempts at aerial combat. He did everything wrong, including: separating from his leader without permission; losing his orientation; flying into his leader's firing position; running out of fuel and then destroying his plane in a crash-landing, without damaging a single enemy plane. Naturally, this undisciplined behavior endangered the rest of the Schwarm, and earned a severe reprimand from Kommodore Hrabak.

Erich was then assigned as Rottenflieger for Walter Krupinski, and Count Punski took the youngster in tow with a more relaxed combat attitude. He taught the tyro to get so close to his adversary before firing that a hit was guaranteed. This lesson, coupled with the fact that Hartmann was a crack shot, enabled Erich to score most of his kills with very little ammunition. Sometimes he downed an enemy with only one cannon shell! It was Krupinski who began calling Hartmann Bubi, or boy, and this nickname followed Erich throughout his career.

Bubi scored his first victory on November 5, 1942. His Schwarm took off at noon to intercept 18 heavily armored Shturmovik ground-attack planes escorted by 10 Lagg-3 fighters, east of Digora. Hartmann

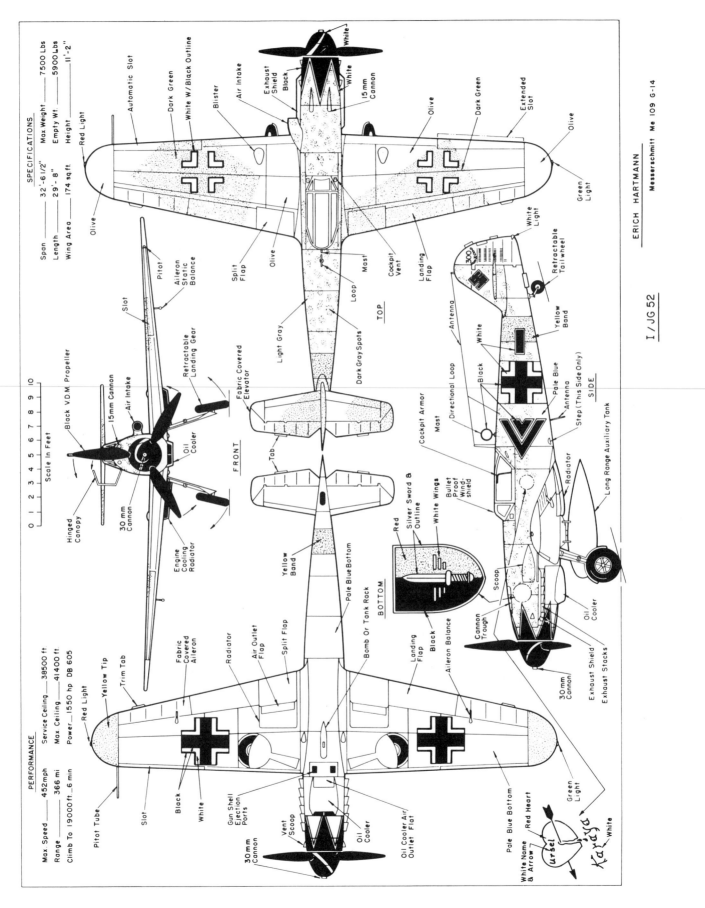

SPECIFICATIONS

Span	32'-6 1/2"
Length	29'-8"
Wing Area	174 sq.ft.
Max Weight	7500 Lbs
Empty Wt.	5900 Lbs
Height	11'-2"

PERFORMANCE

Max Speed	452mph
Range	366 mi
Climb To 19000ft	6 min
Service Ceiling	38500 ft
Max Ceiling	41400 ft
Power	1550 hp DB 605

Scale In Feet
0 1 2 3 4 5 6 7 8 9 10

ERICH HARTMANN
Messerschmitt Me 109 G-14

I / JG 52

TOP

FRONT

SIDE

BOTTOM

Automatic Slot
Dark Green
White W/ Black Outline
Blister
Air Intake
Exhaust Shield
Black
White
15 mm Cannon
White
Olive
Dark Green
Extended Slot
Olive
Green Light
Red Light
Olive

Pitot
Aileron Static Balance
Slot
Retractable Landing Gear
Fabric Covered Elevator
Split Flap
Light Gray
Loop
Mast
Cockpit Vent
Dark Gray Spots
Landing Flap

Black V.D.M. Propeller
15mm Cannon
Air Intake
Oil Cooler
30 mm Cannon
Engine Cooling Radiator
Hinged Canopy

White Light
Retractable Tailwheel
Yellow Band
Pale Blue
Antenna
Step (This Side Only)
Directional Loop
Antenna
Black
White
Mast
Cockpit Armor
Radiator
Long Range Auxiliary Tank
Scoop
Cannon Trough
Oil Cooler
30mm Cannon
Exhaust Shield
Exhaust Stacks

Red
Silver Sword & Outline
White Wings
Bullet Proof Windshield
Black
Landing Flap
Aileron Balance

Yellow Tip
Trim Tab
Red Light
Pitot Tube
Slot
Black
White
Gun Shell Ejection Ports
Fabric Covered Aileron
Radiator
Air Outlet Flap
Split Flap
Yellow Band
Pale Blue Bottom
Bomb Or Tank Rack
30mm Cannon
Vent Scoop
Oil Cooler
Oil Cooler Air Outlet Flat
Pale Blue Bottom
Green Light

White Name & Arrow
Red Heart
Karaya
Ursel
White

"Bubi" Hartmann wears the smile of victory as he emerges from his 109 shown at left. He poses by the tail of his Messerschmitt in the photo on the right, showing 121 victory flashes. Hartmann is the world's greatest ace, with 352 victories.

Erich Hartmann is shown with General Pflugbeil on the Eastern front, where the flyer scored all his victories.

headed directly for the nearest Shturmovik and pulled in close, as he was taught. At 300-ft. range, he began firing, but his cannon shells bounced off the plane's heavy armor. Quickly adjusting altitude to get below his target and aim for the Russian's oil cooler before the escorting fighters could interfere,

he fired again at a closer range of only 200 ft. The tactic worked, for the Shturmovik first belched smoke and then exploded, striking the trailing Messerschmitt with some debris. As Bubi watched his victory crash into an open field, his Messerschmitt began smoking, followed by a muffled ex-

Hartmann, whom the Russians called the "Black Devil," was in a Soviet prison for ten years after the end of the war. Photos show him as he appeared just before he was put into confinement and as he appeared when released from the Soviet POW camp.

plosion as tongues of flame licked the engine compartment. There was no alternative: he had to belly-land his damaged plane not far from the wreckage of his first victim! This was the first of three occasions in which the debris from his victim forced Hartmann to crash-land.

Although Hartmann scored his initial victory within one month of his appearance at the front, he was no fast scorer. By April, 1943, he had made only seven kills, after flying over 100 missions! Bubi began scoring in earnest at the end of April, when he shot down two Lagg 3 fighters on the 30th for his 10th and 11th victories. During the fierce air battles in the July Kursk offensive, Hartmann scored seven victories on the seventh of the month.

On August 19, while Bubi was a temporary escort leader for Stuka pilot Ulrich Rudel's Immelmann Geschwader, about 40 Soviet La-5 and Yak 9 fighters intercepted the attacking force deep over Russian-held territory. Hartmann led 7/JG 52 against the fighters, and flamed a Yak at 300-ft. range. A moment later, his Messerschmitt was disabled by ground fire, and Bubi was forced to belly-land in the

Donitz area. As the Messerschmitt ground to a halt, Hartmann could see swarms of Soviet infantry running toward him, so he decided to feign semiconsciousness and an abdominal injury. The ruse worked and saved him from a possible beating by the angry troops. Four hours later he was riding in the back of an open truck with two armed guards standing over him when the unmistakable whine of a diving Stuka pierced the skies directly overhead. The driver panicked, ran the truck off the road into a ditch, and joined the guards as they ran for safety while Bubi jumped out seconds later and ran in the opposite direction! It was many hours before Erich reached German territory, almost getting shot as an infiltrating Russian by nervous German troops. Meanwhile, in an act of true loyalty and comaraderie, Hartmann's crew chief, Fw. Heinrich Mertens, had taken a rifle and crossed the front lines into Russian-held territory in an effort to save his commander!

Hartmann was given a short leave to marry Ursul Pätch on September 10, and was back at the front after a few days. Upon his return, he had the mechanics paint Ursul's name on his plane's fuselage.

By September 18, 1943, Hartmann had completed 300 missions with 95 victories to his credit. On October 29, he was awarded the Ritterkreuz for his 148th victory. He was now Staffelkapitan of 7/JG 52, and recipient of the Eichenlaub on March 2, 1944, for his 200th victory. With his combat style fully developed, Bubi rode the crest of success in the summer of 1944. After receiving the Schwertern on July 4 for his 239th kill, he scored 59 victories in 16 missions, and downed 78 Soviet aircraft in four weeks. He shot down eight adversaries on August 23, and eleven more on the following day for a total of 301 victories! Oblt. Hartmann was awarded the Brillanten to his Ritterkreuz on August 25. By then 7/JG 52 had shot down 1,200 Soviet aircraft more than any other Staffel in the Jagdwaffe.

Hartmann was transferred to the leadership of 4/JG 52 in October, 1944, and advanced to Gruppenkommandeur of I/JG 52 on February 1, 1945. His score continued to mount, despite the fact that most Russian pilots turned and ran when they saw Hartmann's black-nosed Messerschmitt approaching. Erich's tactic was to strike quickly, getting as close as possible before firing, and then "hit and run," using the Messerschmitt's excellent climbing ability to advantage. Then he would repeat the process, taking advantage of his plane's good diving ability. Unlike Marseille, Hartmann hardly ever scored multiple victories in a single pass. Bubi generally looked for a high cloud behind which to hide between attacks. His tactics were not unlike those of Manfred von Richthofen, the top scorer of the First World War.

During his combat career on the Russian front, Hartmann met U.S. planes over Romania, shooting down seven P-51 Mustangs during these engagements. One of the U.S. units engaged was the 334th Fighter Squadron and it is thought that U.S. Ace Lt. Ralph K. Hoffer (16.5 victories), might have been one of Hartmann's victims.

In the late morning of May 8, 1945, Hptm. Hartmann led the Schwarm over Czechoslovakia to spot the advancing Russian troops. He saw a Soviet fighter performing aerobatics over the town of Brunn, apparently in celebration of the pending Russian victory. Erich struck quickly and the hapless aerobat became his 352nd victory.

As part of the Graf Storm Regiment, Hartmann was turned over to the Russians by the U.S. authorities. Once the Soviets realized that they had the Black Devil as prisoner, he was singled out for especially brutal treatment, including long periods of solitary confinement in total darkness. Using every

persuasive device known, the Russians could not convert Hartmann to Communism and held him in prison for ten years—far longer than other POWs. While he was illegally detained in Russia, Hartmann's 3½-year-old-son, whom he had never seen, died. It was only after Chancellor Adenauer personally visited Moscow in 1955 and arranged for his release that a gaunt and haggard Bubi Hartmann was released by his captors, broken in body but not in spirit.

Hartmann quickly regained his health and joined the new West German Air Force in 1959, becoming Kommodore of JG 71, the new Richthofen Geschwader based at Fliegerhorst Ahlhorn in Oldenberg. JG 71 was the first of the new Geschwadern formed by the Federal Republic's air force. Today he is a tactical advisor to the West German air force and is a frequent visitor to the United States.

GÜNTHER RALL is the world's third leading aerial combat scorer, with 275 official victories to his credit. Like Barkhorn and Hartmann, he is closely associated with JG 52. Born in Gaggenau, Baden on March 10, 1918, Günther graduated from Gymnasium in 1936. He then joined Infantry Regiment No. 13 as an officer candidate and underwent officer's training at the Kriegsschule, or war school, in Dresden. Two years later, he transferred to the Luftwaffe and joined 8/JG 52 in 1939.

Oblt. Rall scored his first kill during the Battle of France and became Staffelkapitan in July, 1940. After scoring his 36th victory, he was seriously wounded on November 28, 1941, which paralyzed him for six months. Rall returned to 8/JG 52 in August, 1942, and was awarded the Ritterkreuz for his 65th victory on September 3. The Eichenlaub followed on October 26, for his 100th kill.

In April, 1943, Rall was promoted to Hauptmann and elevated to Gruppenkommandeur of III/JG 52. The Schwerten was presented on September 12, 1943, for Günther's 200th victory (the third pilot to score that number). Scoring 40 victories during October enabled Rall to become the second pilot to reach a score of 250 victories by November 28.

As with many of the Experten, Rall was transferred to the Western front in the spring of 1944 to combat the U.S. bombers. He was Gruppenkommandeur of II/JG 11 until March, 1945, when as a Major, he became Kommodore of JG 300. Rall was shot down five times in the course of his 621 missions.

In 1956, Günther Rall became a Major in the Bundeswehr Air Arm and was deeply involved in developing combat systems for the Lockheed F-104 jet

The world's third-ranking ace is Günther Rall, who shot down 275 enemy aircraft in 621 missions. He became Inspecteur der Luftwaffe in the West German Air Force.

Hans-Joachim Birkner was Rottenflieger for both Hartmann and Rall. He performed his part in the Rotte with dedication, shooting down 117 victories in 284 missions.

fighters for NATO. Rall became a Brigadegeneral in September, 1966, and one year later was the Kommandeur of the 3 Luftwaffendivision. By April, 1969, he was Chef der Stabes (Chief of Staff) and in October, 1970, became Kommandierender General Luftflotte with the rank of Generalleutnant. In January, 1971, he was appointed Inspecteur der Luftwaffe.

HANS-JOACHIM BIRKNER acted as Rottenfleiger for both Hartmann and Rall, and deserves credit for performing his part in their Rotte with dedication. Born in Schönwalde, East Prussia on October 22, 1921, he joined JG 52 as a Feldwebel in mid-1943. He scored the first of 117 victories on October 1. Less than a year later, on July 27, 1943, he was awarded the Ritterkreuz for his 98th kill. Birkner was commissioned a Leutnant in the field and became a member of the century club on October 14. He was appointed Staffelkapitan of 9/JG 51 in mid-1944 and, while leading his unit on a mission, his engine failed during take-off from Crakow airfield on December 14, 1944. Birkner crashed to his death. This young Expert shot down his 117 victories in only 284 missions.

WILHELM BATZ is little known outside of military aviation circles, despite his ranking as seventh-highest combat scorer and the world's fourth-ranking living fighter pilot. Willi Batz shot down a total of 237 adversaries in only 445 missions. Bamberg-born on May 21, 1916, Batz joined the Luftwaffe in 1935 and passed his tests so well that he was assigned duty as a flying instructor. After 5,000 hours of instruction flying, he was posted as adjutant to II/JG 52 in December, 1942, in response to his repeated requests for combat duty.

Willi scored his first victory on March 11, 1943, and became Staffelkapitan of 5/JG 52 on May 1. He received the Ritterkreuz on March 26, 1944 for his 75th victory, two days after he had already made his 100th kill. Oblt. Batz was consistently downing 3 and 4 adversaries a day by the summer of 1944, scoring 15 kills on May 30 alone. Promoted to Hauptmann, Batz succeeded Rall as Gruppenkommandeur of III/JG 52 in June, and was awarded the Eichenlaub on July 20 for his 175th victory. He was the ninth pilot to reach the 200-victory mark, which he did on August 17, 1944.

Like many of the Experten, Batz experienced six

Wilhelm Batz is the world's fourth-ranking Ace with 237 victories. A last-minute transfer saved him from imprisonment in Russia.

Hajo Hermann was a former bomber pilot who developed the Wild Sau single-engine night fighter idea.

crash landings and was wounded on three occasions, the most serious when a Shturmovik came at him, head on and sprayed his Messerschmitt with machine-gun fire. The instrument panel shattered, filling Willi's eyes with finely powdered glass, because his goggles were not in place at the time.

A February 1, 1945 transfer from Kommandeur of III/JG 52 in Czechoslovakia, to the same position in II/JG 52 in Hungary, greatly affected Major Batz' life. At the war's end he was able to lead his Gruppe from Hungary through Austria, undetected, to Germany, thereby avoiding the fate of the Graf Storm Regiment.

After the war, as with many of his comrades, Batz joined the new West German Luftwaffe and was last known to have the rank of Oberstleutnant.

HAJO HERMANN was the originator of the Wilde Sau, or Wild Boar, single-engine night-fighter tactics. Born in Kiel on August 1, 1913, he began his combat career as a bomber pilot with KG 4. Oblt. Hermann met with exceptional success in sinking British shipping and received the Ritterkreuz on October 13, 1940, for this work. Early in 1941, he was posted with KG 30 as Staffelkapitan, and by the following year his administrative ability brought him membership in the Luftwaffe Operational Staff. It was here, building on his bombing experience, that he developed the Wilde Sau idea. Major Hermann organized JG 300 in mid-1943 to combat the U.S. daylight raids. He then led the 30th and 1st Jagd Division. On August 8, he received the Eichenlaub for his activity in the defense of the Reich. In December, 1943, Hermann was promoted to Luftverteidigung, or Inspector of Aerial Defense, and was awarded the Schwerten on January 23, 1944. Oberst Hermann was leading the 9th Flieger Division by the end of 1944, and created the Rammkommando Elbe in his attempt to halt the massive U.S. bomber offensive.

Despite the fact that his wartime activities were directed against the Western Allies, Oberst Hermann became a POW of the Russians and spent a decade in Soviet captivity after the war.

As a bomber pilot, Hajo Hermann sank a total of 12 ships, totaling about 70,000 tons in about 320 missions, and shot down 9 U.S. four-engined bombers in about 50 missions. Despite these significant accomplishments, Hermann's major contribution to the German war effort was his never-ending develop-

Friedrich-Karl Müller was the most successful
Wild Sau pilot, scoring 23 victories.

ment of radical and innovative schemes to stop the
Allied bombing offensive.

FRIEDRICH—KARL MÜLLER was the most successful single-engine night-fighter pilot in Wilde Sau
operations. Sulzbach, Saar-born on December 4,
1911, Müller flew as a Lufthansa pilot before the
war and, therefore, when hostilities started, he was
assigned as a bomber and transport pilot. He was selected by Hajo Hermann as blind flying instructor
for the Wilde Sau test unit in mid-1943 because of
his night-flying experience. Müller quickly scored
his first Wilde Sau victory on July 4, and shot down
three more bombers over Berlin on the night of August 24.

When JG 300 was organized, Nasen-Müller, or
Nose-Müller, as he was called, became technical of-
ficer and in February, 1944, he was transferred as
Staffelkapitan of 1/NJG 10. Müller received the Rit-
terkreuz on July 7 for his 22nd night victory, and by
November, he was Kommandeur of I/NJG 11.

Major Müller flew a total of 52 night-fighter missions and scored 30 night victories, 23 of which were
shot down during Wilde Sau operations.

KLAUS BRETSCHNEIDER and KONRAD BAUER
were two of the most successful Wilde Sau pilots,
both with Sturmgruppe II/JG 300. Bretschneider
scored a total of 31 victories 14 of which were during 20 Wilde Sau missions. On October 7, 1944, Lt.
Bretschneider shot down three four-engined bombers ramming the last to insure a kill. He was
awarded the Ritterkreuz on November 18, 1944, and
one month later, on Christmas Eve, he was shot
down and killed over Kassel by Mustang fighters.
Bauer flew with JG 51 Mölders in 1942 and 1943,
and on December 15, 1943, shot down six adversaries in five minutes! After a transfer in March, 1944,
to JG 3 Udet to battle day bombers, he was posted to
II/JG 300 in June where his scoring was phenomenal.
The Ritterkreuz was awarded on October 31 for 34
victories. Shot down and wounded seven times,
Bauer ended the war as Staffelkapitan of 5/JG 300.
Oblt. Konrad Bauer flew a total of 416 missions and
scored 68 victories, 32 of which were four-engined
giants.

EINO LUUKKANEN is Finland's third-ranking ace,
scoring the vast majority of his 54 victories while flying the Messerschmitt Me 109. Born on June 4, 1909
on the Karelian Isthmus, he joined the tiny Finnish
air force as soon as he was of age. Eino soloed in August, 1932, in a French-built Caudron C-60 and three
years later was flying British-built Bristol Bulldog
fighters with H Le Lv 26, or Fighter Squadron 26. By
1939, Luukkanen was a flight leader in H Le Lv 24,
flying Dutch-built Fokker DXXI fighters.

Since 1938, the Russians had been trying to make
Finland a Soviet satellite, but the independent Finns
resisted. In October of 1939, Russia invaded
Lithuania, Latvia, and Estonia and, realizing it
would be next, Finland mobilized its diminutive defense forces. After a border incident, the Soviet
giant attacked, and the "Winter War" of 1939/1940
was on.

Eino Luukkanen led the first combat flight of the
war on November 30, scoring his first victory on the
following day. The valiant Finns inflicted considerable damage on the Russians, but were forced to ca-
pitulate on March 13, 1940. Russia took one-eighth
of the Finnish population and one-tenth of the land
area of this tiny country.

When Germany attacked Russia on June 22, 1941,
the paranoid Reds reacted by attacking Finland and
Hungary three days later. The Finns called this new
conflict the Continuation War, and by virtue of their
common enemy, Russia, it brought them into a close
alliance with Germany. One year later, I/JG 54
Grünherz moved into the Finnish Mensuvaara Base,

Eino Luukkanen scored 54 victories and is Finland's third-ranking ace. The pilot is shown in a Gustav; the rudder shows his squadron insignia.

Luukannen (right) discusses the problems of tackling the enormous Soviet air force with Finnish air force brass.

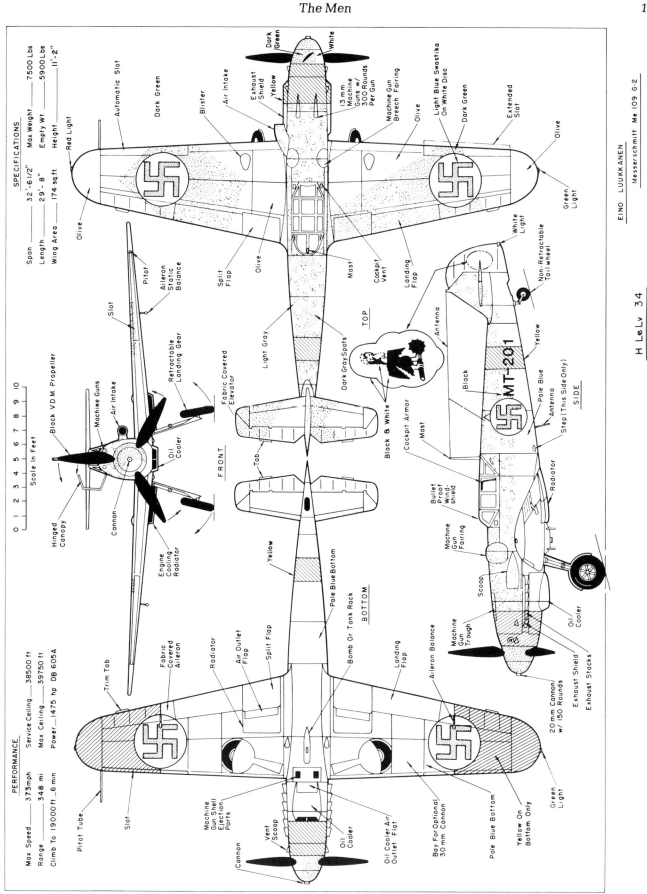

EINO LUUKKANEN
Messerschmitt Me 109 G-2

H LeLv 34

Finnish aces were very successful with the Mersu or Messerschmitt against the Soviets. Four aces from Finland are: top Ace Eino Ilmari Juutilainen, with 94 victories; Haase Wind, 78; and Joppe Karhunen, 31 victories. Aippa Tuominen poses with his Gustav.

north of Lake Ladoga, and by the spring of 1943 German-built Messerschmitt Me 109 fighters were available to replace the obsolete, U.S.-built Brewster Buffaloes the Finns used against superior Russian equipment.

On March 27, 1944, Luukkanen took over H LeLv

34 based at Utti, becoming the youngest Squadron Commander in the Finnish air force. He led the first ferry flight of 16 Me 109G-2 fighters from Wiener-Neustadt, near Vienna, to Malmi. The Finns were very pleased with their Messerschmitts, and called them Mersu.

Eino scored his first victory with the Messerschmitt on May 19, 1943, followed by kills on the 21st, 22nd and the 24th. During a large aerial battle on May 21st, H Le Lv 34 shot down ten of a superior Russian force, and lost only two Messerschmitts. By September 11, the unit had scored its 100th kill. Based at Malmi to protect Helsinki, Luukkanen led six Mersus to intercept a Russian attacking force on May 17, 1944. The Finns met the 27 PE-Z bombers and their 15-fighter escort at 6,000 ft. Before the Russian fighters could interfere, seven bombers were destroyed and the remaining 20 dropped their bombs on a lake and sped for home. The Soviets lost three fighters during the melee, the Finns only one. Eino scored one bomber in this action. On June 4, the Russians launched a massive offensive across the Karelian Isthmus. Three days later all three flights of Luukkanen's squadron relocated to Immola, in order to be based closer to the action.

On June 14, 1944, Luukkanen led twelve Mersus on a mission to destroy two Makkara, or observation balloons, that were directing Soviet artillery. Eino encountered twenty U.S.-built Bell Airacobra fighters protecting the balloons, and at the onset he sent one plunging into a ploughed field. More Red fighters appeared and Luukkanen fired at the closest, an La 5. The Russian continued on course in a shallow curving dive. Eino continued the chase, watching his shells tear off pieces of the Russian fighter and wondering why they had no effect. As he closed in, he saw the pilot slumped over to the side and realized that a dead man had been at the controls from his first burst! H Le Lv 34 scored 11 Soviet aircraft on this day with one loss.

Some Luftwaffe units arrived at the Immola airfield to help defend Karelia, but this made the field so crowded that the Finns moved to Lappeenranta. This proved too small for Messerschmitt operation so they moved again to Taipalsaari, a dusty earth field. The heavy air battles continued, and while the Finns inflicted severe losses on the Russians, they could not replace their own, however small. Luukkanen's unit was down to ten flyable Mersus.

All ten Messerschmitts took off on June 19 to provide cover for retreating Finnish troops, when an artillery observation balloon was sighted in the distance. Eino decided to go after it alone despite heavy flak. As the balloon burst into flames, Luukkanen's engine was hit by the antiaircraft fire, tearing off the cowling and slowing the engine. Eino quickly zoomed up to 2,500 feet before the engine stopped. Located about ten miles inside Russian-held territory, Luukkanen turned toward the front lines and was amazed at how well his Mersu could glide. He then discovered that he was over Summa Forest, one of the many large evergreen forests that cover Finland. There was no other place to land! As the Messerschmitt brushed by the tops of the conifers at 220 mph, sinking deeper into the dense foliage, the wings tore off and the fuselage slithered through the branches dropping closer and closer to the ground. Finally, the tail and fuselage rear snapped off, while the engine–pilot capsule continued its journey through the trees until it struck the ground in a cloud of dust. Luukkanen emerged unhurt, located some Finnish troops and rode back to Taipalsaari in a truck.

Eino scored his 40th kill on May 20, 1944, despite overwhelming Soviet numerical superiority. Between mid-June and mid-July, his sqaudron flew 1,040 combat hours, fired 25,000 13-mm. shells and 11,000 20-mm. shells. He flew almost 19,000 miles during that period. The summer months saw many Luftwaffe units leave Finland for other fronts to consolidate their forces. Luukkanen scored his 54th and last victory, a Yak 9, on August 5, and 21 days later he flew his last operational flight.

Under pressure by Russia, Finland was forced to sever relations with Germany on September 2, 1944, and declared an Armistice with the Soviets two days later.

ALADAR de HEPPES was known as the Old Puma along the central Russian front because, although twice their age, he flew and fought with the best of his pilots. Heppes was the driving force behind the Hungarian fighter operations, and led his unit against 20 to 1 odds to a victory margin of 4 to 1! Born in the western Hungarian town of Arad in 1904, Aladar was the second son of a Supreme Court Justice, who was killed during the opening phases of the First World War. Upon completion of grade school, he entered the K.U.K. Militar Unterralschule (Junior Military School) in Nagykanizsa followed by several years in the M. kir konved Floreal Iskola (Royal Senior Military School) in Budapest. Completing his education in the M. kir Ludovica Academia (Royal Hungarian Military Academy), Heppes joined the secret Hungarian air service which was forbidden by the 1920 Peace Treaty of Trianon. By 1928, Aladar had made his first solo flight, and after a few years as a reconnaissance pilot, he transferred to

Aladar de Heppes was known as the Old Puma all along the Russian front. The Hungarian leader is shown in one official portrait, and laughing at a close brush with death when shrapnel cut his tunic to shreds. (The colonel escaped injury in that instance.)

the 1/3 Fighter Squadron in 1935 as executive officer. He was promoted to the rank of szazados, or captain, and adjutant for I/II Fighter Group in 1939.

When Hungary found itself at war with the Soviet Union in June 1941, the R.H.A.F. had 350 aircraft, all of which were obsolete. Three months later, Heppes commanded I/II Fighter Group, flying Italian-built Fiat CR-42 biplane fighters suitable only for ground-support duties. Early in 1943, Messerschmitt Me 109G fighters began to arrive at the Hungarian squadrons. By April, Heppes' new 5/I Group went into action with their German aircraft, each emblazoned with a snarling red puma insignia designed by Heppes. His code name on combat missions became Oreg Puma, or Old Puma, and the unit's battle cry was "Hajra Pumak" (pronounced hoyrah pumaak), or Onward Pumas. The two squadrons of 5/I Group were assigned to the Kharkov sector of the Eastern front, about 600 miles from the Hungarian border.

On May 30, 1943, Heppes led eight Messerschmitts on an escort mission for Heinkel and Junkers bombers headed for the Vauliki railroad

yards, 80 miles behind Russian lines. The bombing proceeded unmolested; however, during the flight back, the Old Puma spotted several Soviet fighters taking off from the airfield at Kupyansk. Ordering his men to remain with the bombers, he led his wingman to attack the Yak fighters. By the time the duo reached the enemy, 20 of the Soviet fighters had left the ground, a 10-to-1 battle. Early in the melee, the two Messerschmitts became separated and the Russians focused their attention on the Old Puma. With odds like this, the average pilot would speed for home, but not Aladar de Heppes. His duty was to protect the bombers and, as long as he could keep the Red fighters busy, the Heinkels and Junkers had a good chance to escape. Confident in his aircraft's superiority and his own ability, Heppes flew his speedy Messerschmitt again and again through the Yak formation, to scatter it and prevent a concentrated attack on himself. After a few passes, the Old Puma caught one of the Soviets with a well-placed deflection shot, and the Yak plunged earthward in a ball of flame over his own airfield. By this time, the

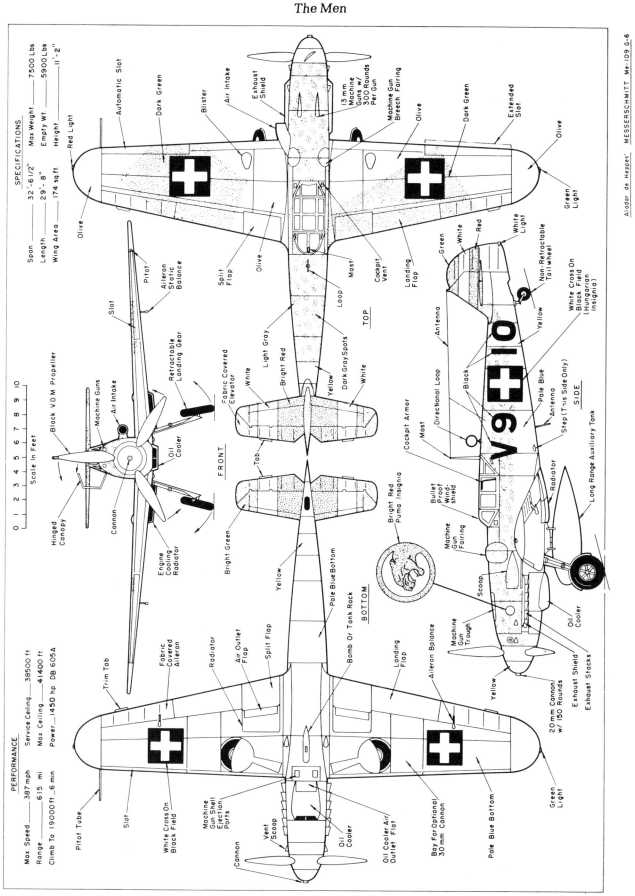

SPECIFICATIONS

Span — 32'-6 1/2"
Length — 29'- 8"
Wing Area — 174 sqft.

Max Weight — 7500 Lbs
Empty Wt. — 5900 Lbs
Height — 11'-2"

PERFORMANCE

Max Speed — 387 mph
Range — 615 mi
Climb To 19000 ft — 6 min

Service Ceiling — 38500 ft
Max Ceiling — 41400 ft
Power — 1450 hp DB 605A

Scale In Feet
0 1 2 3 4 5 6 7 8 9 10

Aladar de Heppes' MESSERSCHMITT Me-109 G-6

5/1 F.G.

TOP

FRONT

SIDE

BOTTOM

bombers were safely inside Hungary, so Aladar decided to run for it. As he turned westward, a Yak flight cut off his escape. The Old Puma quickly maneuvered into position and killed the nearest Russian pilot with a short burst from his cowl-mounted machine guns. The dead pilot fell on his controls, sending his plane directly into the path of his comrades. The other Yaks were forced to take evasive action, therby enabling Heppes to escape!

The Old Puma scored again on July 6, when he downed a Shturmovik near Woltschansk, and again on August 3, when he destroyed a Yak 1 fighter over Belgorod. After the latter victory, Heppes was forced to land near the front lines because his Messerschmitt had run out of fuel. It was almost ten hours before a German Feisler Storch liaison plane brought the Hungarian enough fuel to take off and return to base. When he arrived at the Puma airfield, Aladar learned that he had been presumed dead and this information had been forwarded to headquarters with the weekly report. As a result, an officially dead man commanded the Pumas during the following seven days.

The Pumas spent the late summer and fall of 1943 constantly relocating as the Russian steamroller pressed westward, taking Kharkov, Smolensk, Kiev and other key cities. During this time the Pumas managed to shoot down over 70 Soviet aircraft while sustaining the loss of only six dead and three missing pilots (two of the Hungarian deaths were caused by a midair collision).

The defense of the Hungarian homeland became the prime objective of the R.H.A.F. and Heppes was placed in command of the training school at Tapolca in an effort to increase the number of trained pilots. He was also assigned to write the Royal Hungarian Air Force Combat Training Manual. In March, 1944, the Old Puma was ordered to organize a home defense interceptor unit. This became the 101 Fighter Group based at Veszprem, and included three squadrons, or about 40 Me 109G-6 fighters, plus transports and courier types with about 500 men. It was at this time that Heppes met with Walter Nowotny to discuss advanced training methods and fighter tactics. As Hungary reeled under the Soviets' sledgehammer blows, a greater calamity befell the Magyars: the U.S. Air Force began bombing Budapest and other Hungarian targets on April 3, 1944.

At first the Pumas did not intercept the Fifteenth Air Force Liberators because they were anxious for the Americans to occupy Hungary instead of the Soviets, and wanted to remain on good terms with the U.S. It was only after Mustang fighters shot up the Veszprem airfield that the Old Puma decided to fight back.

Fighting the United States Air Force was an agonizing experience for Heppes and his Pumas. He was used to the relatively small numbers the Soviet Air Force flew on a given mission. The U.S. raids, however, "darkened the sky," according to the Old Puma, with 500 bombers plus a liberal fighter escort. It was an impossible task to combat these armadas with only 40 Messerschmitts, but Heppes led his men repeatedly into the breach in this "David and Goliath" game of death. The Old Puma opened his scoring against the Americans on May 26, 1944, when he shot down two Liberators over Nazyacsad and Mosonszolnok. Four days later he dived on a "box" of B-24 bombers, weathering crossfire from the Liberator gunners smashing into the Messerschmitt cockpit. The .50-caliber slugs narrowly missed the Old Puma, but blew off the cockpit enclosure. The screaming slipstream tore away his unfastened helmet and virtually blinded the pilot. Gasping for air, Heppes broke off the attack, crouched low in the cockpit, and turned for home. Upon inspecting his Me 109 after landing, Aladar found that one of the bullets that caused the canopy to blow away had lodged in the plane's structure. Heppes still has that bullet as a memento of his close brush with death.

The Old Puma was promoted to ornagy (Major) a few days later. On June 16, he led 28 Pumas to intercept a formation of 500 Fortresses and Liberators escorted by Mustangs, Thunderbolts, and Lightnings. After the fighting the wreckages of 22 U.S. planes were found strewn about the countryside, although the men of 101 Fighter group claimed only 10 Liberators, 4 Lightnings, and one each of the Mustangs and Thunderbolts. Thirteen Messerschmitts were destroyed, but only four Hungarians lost their lives, nine having bailed out to safety.

In August, 1944, Romania, which also was allied with Germany, capitulated to the Soviets, and the Russians began pouring into Hungary's neighbor. The entire air defense of Hungary was now placed in the hands of the Old Puma. He was promoted to alezredes (Lt. Colonel) but received a full colonel's pay as a token of his nation's gratitude. Meanwhile, the 101 Fighter Group was enlarged to a full wing, and became the Royal Hungarian 101 Air Defense Fighter Wing. This consisted of the 101/I Group with 40 Messerschmitts based at Veszprem, and 101/II Group with 20 Messerschmitts based at Kenyeri. The six squadrons totaled 1,000 men. By October, the Russians were pouring into Hungary and the front lines extended as far west as Veszprem. The retreating 102 Fighter Group was then absorbed into the Old Puma's command as 101/III.

By the spring of 1945, the Pumas were forced to retreat to airfields at Raffelding, near Lenz, Austria. They flew very few missions due to the shortage of fuel and spare parts. Mustangs strafed the field on May 4 and damaged all but a few Messerschmitts, but the Pumas continued their fight in the face of ever-increasing adversity. Within a few days, the war was over and Aladar de Heppes surrendered his well-disciplined unit to the Americans.

Despite overwhelming odds, the Old Puma had led his men with considerable success during the last year of the war, fighting both Russian and U.S. aircraft. The final tally of this period was 110 Liberators and Fortresses, 36 Lightnings, Mustangs, and Thunderbolts, and 218 assorted Soviet aircraft. While inflicting this loss of 384 Allied aircraft, the Pumas lost 39 men dead and 20 disabled; procurement records reveal that less than 100 Hungarian aircraft were lost. The final score for the Pumas during the war was 454 victories and a loss of 68 men. Heppes scored ten official victories.

During the Communist takeover of Hungary there was considerable unrest. Many heroes, such as Lajos Toth (24 victories), were executed. This forced others to leave their homeland and take residence in Canada, Spain, Austria, the U.S.A., and Argentina. Aladar de Heppes came to the U.S.A., and became an American citizen with his own industrial design business. He died in 1988. All free Hungarians will forever remember the outstanding skill, bravery, and unselfish dedication of Aladar de Heppes, the Old Puma.

Gyorgy Debrody (left), a 26-victory Hungarian ace, and Leslie Molnar (25 victories) relax between sorties. Debrody's victories included B-17 Fortresses, P-38 Lightnings, and P-51 Mustangs.

GYORGY DEBRODY, one of the Old Puma's finest combat pilots and Hungary's second-ranking ace, shot down 26 adversaries. Debrody graduated from the Royal Hungarian Military Academy in 1942 and was immediately posted to Heppes' 5/I Fighter Group. When the Messerschmitts began arriving in early 1943, Debrody was attached to II/JG 51 Mölders for indoctrination to the modern fighter.

Flying with 5/1 Squadron, he scored his first kill on July 5, during the Kursk offensive, when he shot down an La-5 fighter. By the first week of August, Debrody had six official victories to his credit, and by year's end he was one of Hungary's leading aces, with 16 confirmed victories. He then transferred to 5/2 Fighter Squadron based at Uman.

In late February, 1944, Debrody's Schwarm was escorting a formation of Junkers transports carrying supplies for a surrounded German battalion. After the supplies were delivered, a formation of Yak-1 fighters appeared in the distance and sped for the transports. Gyorgy ordered one Rotte to remain with the Junkers while he led his wingman, Miklos Kenyeres, to engage the Yaks. As Debrody closed in for a kill, another Soviet fighter scored a hit on the Daimler-Benz engine, stopping it instantly. Gyorgy quickly dived away from the fight and belly-landed on a pasture. He set fire to his Messerschmitt and was about to run to a wooded area, when he saw the Yak that had just shot him down destroyed by Kenyeres. Gyorgy waved a final farewell to his wingman but, to his surprise, Kenyares was lowering his flaps and landing gear: he was going to land! By this time squads of Russian troops began to appear in the distance and Debrody could hear small-arms fire.

144

Kenyares' Me 109G touched down about 400 feet away from his leader and taxied toward Debrody. Both men were, meanwhile, removing their parachutes and heavy flying jackets because the Messerschmitt cockpit was not built for two men. The two Hungarians squeezed into the tiny space, with Kenyares sitting on Debrody's lap. While Debrody operated the rudder pedals, Kenyares handled the control stick, and with amazing coordination the pair made it back to their airfield!

After scoring his 17th and 18th victories, Debrody returned, once again, to the command of the Old Puma in 101 Fighter Group. Debrody first scored against the U.S. Air Force on June 14, 1944, when he shot down a Lockheed Lightning fighter. Two days later another P-38 fell before his guns, and during July Debrody scored two Fortresses and a Mustang. After destroying a B-24 Liberator in November, Debrody was seriously wounded on the 16th when a partly spent cannon shell hit him in the stomach. Despite the loss of tremendous amounts of blood, Debrody made his way back to Hungarian-held territory and landed near a friendly artillery battery. He

was taken to a Budapest hospital, and little hope was given for his survival. But his recuperation was amazingly short, and upon returning to the Pumas, he was promoted to the rank of Szazados, or captain. He was also given command of 101/1 Group of the Puma Wing or Regiment. Debrody saw no more action due to his wound and command responsibilities.

During 240 missions, Debrody shot down 20 Soviet aircraft and 6 American planes. Like the Old Puma, Gyorgy Debrody escaped the Communists' wrath and settled in Canada. He now lives on the eastern coast of the U.S. and is employed by a prominent U.S. airline.

The men we have just met had much in common. They were brave and chivalrous foes, dedicated airmen who flew and fought valiantly for their country, and talented marksmen, pilots and leaders. Moreover, they all used the same weapon, as they cut through the skies over most of Europe, the Mediterranean and North Africa: the Messerschmitt Me 109 fighter, which remained on active duty longer than any other fighter plane in the history of combat aviation.

PART THREE

The Weapon:
The Classic Ein-Hundert-Neun

The Messerschmitt Me 109 was flown by every major Luftwaffe ace and is probably the most successful fighter plane ever built. More victories were scored in it than any other type. The very term Messerschmitt has become a household word since the Second World War, recognized by the average "man on the street". It was the first major World War Two fighter to be placed in production, the first to see service, first to taste combat, and the last to be in service! About 35,000 of the Me 109 were built, more than any other fighter plane, and it was used by more countries than any of its contemporaries.

Simplicity was the keynote to its design, and the watchword of the engineers was KISS: Keep It Simple, Stupid. It has been said that the club is the ultimate weapon because it has the fewest working parts. Similarly, the Messerschmitt was the simplest, smallest, and cleanest fighter that could be designed in 1934, and it proved to be one of the most adaptable planes in combat aviation history. In ten years, from 1935 to 1945, it increased in power from 610 to 2,000 horsepower; top speed rose from 292 to 452 miles per hour; gross weight increased from 4,850 lbs. to 7,438 lbs.; armament went up from three rifle-caliber machine guns to two 15-mm. and one 30-mm. cannon; rate of climb improved from 2,700 to 4,850 feet per minute; and the ceiling went up from 29,500 ft. to 41,400 ft. Because of the increased power and weight the 109's endurance went down from 90 minutes to 50 minutes. The compact design had its limits to modifications, however, and the small airframe could not adapt to every fighter-plane improvement developed during the ten-year period. It could not avoid obsolescence forever, yet its tremendous capacity for progressive development without major redesign guaranteed the

Me 109 its place as the Luftwaffe's standard fighter plane in Europe throughout the entire Second World War.

In appearance it possessed an aura of vitality: lean and hungry, almost predatory and sharklike. It certainly appeared efficient, brutal, and ruthless: simplicity with no frills. It was all weapon, yet retained a sense of mysterious beauty.

The most remarkable fact regarding the Me 109 design is that its designer, Willi Messerschmitt, had never before worked on a military craft. Yet his first venture into fighter plane design became one of the classic military aircraft of all time! This talented engineer also designed the world's first production military jet fighter, and the world's first rocket fighter.

Willi Messerschmitt was born in Frankfort-am-Main on June 26, 1898, the son of a wine merchant. He became interested in aircraft at an early age and was building model airplanes by the time he was 11. In 1910, the family moved to Bamberg in Bavaria and it was here that Willi met Friedrich Harth, a glider pioneer. Young Messerschmitt began helping Harth with the construction of his gliders, and actually completed one by himself after Harth joined the army in 1914. In the postwar years, the Harth –Messerschmitt designs gained considerable attention in gliding circles by establishing altitude and endurance records. Willi studied engineering at the Technical Hochschule in Munich, and while still in attendance he broke with Harth and organized his own company in Bamberg: Messerschmitt-Flugzeugbau. By 1923, he was a graduate engineer and was the only student at school who was permitted to build a glider as part of his thesis.

Messerschmitt-Flugzeugbau concentrated on very

This sleek Messerschmitt Me 108B Taifun light transport provided much design data and experience which was applied to the development of the 109 fighter design.

Willi Messerschmitt just before the war. By designing the 109, he produced the most famous and successful fighter plane ever.

This Me 109V-4 was the fourth prototype and the first to be fitted with an engine-mounted gun firing through the propeller hub. Notice that the craft bears civil registration identification in lieu of Luftwaffe crosses.

Willi Messerschmitt is seen explaining a point about his ein-hundert-neun to Gen. Ernst Udet during preliminary testing of the new fighter.

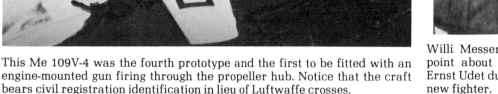

low-powered light planes until the firm obtained an order for a small economical transport plane. The success of the Messerschmitt M-18 transport enabled the company to expand into a corporation, and

led Willi to request a subsidy from the Bavarian government. No funds were available, however. It was suggested that Messerschmitt merge with the ailing BFW or Bayerische Flugzeug Werke (Bavarian

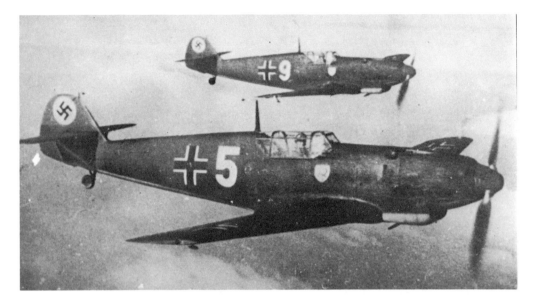

The International Flying Meet at Zurich was dominated by Messerschmitt performance. The Me 109B-2, shown flying in JG 2, won the Alpine Circuit for Formations and the International Circuit of the Alps. The Me 109V-13, shown at rest in Zurich, won the climb and dive competition and later established a new world's landplane speed record.

Airplane Works) with an unusual arrangement: BFW was to produce only Messerschmitt designs while Willi must give BFW the first priority to produce his designs. In 1931, BFW declared bankruptcy and Messerschmitt obtained control of the firm.

Two years later, BFW rose like the Phoenix and was reorganized as BFW G.M.B.H. Simultaneously, Willi Messerschmitt became technical director of Bayrische Flugzeug A.G. The new Nazi government complained to Messerschmitt that he had accepted a Romanian order for his M-36 Transport when Germany needed the planes and resources of every manufacturer. When Willi explained that he needed the order to stave off bankruptcy, the RLM (Reichsluftfahrtministerium), or German Aviation Ministry, invited Messerschmitt to enter the forthcoming competition for the new single-engine fighter contract. In view of the fact that Messerschmitt had no previous experience with military aircraft, and experienced firms such as Heinkel, Arado, and Focke-Wulf had also been invited, it was generally

The deep-chin radiator/oil cooler was retained in the Me109 C, but underwing radiators were fitted to the D. The C variant (top) was powered by the 640-hp. Junkers Jumo engine and carried 4 or 5 guns. The D variant (bottom) was powered by the 960-hp. Daimler-Benz 600 A engine and carried three guns; they paved the way for the Emil.

felt that Messerschmitt had no chance at all.

Fortunately for Willi Messerschmitt he was at this time designing the Me 108A Taifun, a sleek 4-place low-wing cabin monoplane. The craft was extremely advanced, and besides its all-metal construction, it featured a retractable landing gear, leading-edge slats, and slotted landing flaps. This design became the basis for Messerschmitt's fighter competition entry and, with the able assistance of Walter Rethel, work began with the objective of designing the smallest possible airframe for the largest available engine.

Some of the basic objectives which emerged as the design progressed were: construction aimed at mass production and economy; forged 2-piece engine mounting for quick engine changes; simplified construction to utilize unskilled labor, such as single spar wing and bulkhead/skin section subassemblies; landing gear attached to fuselage structure keeping wing as light as possible (this produced a very narrow-track landing gear which later caused many accidents during takeoff and landing); self-sealing fuel tank located behind pilot for safety; heavily framed, hinged cockpit canopy in lieu of sliding type for easier construction, safer nose-overs and fewer jammings due to fuselage distortion; Handley–Page automatic slats which opened at about 100 mph and enabled the plane to fly at slow speeds; high ground angle as a safety measure in the event of heavy braking while taxiing; pilot arranged with feet very high to withstand g-forces of sharp maneuvers without losing consciousness.

The prototype Me 109 V1 made its maiden flight in September, 1935. The craft was powered by a 695-hp. Rolles-Royce Kestral V engine, because the specified Junkers Jumo 210 engine was not available. Gross weight of the V1 was 4,195 lbs. and top speed 292 mph. In the following month, the four competitors met at Travemünde with their entries. The Arado and Fock-Wulf prototypes were rejected at once because the former failed to include a retractable landing gear, while the latter had an archaic parasol wing, mounted above the cockpit on struts. Although the Heinkel He 112 was favored, its complex structure caused production problems. The RLM ordered ten prototypes of the Heinkel and Messerschmitt designs and, upon further testing, Heinkel was awarded a limited production contract while Messerschmitt's design was selected for mass production as the Luftwaffe's standard fighter!

Meanwhile, Willi had cultivated a friendship with the air-minded Rudolf Hess, the No. 3 Nazi at the time. Hess won the Zugspitz trophy in 1934 while flying a Messerschmitt M 34, and was very impressed with Willi and his designs. Hess also demonstrated the Me 108 B Taifun in an aerobatics display near Berlin. This influenced the RLM to award Messerschmitt a contract for 35 Me 108 B's for use as a trainer and personal transport for military brass.

The second prototype Me 109V2 was first flown in January, 1936, fitted with the 610-hp. Junkers Jumo 210 A engine. Six months later, the third prototype, Me 109V3, appeared. Advanced as the design was,

its armament had progressed no further than the two World War One cowl-mounted rifle-caliber machine guns. When the RLM discovered that the Royal Air Force was planning to equip their new Hurricane and Spitfire designs with four to six machine guns, it revised its specifications to require at least three guns. The V4 had one additional machine gun mounted between the cylinder banks of the V-type engine, firing through the hollow propeller shaft. During the tests, a 20-mm. cannon replaced the engine-mounted machine gun; however it was removed due to the severe vibrations it generated. In December, 1937, the V4 was sent to Hannes Trautloft in Spain for combat assessment. The next prototypes, V5 and V6, followed the V4 to Spain. The eighth prototype, Me 109 V8 carried four machine guns, two in the upper cowling synchronized to fire through the propeller arc and two mounted in the wings. The Me 109 V9 replaced the wing machine guns with 20-mm. MG FF cannons. The propeller was a primitive two-bladed wooden type manufactured by Schwarz. Engine power was increased slightly and the design appeared ready for quantity production.

The BFW Augsburg plant was able to supply the Me 109B-1 initial production model to the Luftwaffe by the spring of 1937. JG 2 Richthofen, based at Döberitz near Berlin, was the first unit to be equipped with the Messerschmitt.

Powered with a 635-hp. Junkers Jumo 210 D, the B-1 had a gross weight of 4,857 lbs., and attained a top speed of 292 mph at 13,000-ft. altitude. The range was about 350 miles and ceiling was 29,500 ft. The wooden two-bladed Schwarz propeller remained, but armament reverted to the three 7.92-mm. machine guns of the V4. The Me 109B-2 was an improvement over the B-1 because it was fitted with a two-bladed Hamilton–Standard variable-pitch metal propeller.

The Messerschmitt Me 109 astounded the aviation world at the International Flying Meet in Zurich, Switzerland during the summer of 1937. When the performance of the Me 109 was revealed several competition entrants, including the British, withdrew. Germany proved that it possessed the finest fighter plane then in production by winning the following events:

1. The speed competition, in which individual entrants flew four laps around a 3½-mile circuit. A Messerschmitt 109B-2 won with an average speed of 254 miles per hour. The pilot was Dipl. Ing. Franke.
2. The Alpine Circuit for formations of three air-

planes was won by three Me 109B-2 fighters piloted by Hptm. Restemeier, Lt. Schleiff, and Lt. Trautloft. This 228-mile flight was completed in 58 minutes and 53 seconds.

3. The International Circuit of the Alps was won by Major Hans Seidemann flying an Me 109B-2. He covered the 228-mile course in 56 minutes and 47 seconds in a flight which included two landings.

4. The Climb and Dive Competition was won by Dipl. Ing. Franke in an Me 109 V13 powered by a Daimler-Benz DB-600 engine. His time to climb from an altitude of 1,000 ft. to 9,800 ft. and then dive back down to the starting height was 2 minutes and 5 seconds.

As though the triumph at Zurich was not enough, Willi Messerschmitt began preparations for an assault on the world's landplane speed record! Using the Me 109V13, which had already won at Zurich, he installed a special Daimler-Benz DB 601 engine, capable of as much as 1,650-hp. for only a few minutes at a time. Dr. Hermann Wurster flew the plane in the required 100-km. closed circuit on Nov. 11, 1937 and established a new record of 379.38 mph!

By 1938, Willi Messerschmitt was acknowledged as one of Germany's most gifted aircraft designers and, with the government's approval, the BFW name was changed to Messerschmitt A.G. Willi became general director and chairman of the board. The entire German aircraft industry was then in the process of reorganization, and several firms were ordered to undertake the production of the Me109 in order to insure an adequate supply. It was later discovered that the need was greatly underestimated. The affected firms were: Arado in Brandenburg, Warnemunde and Anklam; Erla Maschinenwerke in Leipzig; AGO in Oschersleben; Feisler in Kassel; and Wiener-Neustadter in Weiner-Neustadt. Messerschmitt A.G. plants were in Augsburg, Regensburg-Prufening and Regensburg-Obertraubling. Of the 1,540 Messerschmitts delivered in 1939, less than 150 were made at the Messerschmitt plants!

The Messerschmitt Me 109C and D models differed mainly in armament and increased power, but the Me 109E, known as the Emil, was the milestone design which saw considerable action in the Second World War.

Developed in late 1938, the Emil first saw action in the Polish Campaign. It was the first Me 109 to be mass produced, once the Luftwaffe decided to put all their eggs in one basket and place their fate in one design. This variant equipped JG 1, JG 2, JG 3, JG 26, JG 51, JG 52, and JG 53, and about 15 were sent to Spain in the spring of 1939. This model was powered with the inverted-V 12-cylinder, 1,100-hp. liquid-cooled Daimler-Benz DB 601 A engine, swinging a VDM 3-bladed metal variable-pitch propeller. This advanced and efficient power plant featured direct fuel injection and much-improved supercharging. The most widely built of the Emils was the Me 109E-3 which entered service in the fall of 1939. Loaded, it weighed 5,523 lbs. and maximum speed 354 mph. The normal range was 412 miles and the service ceiling 36,100 ft. Armament consisted of five guns: two 7.9-mm. MG 17 machine guns in the wing; and two machine guns in the upper engine cowling; and one 20-mm. cannon firing through the propeller shaft. The engine cannon still caused considerable vibration and was seldom used, while the 110-gallon self-sealing fuel tank proved too small for Battle of Britain operations. Another problem was the jamming of the wing guns after firing only a few rounds. Investigation revealed that moisture on the gun's moving parts froze at high altitudes, and it was necessary to devise a method of keeping the gun breeches warm.

Over 1860 E-3 variants were delivered in 1940. In addition, many were exported: 73 to Yugoslavia; 16 to Slovakia; 19 to Bulgaria; 80 to Switzerland; 40 to Hungary; and, surprisingly, 5 to Soviet Russia. In addition, 2 were sold to Japan where the Kawasaki aircraft manufacturer planned to produce the design under license, a scheme later abandoned. Germany's need for foreign currency was the principal reason for exporting its premier fighter plane to friend and foe alike.

As the E-3 fought in the skies over England, another variant was being developed at Augsburg, and shortly would be ready for delivery to the Jagdwaffe; the Me 109 E-4. This was a basic E-3 with such minor modifications as improved armor protection and pilot visibility and a major refinement in the armament. The troublesome engine cannon was eliminated, and the wing machine guns were replaced by 20-mm. MG FF cannons with 60 rounds per gun. The cowl machine guns were retained with 1,000 rounds per gun. The engine was a slightly improved Daimler-Benz DB 601 Aa, which was rated at 1,150-hp. at 2,400 rpm. The craft was lighter than the E-3 by about 300 lbs., and coupled with its increase in horsepower the E-4's top speed rose to 357 mph at 12,300 ft. The range and service ceiling remained the same as the E-3.

Messerschmitt construction was all metal with fabric-covered ailerons, elevators, and rudder. The fuselage was made in two halves, left and right, and joined on the vertical center line. It was of flush-riveted monocoque design with the metal skin taking

The Me 109-E, or Emil, was the first real milestone variant of Messerschmitt development. Many were exported to Switzerland (above) and Yugoslavia. Observe that the landing gear is attached to the fuselage, thereby accounting for the narrow track.

the stress. The wings were single spar, cantilever, of a flush-riveted, stress-skin design. The wing panels were attached to the fuselage at two spar locations and at the leading edge. The entire trailing edge was hinged to form slotted ailerons outboard and slotted flaps inboard. The landing gear retracted via hydraulic jacks with a manual handwheel in the cockpit for emergency operation. This hydraulic operation had no locking device, and very often a hit in the hydraulic system caused the landing gear to fall away, reducing the plane's speed and controllability. The wheel-well sides were zippered leather,

providing a ground-mechanic access to the inside of the wing. The horizontal tail surfaces were mounted on the vertical fin and strut-braced to the fuselage.

Many Me 109 E-4 machines were modified for Jabo duty by Staffel mechanics in the field, using kits of specially prepared parts called Rüstsatz.

Variants E-5 and E-6 were reconnaissance fighters with wing armament removed and a camera installed behind the pilot's seat. The E-7 was basically an E-4 with a jettisonable 66-gallon (Imperial) streamlined belly tank, and was used over the Balkans, Greece, and Malta. In Africa, the Me 109E-

The Messerschmitt Augsburg plant with the E-3 in production. Closeup shots show the installation of wing, wing gun, and instruments.

7/U2 was fitted with extra armor plate under the engine and radiator, because it was used extensively in a ground-attack role.

In general, the "E" variant was superior to most contemporary fighters above 20,000 feet, even the vaunted Spitfire. Although the Spitfire had the edge in maneuverability and relatively short climbs, the Emil surpassed the British fighter in extended climbs and diving speed. A seldom-mentioned advantage was afforded to the "E" variant by its fuel-injected engine. During climbs and level flight the pilot of the Emil could push the control column forward and bring the nose down abruptly without any effect on engine speed or power. Carburetor-equipped engines, such as the Spitfire's Rolls-Royce Merlin, tend to lose speed and power momentarily during the same maneuver, enough to make the difference between being the victor and the vanquished. The number of Messerschmitts constructed through the Emil variant consisted of almost 23% of the total Me 109 production, or about 7,600 aircraft. The success of the Emil led the Messerschmitt design team to produce a more advanced version, employing the newly-developed and more powerful 1,300-hp. DB 601 E engine to better advantage. This was to be the Me 109F or Franz as it was known in the Jagdwaffe.

During the spring of 1940, an Emil was fitted with the new engine, a larger, well-rounded propeller spinner, and a new symmetrical engine cowling. The supercharger intake scoop was also redesigned to create less turbulance. This cleaned up the entire nose and gave the craft a smooth and more streamlined appearance. The underwing radiators were shallower to further reduce resistance and featured boundary-layer bypasses, which like many Messerschmitt features was a novel development. Some models featured a semiretractable tailwheel to improve streamlining. This craft was first flown on July 10, 1940, and although the results were gratifying, the engineers decided to go back to the drawing board. An entirely new wing was designed with beautifully rounded tips replacing the squared-off tips of the Emil. This was fitted on the next two test models as was an unbraced horizontal tail. A major point of controversy was the armament. Werner Mölders favored light armament because it meant less weight and a more agile aircraft, while Adolf Galland felt that the light armament was useless against contemporary aircraft and that cannons would be more effective for the novice. The result was one 15-mm. MG 151 engine cannon firing through the propeller shaft, and two 7.9-mm. MG 17 machine guns in the upper cowling. It was, at best, a compromise, but by contemporary standards inadequate. Walter Osau was violently opposed to this armament, yet other Experten thought it sufficient. In fact, some only used the rapid-fire MG 151 cannon and hardly ever used the two fuselage machine guns.

The first Me 109F-1 aircraft were supplied to the Jagdwaffe in early 1941. After only a few weeks of service, several "F" variants crashed mysteriously when their tails tore off in flight. Investigation revealed that at specific engine revolutions, sympathetic vibrations caused the tail bolts to shear and the rivets to loosen. The unbraced tail was then redesigned and the fault corrected. Several wing failures were also reported, such as in Balthasar's last flight. This was remedied by reinforcing the fuselage bottom to prevent the skin from wrinkling under stress.

The Franz appeared in six versions, F-1 through F-6. The F-3 of 1942 was powered by the DB 601 E engine, which gave the craft a top speed of 390 mph at 22,000 ft. Service ceiling was 37,000 ft. and range 440 miles. The cruising speed was 310 mph at 16,500 ft. Loaded weight went up to 6,054 lbs. and empty weight was 4,330 lbs. It carried 200 cannon rounds and 500 rounds for each machine gun. The Franz was the favorite of many of the Experten, the most outstanding exponent being Hans-Joachim Marseille. The Jagdwaffe pilots enjoyed exceptional success on all fronts when flying the Me 109F, and flew this thoroughbred of fighter planes with great enthusiasm.

The Franz was a beautiful airplane, truly the high point of Me 109 development, and the last pure fighter in the ein-hundert-neun series. This most beautiful and agile of the Messerschmitts comprised only 7% of the total production or about 2,300 planes, a victim ultimately of the long-time argument between armament and performance. The demand for heavier armament produced a kit to retrofit a 15-mm. MG 151 cannon under each wing, housed in a streamlined enclosure. This increased the Franz's effectiveness against bombers, but destroyed the speed and agility so necessary in fighter-to-fighter combat. From this point onward the variants became encumbered with bigger and better guns, which were required to effectively destroy the increasingly-destructive Fortress and Liberator bombers.

The Me 109 F had virtually disappeared from the skies of Europe and Africa by the end of 1942, giving way to the next variant, developed as a bomber killer, the Gustav Me 109G.

Developed in accordance with the demand for increasingly heavy armament, armor, and power, the

Me 109 F-4

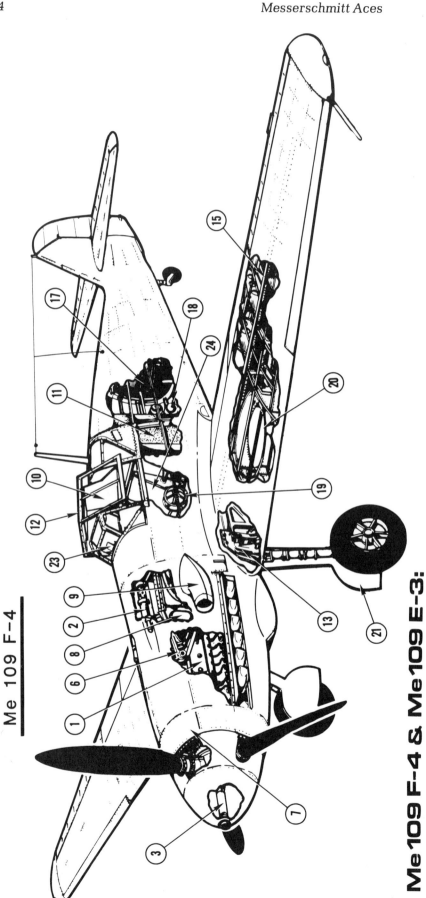

Me109 F-4 & Me109 E-3:

(1) Daimler-Benz V-12 inverted engine; (2) 7.9-mm cowl-mounted machine gun; (3) 15-mm. engine cannon; (4) 20-mm. engine cannon; (5) 7.9-mm. wing-mounted machine gun; (6) Forged engine mount; (7) Oil tank; (8) Machine gun magazine; (9) Supercharger intake scoop; (10) Cockpit armor; (11) Self-sealing fuel tank; (12) Hinged cockpit cover; (13) Landing-gear attachment to fuselage; (14) Landing-gear worm-gear-drive retracting mechanism; (15) Wing main spar; (16) Wing attachment to fuselage; (17) Radio equipment; (18) Oxygen flasks; (19) Landing-gear emergency retracting hand wheel; (20) Landing-gear well; (21) Landing-gear cover; (22) Control surface static balance; (23) Reflector gun sight; (24) Seat.

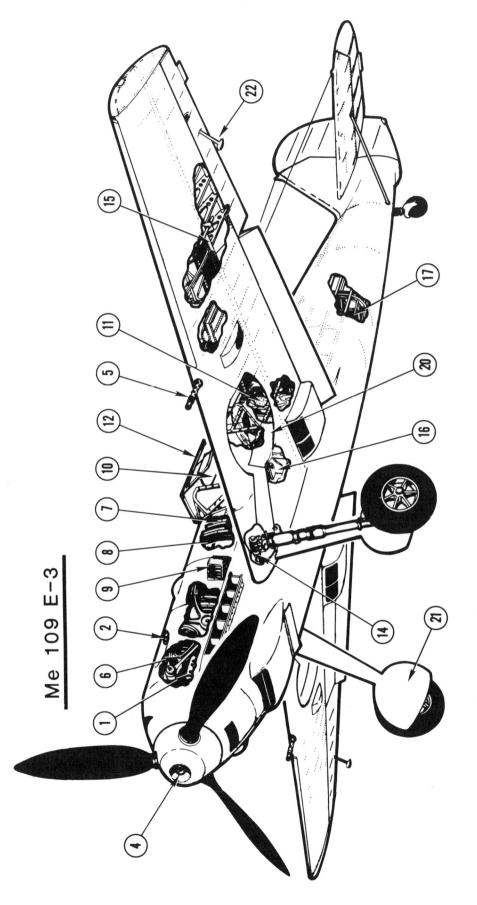

Me 109 E-3

The high point of Me 109 development as a pure fighter was the Franz. This was the most beautiful and agile of all the variants. The belly-landed machine is from JG 27; the other is from JG 26. The clean lines of this design are readily apparent.

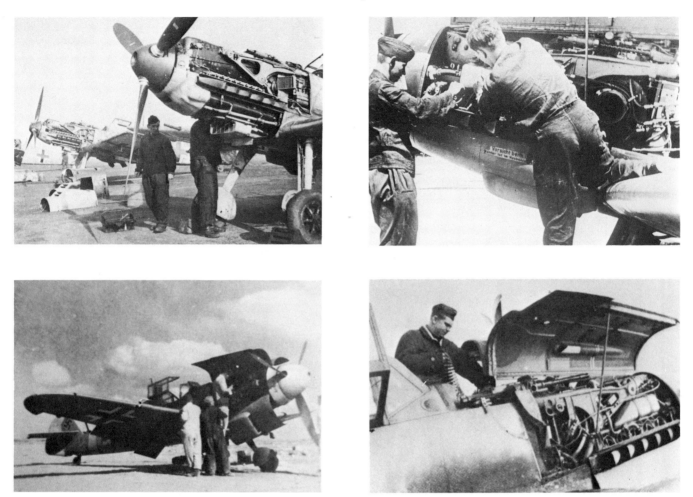

Willi Messerschmitt took special interest in simplified maintenance procedures as well as in rapid production. Notice how the entire engine cowling of the Emil was removed in three sections, and improved on the Franz and Gustav by employing three-hinged panels. Observe the forged engine mount and turbo-supercharger.

Me 109 G variant was no longer a first-class fighter plane. The addition of more cannon and heavy-caliber machine guns required bulges and large fairings, destroying the smooth lines the Gustav had inherited from the Franz and greatly reducing its agility. Despite this, the Luftwaffe had no other choice than to continue with Messerschmitt variants, because an entirely new fighter design would take over a year to develop. Further, the Focke-Wulf 190 had not fulfilled its expectations, especially at high altitudes, and required considerable refinement. More Gustavs were constructed than any other Messerschmitt variant, almost 70% of the total production, or about 23,000 aircraft.

The Gustav was developed during the winter of 1941/42, and the early models were virtually identical with the Franz except for the power plant. The application of bigger superchargers, fuel additives,

higher compression ratios and 96-octane fuel increased the Daimler-Benz power to 1,475 hp. in the DB 605 A. This engine was fitted with the GM-1 power-boosting system, whereby nitrous oxide was injected into the supercharger to increase the power at extreme altitudes. The cockpit was redesigned so it could be pressurized, requiring a reinforced structure and heavier canopy frame. The first Gustavs were delivered in May, 1942 to 11/JG 2 for high-altitude interception of American bombers.

The most important and numerous Gustav was the Me 109G6. It was the first to be fitted with the heavy weapons that became closely associated with the variant. Armament consisted of a 20-mm. MG 151 engine cannon firing through the propeller shaft, provided with 150 rounds; two 13-mm. MG 131 machine guns mounted in the cowl above the engine, provided with 300 rounds per gun; and one 20-mm.

The Me 109G-6 shown here was flown by III/JG 3 Udet. Note the large wing cannon fairings and the eye painted on the gun-breach cowl bump. The Gustav cockpit was well arranged; observe the handgrip on the windshield and the engine-boost solution handles on the instrument panel.

MG 151 mounted under each wing, enclosed in pod-shaped fairings and provided with 120 rounds per gun. Some G-6 variants were fitted with the 30-mm. MK 108 engine cannon, while the G-6/U4 mounted this cannon in the underwing nacelles instead of the standard issue 20-mm. cannon. The larger caliber machine guns were actually too bulky for the cowl, and a bump was formed in the fuselage to clear the breech and ammo tracks. This cowl bump became one of the identifying characteristics of the Gustav, and the nickname of "Beule," (bump) was often used for future G variants by the Jagdwaffe. This heavy punch proved very effective against the big bombers; however, the added weight and resistance severely reduced the 109G's effectiveness against fighters. Although the underwing cannons were standard G-6 equipment, units in the field often removed the wing guns. It was found that the muzzles and fairings reduced the G-6's speed by 20 mph, and the 150 lbs. under each wing drastically reduced maneuverability. Further, the fairings caused the G-6 to porpoise at cruising and higher speeds. At times, the wing cannon was replaced by a 210-mm. rocket-launcher tube. Each stovepipe tube fired one W Gr. 21 Dodel missile as an antibomber or ground-

attack weapon. Dodel rocket tubes were used by JG's 3, 11, and 26.

A streamlined, jettisonable 65-gallon fuel tank could be carried under the fuselage for long-range missions, while a Jabo variant, G-6/R1, was equipped to carry a 550-lb. or 1,100-lb. bomb in the under-fuselage rack.

In an attempt to save precious raw materials, wood was utilized for the fin and rudder construction during the Gustav's development. Surprisingly, this proved heavier than the conventional dural and plastic tail, and it required a weight bolted in the nose to keep the plane in proper balance! The already weak narrow-track landing gear groaned under the loaded weight of 7,500 lbs., and landing accidents with the Gustav became commonplace despite some strengthening of the landing gear. After its debut in combat, the Gustav was plagued by mysterious oil cooler fires. As was previously recounted, it was an oil cooler fire that caused Hans-Joachim Marseille's death in September, 1942, and shortly thereafter JG 1 and other units reported numerous oil cooler fires.

The 1,475-hp. Daimler-Benz DB 605 A-1 12-cylinder, liquid-cooled, inverted-V engine gave the

The Me 109G 16 (top) was a stepping stone to the K 4, which was one of the last production variants, developed late in 1944 and supplied to only a few units. Performance of the two variants was virtually identical.

Me 109 G-6 a maximum speed of 387 mph at 22,970 feet, and 338 mph at sea level. The craft had a range of 450 miles at 330 mph and 615 miles at 260 mph, both at 19,000 ft. The G-6 could climb to 19,000 feet in six minutes. Service ceiling was 38,500 feet and maximum ceiling 39,750 ft.

Some G-6 variants were fitted with an MW 50 water-methanol injection instead of the GM-1 nitrous oxide injection. The MW 50 boost could increase the engine power to 1,800 hp for short periods when used with 100-octane fuel! At this power, the plugs lasted only 15 to 20 hours! In 1942, the DB 605 could operate for 100 hours before an inspection

was necessary. As the war progressed and maintenance deteriorated, the time between inspection/overhauls lengthened to 200 hours, and eventually 300 to 350 hours became normal. This reduced the engine dependability and caused many accidents. In order to combat this problem, the standard procedure by 1945 was to replace the engine after only 20 hours of operation. Often this was necessary after only five hours of operation! Inadequate maintenance and neglect in the field, as well as an overdevelopment of the basic engine design for increased power, were at the root of the situation. Of course, inferior production standards and overuse of the booster installa-

The ground crewman is sitting on the wing and signaling the pilot of this taxiing Emil because the pilot's forward vision is greatly impaired in this nose-up attitude.

tion added considerably to the problem.

The last production Messerschmitt Me 109 variant was the "K", developed in early autumn of 1944. The DB 605 ASCM/DCM engine of 1,550 hp. could be boosted to 2,000 hp. with the MW-50 injection, enabling the Me 109 K-4 to attain 452 mph! Pilot visibility and streamlining were greatly improved by the new "Galland Hood," named for the General who suggested the design. The "K" variant featured something previous Me 109s did not have: a fully retractable tailwheel. The vertical fin and rudder were increased in height, which eliminated much of the curvature in the rudder.

The Me 109 K-4 was fitted with two 15-mm. MG 151 cannons mounted in the upper engine cowl, plus one 30-mm. MK 108 engine cannon firing through the propeller shaft. This centrally located armament was very effective against bomber and fighter alike. The maximum speed was 452 mph at 19,685 ft. At sea level the maximum speed was 377 mph. The K-4 could climb to 16,400 ft. in only three minutes, and to 32,800 feet in six minutes. Service ceiling was 41,000 feet. The range of the Me 109 K-4 was 366 miles and endurance was 50 minutes. Maximum loaded weight was 7,438 lbs.

When flown by an experienced pilot the K-4 variant proved itself a suitable adversary, even for the vaunted Mustang. Its major disadvantage was the short flight duration which forced pilots to break off from dogfights to land and refuel! In the hands of an

expert the K-4 was a potent weapon against bombers, but less successful when attacked by the escorting fighters. The war ended before more than two or three Jagdgeschwadern were equipped with "K" variants.

The majority of the Experten preferred the 109 even though the design had been stretched to the limit as the war progressed. They all agreed that the Franz was the best variant, despite the heavier armament of the Gustav and higher speed of the K variant. Barkhorn, who led a Focke-Wulf 190 D-equipped unit late in the war, preferred to lead them on missions flying a Gustav! The Me 109's most laudable design characteristic was its steady handling in all flight regimes. It could fly and fight fast or slow at all altitudes. It was a very stable airplane and therefore an excellent gun platform.

What was it like to fly the Messerschmitt Me 109? Gerhard Barkhorn and other surviving Experten generally agree with the following description of the Me 109 G-6 Gustav.

The initial impression of the plane when approached on the ground is that it appears unusually small. It sits at a very steep angle on the runway with its nose pointing skyward, resembling a missile ready for launching. The cockpit must be entered from the left side because the canopy hinge is on the right. Climbing on the port wing root from the trailing edge, you must walk up gently until abreast of the windshield, and then grasp the windshield hand-

Of interest in this view of a Hungarian Gustav is the cockpit armor on the canopy and the engine emergency starting crank, protruding from the cowling just forward of the cockpit.

grips as you swing your right leg into the cockpit. As your body is brought over the seat, you must take care to duck under the open canopy and its suspended armor slab. As you slide into the seat, still grasping the windshield handgrips, you find that the cockpit is far from spacious, yet comfortably efficient.

Your legs are almost horizontal as they reach the rudder pedals, fitted with a mesh socket for the heels and a strap across the insteps. The windshield seems small and the heavy frame is annoying, like wearing heavy-rimmed eyeglasses for the first time. Just ahead of the windshield extends the long engine cowl, effectively blocking forward ground vision. The two cowl cheek bumps, or Beule, add to the forward vision obstruction. The instrument panel is conventional except, of course, the graduations are in the metric system. Instruments not included on earlier variants are the radio compass, MW-50 boost pressure, and an artificial horizon. Messerschmitts had no manifold pressure gauge. Propeller pitch control and MW-50 boost button are found on the instrument panel, while engine throttle and fuel/air mixture controls are on the left side of the cockpit, within easy reach of the left hand.

When you are ready, a member of the ground crew closes and locks the heavy canopy, a task that the pilot would find very difficult to accomplish.

With switch and magnetos on, propeller pitch at full increase, and fuel/air mixture set at full rich, you signal the ground crew to stand clear and push the starter. The Daimler-Benz engines fire promptly (in the bitter cold of the Russian front pre-heating the engine and adding kerosene to the lubricating oil were necessary). After a jerk or two the propeller spins to life, and black smoke puffs out of the stubby exhaust stacks. Should the battery fail to start the engine, a member of the ground crew will crank the inertia starter from the right, or starboard, side of the cowl. When the inertia wheel is up to speed and the crew has removed the crank, you can again push the starter.

The throttle must be opened slowly, because we have a lot of horses pulling. Unlike American aircraft, the Messerschmitt throttle is pulled back to accelerate and pushed forward to slow the engine. As you taxi, you must take care with the sensitive toe brakes, although a fast taxi is not dangerous. Turns, however, must not be made abruptly because, due to the narrow-track landing gear, the plane is prone to ground looping. As you taxi onto the 2,000-ft. grass runway, the stiff landing gear transmits every bump to the pilot, at times making your teeth chatter. After a quick cockpit check you set the flaps and stabilizer. Both are adjusted manually by means of vertical wheels at the left side of the cockpit. The

"Don't gun the engine too close to the ground during landing, and touch down softly because the landing gear is notoriously weak." These photos lucidly illustrate the results when such rules are either ignored or forgotten by 109 pilots.

flaps are set at 20 degrees and the stabilizer at takeoff setting. As the throttle is opened, the acceleration is awe-inspiring, pressing you hard against the back of the seat. You must apply full right rudder judiciously to keep the Gustav tracking straight as it speeds down the runway. Slight forward pressure on the control column raises the tail, and as the nose drops to the horizontal you can, at last, see ahead! You must keep the fighter on the ground until about 115-mph air speed is reached. At that point it will almost fly off on its own. The climb is spectacular as you flip the landing gear lever, again with the left hand, and wind up the flaps. Controls are virtually frictionless and the engine responds instantaneously to throttle settings. You are climbing at about 3,000 feet/min., with an indicated air speed of 160 miles per hour.

At 20,000 ft. you level off and try a few checks. First you induce a stall by easing the throttle and pulling the control column back to an I A S of about 130. The automatic Handley-Page slats slam out, and the control column swings from side to side. At 115 I A S, the craft is gripped with severe buffeting and tries to drop the left wing, which requires compensation in the rudder and aileron. The slats prevent an actual stall break, but as the speed drops to 105 I A S, the wobble increases beyond control and all you can do is open the throttle again. Despite exceptional lateral stability and the tendency of the design not to spin, you shouldn't advance the throttle too quickly at this slow speed. If you do, the port wing will drop, despite the application of full rudder and aileron, and fall into a left roll. The Gustav handles not as a machine, but as if it knows what

Willi Messerschmitt as he appeared in 1963, when he returned to Germany from Spain and resurrected the Messerschmitt firm. He organized the first West German Aerospace company. The designer died in 1978.

After Willi Messerschmitt was found innocent of being a Nazi, he designed and built this mini-automobile, the F.M.R. Tiger. The car could attain 80 mph with a 500-cc-displacement engine; it also utilized a steel-tubing chassis. It was sometimes called the Messerschmitt Bubble Car or Messerschmitt Cabin Scooter.

Spanish-built version of the Messerschmitt: Hispano Aviacion HA 1109, built in 1945 with dimensions identical to the Gustav.

The postwar Czechoslovak version of the 109 was the Avia C210 powered by a 1,340-hp Junkers Jumo 211 F engine. Note the paddle-bladed propeller. During May, 1948, 25 of the machines were sold to Israel; the Israelis operated them against Egyptian Spitfires!

you want to do. At cruising power, we drop the nose, and in less than a dozen seconds, the airspeed is up to 450 mph! Half-snap rolls, sudden dives and extended climbs are no problem with the tough Me 109, because it can take anything its pilot can endure! The controls appear heavier than in other fighter planes, but the craft responds well and there is good feeling in the rudder pedals and control column. Speed checks tell us that fuel consumption is far greater than the operating manuals admit, and that use of the MW-50 speed booster increases fuel consumption from the cruising rate of 85 gal-

The peace treaty allowed Finland to own and operate only 60 fighter planes; the Finns selected their trusty Mersu. Gustavs like this were flown by the Finnish air force until 1955.

lons/hour to 169 gph! With this consumption, the 110 gallons in the tank can't last long. It is a pleasant airplane to fly with no bad habits, yet extreme care must be taken in landing (about 5% of the Messerschmitt production was lost in landing accidents).

Approaching the grass runway and throttling down to just below 180 mph, you can lower the landing gear and then crank down the flaps to a full 40 degree position. Once this is complete, nose-up trim is adjusted to the stabilizer. Approach should be made at about 155 mph, and alignment with runway down to about 140 mph. As speed drops to 120 mph you must keep the nose high and power on. You must be alert as speed drops through 100 mph, as the port wing gets awfully heavy at this point and can cause trouble. You can't gun the engine if the speed drops too quickly, because a sudden burst of power will cause the left wing to drop even further. Maintaining power, you touch down at about 85 mph. With the three wheels on the ground you are again virtually blind, and taxi to the dispersal strip where you cut the switch. You must wait for the ground crew to open the canopy and help with the harness. As you emerge from the cockpit, jump on the ground and walk away, everything seems so mundane and uninteresting compared to a flight in such a magnificant machine!

Willi Messerschmitt was arrested by the Allies in 1945 because of his involvement with the Nazi regime. He was interned, and three years later a de-Nazification court in Augsburg tried Professor Willi on charges of being a compatriot of the National Socialists. Messerschmitt was found innocent, and the court ruled that he was a reluctant beneficiary of the regime. With aircraft production prohibited by the Allies, Messerschmitt retooled his Augsburg plant to manufacture sewing machines, prefabricated houses and a mini-automobile sometimes called the bubble car.

The urge to design airplanes was too powerful for him to resist so Messerschmitt went to Spain in 1952 to return to his first love. There, Messerschmitt developed passenger aircraft in cooperation with the Spanish, as well as a supersonic jet fighter for Egypt.

When the aircraft production ban was lifted, Willi Messerschmitt returned to Germany in 1963 and reconstituted the Messerschmitt A.G., concentrating on jet transport projects. Messerschmitt's firm combined with Boelkow in 1968 to give West Germany an aerospace company which could be competitive in European markets. The following year saw the Hamburger Flugzeugbau Gmbh join the group. Messerschmitt-Boelkow-Blohm Gmbh was now the largest German aviation company. With Willi Messerschmitt as honorary chairman, the firm produced jet fighters, transports and extensive subcontracting work, in addition to satellites, helicopters, highway and rail vehicles, traffic systems and deep sea equipment.

Willi Messerschmitt also became an adviser to Hispano Aviacion of Spain, and moved to Estepona near Malaga, Spain. On Sept. 15, 1978, at the age of 80, Willi Messerschmitt died in Munich, Germany after a major surgical operation. He was survived by his wife, the former Lilly von Michel-Raulino.

Variations of the basic Me 109 continued to be constructed in Czechoslovakia and Spain long after the war was over and the design remained in service in the air forces of Rumania, Hungary, Finland, Spain, Czechoslovakia, Switzerland and Israel long after the Jagdwaffe ceased to exist.

Upon the successful conclusion of the Spanish Civil War, Franco's air force still had 60 Me 109 fighters in service. After buying ten Franz airframes from Germany in 1942, Spain decided to build her own and gave the task to Hispano-Aviacion SA. The prototype was fitted with the 1,300 hp Hispano HS-12-Z-89 engine instead of the Daimler-Benz, and was first flown on March 2, 1945. Tests demanded tail modifications, and the installation of a Swiss Escher-Wyss propeller to replace the Hamilton. The first production model, designated Hispano HA-1109-J1L, was delivered to the Spanish Air Force in January 1946. The machine was not a success and a new design was started at once, the HA-1109-K1L, which was test-flown in May 1951. Dimensions were identical to the Gustav, with a performance of 404 mph maximum speed and loaded weight of 6,034 lbs. Range was 373 miles. Two 20 mm Hispano cannon were installed.

In the Summer of 1953 experiments were conducted with 1,400 hp Rolls-Royce Merlin engine installations. Success with this model led to the initiation of large scale production using the British power plant. Designated HA-1112-M1L, the craft was fitted with a four-bladed propeller, two 20 mm Hispano cannons mounted in the wing and four 80 mm Oerlikon rockets beneath. The maximum speed of this 7,011 lb. loaded-weight fighter was 419 mph. Range was 475 miles. The craft remained in service into the seventies and many were used in motion pictures masquerading as Jagdwaffe fighters.

The R.L.M. ordered the Avia aircraft factory near Prague to tool up for Me 109 G-14 production in 1944. Deliveries began in the Spring of 1945, just as the European war ended. With this production capability in their possession, the Avia works at Cakovice began production for the new Czech Air Force. Avia called the plane C. 10, but the military designation was S-99. Production came to a halt when the original supply of 22 Daimler-Benz engines had been used. Re-engining with the heavier 1,340 hp Junkers Jumo 211F engine was the only alternative. This engine drove a large paddle-bladed propeller, and the tremendous torque created by the blades caused the plane to swing heavily on take-off. This new model was the Avia C. 210, known as the S-199 in the

Czech Air Force. Maximum speed was 367 mph with a loaded weight of 7,717 lbs. and range with 528 miles. Only a handful of the S-199s were delivered to the Czech Air Force before a revolution delivered the country to the Communists. The Air Force was then quickly re-equipped along Soviet lines and the S-199 was replaced with MiG 15 jet fighters.

On May 14, 1948 the Israeli-Arab war erupted, and Israel was desperate for fighter aircraft. Arrangements were made with Czechoslovakia to sell 25 Avia C.210 fighters to Israel for a price of about 150 thousand U.S. dollars each. Delivery was made on May 20 and by June the force was operational. The Egyptain Air Force was equipped with a number of Spitfires and here, again the two adversaries met in combat, recreating the roles they originated 18 years before! The Messerschmitt descendants were flown by the Israeli Defense Air Force until 1949.

Finland was permitted only 60 fighter planes by the terms of the peace treaty. The Gustav was selected and all other planes were destroyed. The Finnish Air Force flew the Me 109 G until 1955.

Hungary and Romania used the Gustav in their air forces until the mid-fifties when Soviet jets replaced them.

Despite the fact that more Messerschmitts were built than any other fighter plane in the history of aviation, there are only 13 German-built machines still in existence. None is in flying condition except, perhaps, the G-2 in Wattisham, England, and it has been refused an Air Ministry permit to fly. The last 13 are distributed all over the world, and if the opportunity presents itself it would be well worth seeing at least one example of this most famous of all fighter planes.

Me 109 G	National Air and Space Museum Smithsonian Institution Washington, D.C. U.S.A.
Me 109 G	John W. Caler (Private owner) 7506 Clybourn Sun Valley, California U.S.A.
Me 109 G-10/U4 Werke Nr. G11943	Air Museum Claremont, California U.S.A.
Me 109 E-4 Werke Nr. 4101	Royal Air Force Museum Henlow near Royston

Marking + 12	Central Fighter Establishment—Duxford, England	Me 109 G-6 Marking MT 507	Finnish Air Force Rissala, Finland
Me 109 E-3 Werke Nr. 1190	P.G. Foote (Private owner) Bournemouth, England	Me 109 G-6 Werke Nr. 163824	Sidney Marshall (Private owner) Bakstown Airport Sydney, Australia
Me 109 G-2 Werke Nr. 10639	Royal Air Force Wattisham, England	Me 109 G	Military Museum Belgrade, Yugoslavia
Me 109 E-1 Werke Nr. 750 Marking AJ + YH	Deutsches Museum Munich, W. Germany	Me 109 E-3 Werke Nr. 2422	Verkehrshaus der Schweiz Luzern, Switzerland
Me 109 G-6 Werke Nr. 165227 Marking MT 452	Finnish Air Force Rissala, Finland	Me 109 F	South African War Museum Johannesburg, South Africa

PART FOUR
Conclusion

SYNOPSIS OF THE JAGDWAFFE'S ROLE

The story of the Jagdwaffe, vastly outnumbered yet able to inflict considerable damage on the enemy until the end, has no parallel in military history, except perhaps Leonidas and his 300 Spartans at the pass of Thermopylae, who held off tens of thousands of Persian soldiers, annihilating all who challenged them until the 300 perished due to the overwhelming numbers sent against them. The soldiers of the Jagdwaffe were powerless to change the political situation leading their country to ruin, but were determined to stop, or at least reduce, the military tragedy engulfing their homeland. The Jagdfliegern were involved in a 5½-year struggle against enormous forces on three fronts. In this battle, they reached the zenith and nadir of their existence.

Once Britain and France, and Germany were in a state of war, both sides exercised the utmost restraint in the air. Neither the British nor the German air forces bombed enemy territory. The Germans, who did not entertain a war with the West, hoped this would encourage Britain to make peace. The British, on the other hand, didn't feel that the RAF was strong enough to start an offensive. Both sides, therefore, attacked each other's ships with limited success. In the first major air engagement of the war on December 18, 1939, unescorted British bombers were mauled by the defending Messerschmitts over Helgoland Bight in northwestern Germany. The British learned their lesson well: that only with a fighter escort could the bombers get through, and the absence of fighters meant an enemy victory. The Oberkommando der Luftwaffe did not learn from this experience and failed to accelerate fighter production.

The lightning defeat of France owed much to the Jagdwaffe which not only protected the Stukas and larger bombers, but shot up the French and the British Expeditionary Force airfields as well. The Panzers' rapid advances would not have been possible without the Luftwaffe, which not only prepared the way for the armor by pulverizing enemy supplies, communications, and armor, but also safeguarded the long, exposed flanks. Despite the fact that the Jagdwaffe defeated the Armee de 1'Air with relative ease, the small force needed rest and regrouping. It now had to build the necessary ground organization for the attack on Britain.

Even though the losses suffered in the Battle of France had yet to be replaced, the Jagdwaffe was ordered to engage Fighter Command a few months after France fell. Up to this time the fighter-versus-dive bomber controversy still raged within the Luftwaffe. Many had cast their loyalties to the dive-bomber, little realizing the impotence of this weapon without a fighter escort. Only the pilot leaders in the field realized that the Jagdwaffe had to accelerate fighter production, as well as pilot training, if the air war was to be brought to a successful conclusion.

During the opening phases of the Battle of Britain, the Jagdwaffe consisted of about 800 first-line fighters, which was about the same as the RAF. The size of the Jagdwaffe was totally inadequate for the dual role of engaging the British fighters in open combat and providing close escort for bombers and Stukas. The limited range of the Messerschmitt placed London at the farthest distance for daylight bombing, and the absence of a heavy four-engine bomber prevented attacks on aircraft manufacturing centers north of London, as well as the Fighter Command airfields of 12 Group. This enabled the British fighter force to remain strong while the Jagdwaffe was hard pressed to replace its losses.

The use of Freie Jagd, or freelance missions, became a necessary tactic in the efforts to lure Fighter Command into combat. These were the most popular missions with the confident and eager Jagdflieger, but when later carried to other fronts of the war, the Freie Jagd proved to be inefficient and

This Polikarpov I-15 Chato sports post-civil-war Spanish markings. It was the first aircraft type to meet the Messerschmitt in combat.

The Experten claim that the Polikarpov I-16 Moska was the most difficult Soviet plane to shoot down because of its extremely small turning radius and slow speed.

The Morane-Saulnier M.S. 406 was France's most widely used and most famous fighter of WWII, but posed no challenge to the Me 109 E in the Battle of France.

wasteful. The combat tactics used by each side were dictated by the aircraft and its performance. The British took advantage of the low wing-loading, tight turning-radius, and aerobatic qualities of the Hurricane and Spitfire by engaging in dogfights. The Messerschmitt pilots were forced to hit and run, taking advantage of their aircraft's climbing and diving ability and speed.

The German government had decided to attack the Soviet Union as early as July, 1940. Preparations for this enormous undertaking usurped all priority from the Battle of Britain, which had just begun and would continue half-heartedly for a year! Despite the many difficulties facing the Jagdwaffe in its battle with Fighter Command, the supply of equipment to this hard-pressed force was virtually cut off. Vital

The American-made Curtiss Hawk 75 A performed yeoman service for the Armee de l'Air and scored the first French victories of WWII.

British Battle-of-Britain ace Robert R.S. Tuck leads his Hurricanes to intercept a Luftwaffe attack. The Hurricanes shot down more Luftwaffe planes during the Battle than all other planes and flak combined.

It is generally conceded that the Spitfire was very evenly matched with the Messerschmitt; victory could often depend on luck.

The Illyushin I1-2 Shturmovik was the Allied plane most difficult to shoot down, according to German fighter pilots, because this Soviet ground attack plane had a strong armor shell protecting the engine, oil cooler, radiator, crew, fuel tanks and other vital parts. It was made in one- and two-man crew models. Two-man version shown.

The U.S.-built Curtiss P-40, or Kittyhawk, was flown by the RAF, Commonwealth Forces, and the U.S. Army Air Corps against the Messerschmitt in the skies over the North African desert. U.S. P-40 is shown at La Senia Air Base. Insert shows a Kittyhawk of 112 Squadron RAF and famous desert Ace Clive "Killer" Caldwell at right.

lessons were being learned, but Göring refused to listen to his battle-weary combat leaders' pleas for boosted fighter production and pilot training. He also changed constantly from one objective to another, splitting the available forces instead of con-

centrating them on one point of effort. Unknown to the Germans, they had the RAF Fighter Command close to defeat on several occasions. But the Jagd-waffe could never follow through, due to a shortage of equipment and inferior High Command leader-

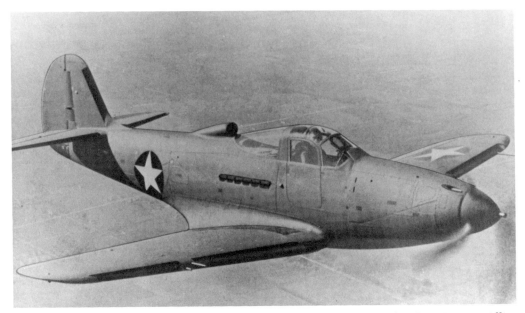

The sleek U.S.-built Bell Airacobra was considered a dismal failure by the Western Allies because of its low-altitude performance. However, it met the Soviet requirements and proved successful on the Eastern front.

The Yak-3 was superior to the Gustav at altitudes up to 20,000 ft.; it was the most troublesome Soviet fighter, according to many Experten.

ship. While the Battle of Britain was at its peak, the Jagdwaffe was called upon to serve in the Balkans and Greece, where it rescued the Regia Aeronautica. The Messerschmitt Jabo performed magnificently, ensuring the conquest of Yugoslavia and the eviction of the British from Greece and Crete. This was the first air/sea conflict in history, and ended with a resounding victory for the Luftwaffe as it forced the British Mediterranean fleet to withdraw from the area. The Jagdwaffe also moved to Africa while the "Battle" was still raging. When the Battle of Britain effort was finally ended in the late spring of 1941, the main strength of the Jagdwaffe was transferred to the East. With a minimal resting and

The Lavochkin La-7 could make such tight turns at low altitudes that many of the pursuing Messerschmitts stalled and crashed, or skidded into the ground or into trees.

This American Lockheed P-38 Lightning was one of the most unusual single-seat fighter designs of WW II. The two engines made it less maneuverable than the Messerschmitt.

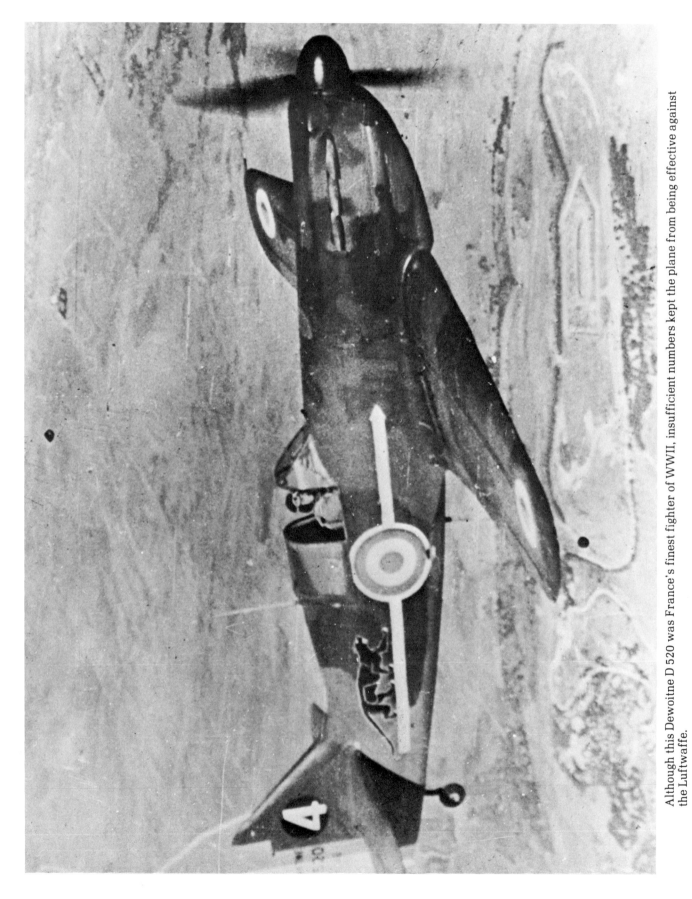

Although this Dewoitne D 520 was France's finest fighter of WWII, insufficient numbers kept the plane from being effective against the Luftwaffe.

The Thunderbolt was one of the very few planes that could outdrive the Messerschmitt. It was the heaviest and largest single-engine fighter of WWII.

The Mustang was faster and more maneuverable than the Messerschmitt above 20,000 ft.; however, this advantage disappeared below a 15,000-ft. altitude.

reorganizing period, the Jagdwaffe was thrust against the Soviet giant! At the same time, selected units of the Jagdwaffe were sent to North Africa to help Rommel in his drives toward Cairo.

Luftwaffe forces in Africa were drawn mainly from those in the Balkans, Sicily, and Greece. The air war in Africa again became a fighter-vs.-fighter conflict, because the Jagdwaffe flew mostly Freie Jagd. This was a mistake. It should have concentrated its attacks on vehicles, airfields, and troops, as the Commonwealth Forces did. It was customary for the small Jagdwaffe patrols to meet 30 to 50 RAF, SAAF, or Free French aircraft and, out of necessity using their hit-and-run tactics, scoring only a minimal loss to the enemy. The fact that the Commonwealth squadrons flew lower than the Germans enabled the Jagdwaffe pilots to surprise their adversaries by utilizing the high diving and climbing speeds of the Messerschmitt. According to several Jagdwaffe pilots, the large Commonwealth fighter formations in Africa usually milled about in confusion after a surprise attack. They then formed defensive circles and headed for home. After this, the progress of the battle depended on fuel consumption and the aggressiveness of the attackers. Frequently, an Allied plane bolted from the defensive circle in panic disintegrating the circle and inviting further losses.

The average Jagdwaffe pilot in Africa was well trained and had a positive fighting spirit. He had the will to destroy his adversary. Two slogans were used and admired above all others in "Afrika": "Der Geist macht's" (or "It's the spirit that counts"), extolling a good esprit de corps; and "Den Letzten beissen die Hund" (or "The last is bitten by the dogs"), referring to the hit-and-run tactics, where the laggardly attacker places himself in jeopardy.

During Operation Barbarossa, it was the Jagdwaffe that smashed the Soviet Air Force in 1941, paving the way for the advancing armor. However, the declining material and trained personnel strength was not replaced at the rate of loss, with the result that, as the campaign progressed, the Jagdwaffe became weaker in the face of an enemy that rapidly grew stronger!

The initial military objective of crushing Russia in a six-week campaign failed. Then, the mud and frost of winter intervened. As in the Battle of Britain, no strategic air offensive was launched, leaving the task of destroying the Soviet air force phoenix to the Jagdwaffe. Again, the fighter arm was forced to perform both the strategic and the tactical roles, while the bombers were tied to the Wehrmacht and used as artillery! The years of 1941 and 1942 were wasted by the Oberkommando der Luftwaffe, with no effort made to strengthen the Jagdwaffe.

The Focke-Wulf Fw 190 was a favorite with the younger and less experienced Jagdwaffe pilots. Unfortunately, performance began to fall off above 20,000 ft.

After serving his country well in two terrible wars, Theodore Osterkamp went into semiretirement. He is shown here in 1967 on his 75th birthday.

Despite the enormous size to which the Red air force had grown by 1943, the Jagdwaffe held its own and inflicted tremendous destruction on the Soviets with a fighter that had outlived its normal service life. Despite consistent tactical victories, the Jagdwaffe found it impossible to defeat the overwhelming production ability of the Red air force. This spelled defeat for the 600-plane Jagdwaffe, suffering a shortage of spare parts, fuel, and ammunition. The Soviet air force had become so huge that when a puny Nazi Schwarm attacked a Russian armada, the Reds actually ignored the Jagdwaffe assaults even as the Jagdfliegern were scoring victories. The Reds had so many planes and pilots that any losses caused by the Germans were insignificant! The war on the Russian front was a harrowing experience for the Jagdwaffe, much more so than in the West or the Mediterranean combat theaters.

While the Luftwaffe was bogged down battling the Russian giant, Britain and the United States were feverishly preparing for the bombing of Germany. By 1943, the Battle of Germany had started. Again the Oberkommando miscalculated, by assuming that a small force of fighters could halt the bombers, never

imagining the sheer number of bombers that would darken the skies over Germany. Prompt and effective action by the Luftwaffe High Command could have enabled the Jagdwaffe to effectively halt the Allied bombing.

The Allied victory resulted from their overwhelming numerical superiority, and the strategic bombing of fuel production and transportation. In the twilight of their existence, the Jagdfliegern could only look back at the years of official neglect they suffered, despite their clearly decisive role in the war as early as 1940. Regardless of how many of the enemy they destroyed, they could not win! The number of Experten who scored over 100 victories are almost too numerous to list, however, starting in 1944, the Allies had dozens of fighter pilots available to combat each one of these Experten! Hypothetically, if each of these Allied pilots scored as few as two or three victories, the Jagdwaffe would cease to exist.

Numbers won the war on all fronts. Overwhelming aircraft production and abundant numbers of trained pilots won the war for the Allies. History is testimony to that fact.

PRODUCTION AND TRAINING: THE SECRETS OF VICTORY

When the Nazis came to power in 1933, the Soviet air force consisted of 1,500 planes, with production rates increasing that number by 2,000 planes a year. During Operation Barbarossa, the Soviets had 17,000 first-line aircraft, of which 5,000 were fighters. By the fall of 1944 Russian factories had produced almost 100,000 aircraft! The Soviets had also received over 8,800 planes from the United States and over 6,000 from Britain. Of this total, about 4,900 were fighters. A three-year aircraft production comparison between Germany and Russia is interesting:

1941—Germany 12,401/Russia 15,735
1942—Germany 15,409/Russia 25,436
1943—Germany 24,807/Russia 35,000

It is evident that the Soviet's production advantage increased as the war progressed.

In view of the fact that the present volume concerns fighters, we will concentrate on fighter-plane production: The United States produced 101,460 single-seat fighters; about one-third were deployed in the Pacific theater, leaving 67,460 to combat the Jagdwaffe. Britain produced 39,310 single-seat fighters and sent about one-fifth to the Pacific, deploying the remaining 31,450 to fight the Jagdwaffe in Europe and Africa. Russia made 34,000 single-seat fighters and received an additional 4,900 from the U.S. and Britain, deploying all 38,900 against the Jagdwaffe. Germany produced 30,570 Messerschmitt Me 109's and 20,000 Focke-Wulf Fw 190 single-seat fighters, or 50,570 planes. They were deployed in a dozen countries on two continents. In summary:

Russia	38,900 fighters
U.S.A.	67,460 fighters (Europe)
Britain	31,450 fighters (Europe)
Allies	137,810 fighters
Germans	50,570 fighters

It has been estimated that the Red air force should have had at least 140,000 aircraft in consecutive operation during the length of the war.

In 1941, Russian factories produced about 7,500 fighters, while the Germans turned out only 3,744. By the spring of 1942, the battle of material had decisively turned against the Jagdwaffe, never to return. This should not have come as a surprise to the Luftwaffe who were afforded first-hand knowledge of the Russian capability as early as the spring of 1941. At this time General Heinrich Aschenbrenner, a member of the German embassy staff in Moscow, arranged for a group of prominent German engineers to tour Soviet aircraft factories. This was after the Germans had made plans for the attack on Russia, and it was an excellent opportunity to appraise Soviet aircraft production capabilities which, they observed, were enormous. In addition, the visitors were warned that Russia would destroy any nation who dared attack them! This warning, and the Soviet production expertise, was ignored, and the plans for Operation Barbarossa remained unchanged!

Fighter production was not the only segment of air power in which the Western Allies and the Soviets overwhelmed the Luftwaffe. In 1933, Josef Stalin ordered a pilot training program developed to have a force of 100,000 pilots available at all times! This ambitious objective was put into operation without delay. By the time of Operation Barbarossa, the 100,000 pilot goal had been achieved, and this pool of well-trained pilots remained at that specified level throughout the war. Training began in a government-operated flying club, attracting the youth with glider and powered-flight training. After passing the club courses, graduates joined the Soviet air force and underwent five more years of training! The Soviet Union was able to produce pilots as fast as they manufactured aircraft.

In 1938, Adolf Hitler ordered the Luftwaffe to expand production and training, but Oberkommando der Luftwaffe failed to follow through. Germany had depended upon a peacetime-trained prewar elite, and entered the war with only one Jagdwaffe pilot training school! Only 300 pilots were trained for the Jagdwaffe in 1941, and about the same number were turned out in 1942. The Germans trained a total of only 28,000 Jagdwaffe pilots. When training finally was accelerated in response to the fighter leaders' demands, the quality had deteriorated. Graduate pilots were sent to the front without having been taught to shoot properly!

In early 1942, Franklin D. Roosevelt ordered the training of 100,000 pilots, and by 1945 the United States Army Air Corps had a pool of almost 160,000 pilots!

The Soviet's determination to achieve air supremacy through concentrated aircraft production and comprehensive pilot training actually saved Soviet Russia. Operation Barbarossa would have easily defeated an average country, but the superbly prepared Soviets were able to weather the attack and bounce back with men and machines to eventually overwhelm the invaders.

THE ADVERSARIES: PRINCIPAL ALLIED FIGHTER AIRCRAFT

The adversaries of the Jagdfliegern and the Messerschmitt Me 109 are presented in chronological order:

Polikarpov I-15 Chato (Flat-nosed one): The first plane to engage the Jagdwaffe and the Messerschmitt. Over 500 I-15 fighters were sent to Spain in 1936 to help the Republican, or Loyalist, forces in the Civil War, and it was here that the two fighters met.

The Soviet air force's tactical theory of the early thirties was based upon the closely coordinated simultaneous operation of biplane and monoplane fighter formations. The faster monoplanes were to intercept the intruders, keeping them engaged until the slower but more maneuverable biplanes arrived. The maneuverable biplanes were then expected to finish off the enemy with dogfighting. When tested in Spain this theory was an abject failure, especially against the new German tactical formations.

Work began on the I-15 in 1932, and it began to appear in Soviet fighter units by 1934. On November 21, 1935 a new altitude record was established by V.K. Kokinaki, flying a light-weight version of the I-15 to 47,818 ft. Construction consisted of a fabric-covered wood and metal framework. Exceptionally maneuverable, the I-15 had a maximum weight of 3,027 lbs. and a top speed of 224 mph when powered with a 715-hp. copy of the American Wright Cyclone 9-cylinder air-cooled radial engine. Armament consisted of two cowl-mounted 7.6-mm. machine guns. Combat range was 450 miles.

On paper; the Chato was completely outclassed by the Messerschmitt Me 109B, yet, its slow speed and outstanding maneuverability made it a difficult target for the faster Messerschmitt.

Polikarpov I-16 Moska (fly): The first low-wing, single-seat fighter with retractable landing gear to see service with any air force. The I-16, also known as Rata (rat), was developed in parallel with the I-15 as the monoplane half of the monoplane/biplane tactical theory.

The I-16 Type 10 of 1937 was powered by a 750-hp. M-25 V air-cooled radial engine, enabling the craft to attain a speed of 280 mph with a loaded weight of 3,782 lbs. Service ceiling was 26,250 ft. and range 480 miles. The design was exceptionally rugged and could absorb considerable punishment. The I-16 take-off run of 755 ft. and landing run of 985 ft. made it necessary to lengthen the runways of all the Soviet fighter airfields. Although its maneuverability and rate of climb was excellent, the I-16 was very unstable in long turns and long climbs.

The I-16 first met the Messerschmitt in Spanish skies. It was here that the stubby fighter earned its nicknames Mosca, or Fly, from the Loyalists, and Rata, or Rat, from the Nationalists. The I-16 Type 10 surpassed the Me 109B in general performance, but in extended dives, climbs, and 180-degree turns the Messerschmitt was demonstrably superior. The I-16 bore the brunt of Operation Barbarossa, and continued in service until early 1943. Despite its on-paper inferiority, many Experten, including Gerd Barkhorn, claim that the I-16 was the most difficult Soviet plane to shoot down. Its low speed and very small radius on short, evasive turns, made it a superior foe.

Morane-Saulnier M.S. 406: France's principal and most numerous fighter in September 1939, and it is considered the most famous French fighter of the war. It was the first fighter in the Armee de l'Air to exceed 250 mph, and 1,080 of the design had been delivered by June 20, 1940.

Designed in 1934, the prototype first flew in the summer of the following year. An order for 1,000 of the fighters was placed by the Armee de l'Air in March, 1938. Construction was unique and not easily adaptable to mass production. The all-metal framework was covered with sheets of bonded plywood and aluminum, called Plymax. The entire plane aft of the cockpit was fabric covered.

Powered by an 860-hp. Hispano-Suiza 12Y-31 12-cylinder liquid-cooled engine, the 5,364-lb. craft could attain a maximum speed of 302 mph. Service ceiling was 30,800 ft and range was 497 miles. Armament consisted of one Hispano-Suiza HS-404 20-mm. engine cannon firing through the propeller hub, supplied with 60 rounds, plus two 7.5-mm. MAC 1934 machine guns located in the wings outboard of the propeller arc, fitted with 300 rpg.

Though the M.S. 406 was reliable, maneuverable, and easy to handle, it was not an outstanding design. While it posed no serious challenge to the Me 109E in the Battle of France, French pilots flying the M.S. 406 claimed 269 victories, including numerous Emils.

Dewoitine D. 520: France's finest fighter of the Second World War. Unfortunately, insufficient numbers were delivered to the Armee de l'Air to alter the course of the Battle of France. Designed by a team led by Emile Dewoitine in 1937, the prototype first flew in October of the following year. This craft was initially fitted with leading-edge slots, as was the Messerschmitt, but when found to be unnecessary they were removed in the production model.

The first eight production models were supplied to the Armee de l'Air on February 1, 1940, the total rising to 31 one month later and to 312 by June 20. When the German blitz on France began in May, 1940, there was only one D.520-equipped Groupe de Chasse: GC I/3. However, GC II/3 converted to the D 520 by May 18, followed by GC III/3, GC III/6, and GC II/7 during June. Although designed for mass production, the Armee de l'Air technical department insisted upon a large number of modifications between April and November 1939, delaying delivery of this fine plane.

A 910-hp. supercharged Hispano-Suiza 12Y-45 12-cylinder V liquid-cooled engine drove the 6, 129-lb. plane to a maximum speed of 329 mph. Service ceiling was 36,090 ft. and range 620 miles. Armament consisted of one Hispano-Suiza 404 20-mm. engine cannon with 60 rounds, and four MAC 1934 7.5-mm. machine guns located in the wing outside of the propeller arc, with 500 rpg.

Although the Emil's maximum speed was greater by about 20 mph, the D.520 was extremely maneuverable and easy to handle. Except for diving speed, the craft was equal to or superior to the Emil, and could easily out-turn the Messerschmitt. Despite the fact that they were equipped with the Dewoitine late in the Battle of France, Groupes de Chasse I/3, II/3, III/3, III/6, and II/7 claimed a total of 147 victories, 114 of which were officially confirmed.

Curtiss Hawk 75 A: Scored the first victories for the Armee de 1'Air over the Western Front, when five of the American-made fighters from GC II/4 shot down two Emils on September 8, 1939.

A French purchasing commission placed an order for 100 Hawk 75 A fighters in 1938, and these were delivered by the end of the year. Additional orders in 1939 brought the total to 730, however, only 291 Hawks had been delivered before France surrendered.

The Curtiss Hawk 75 A was an export version of the Curtiss P-36 fighter which had been delivered to the U.S. Army Air Corps. The design was initiated as a private venture by the Curtiss–Wright Corporation Airplane Division in 1934, and was a contemporary of the Me 109. The Curtiss Design No. 75 was first delivered to the USAAC in April, 1938. U.S. strategy in the thirties concentrated on coastal defense, and so high-flying fighters were deemed unnecessary. The concept stressed rugged ground-attack fighters, similar to Soviet reasoning, and therefore U.S. fighters developed in the mid-thirties found it difficult to compete with modern West European high-flying fighters. The Hawk 75 A-3 was powered by a 1,200-hp. Pratt and Whitney R-1830-17 Twin Wasp 14-cylinder radial engine, driving the 5,734-lb. plane to a maximum speed of 311 mph. Service ceiling was 33,700 ft. and normal range was 820 miles. Armament consisted of four 7.5-mm. machine guns in the wing outside of the propeller arc and two more in the upper cowl. Besides the armament change, the French versions required metric instruments, a modified seat to accommodate a back parachute, a different radio and oxygen system, and a different gun sight. The Hawk 75 A was of all-metal construction, except for fabric-covered control surfaces. The landing gear retracted rearwards into the wing, rotating 90 degrees as it moved into position.

Although its speed was much less that of the Emil,

the Curtiss Hawk 75 A had a lighter wing loading and had the edge in maneuverability. Its short climbing ability was comparable to the Emil, and its range greater; however, the Messerschmitt excelled in long climbs and diving speed.

The Curtiss Hawk 75 A was flown by Groupes de Combat I/4, II/4, I/5, II/5, and II/2, who claimed 230 victories and 81 probable kills in the Battle of France before June 24, 1940. Marin La Meslee of I/5 scored 15 confirmed and 5 probable victories while flying the Hawk 75A.

Hawker Hurricane: Shot down more German aircraft during the Battle of Britain than did all other British aircraft and ground defenses combined! The Hurricane was the creation of Sidney Camm, chief designer for Hawker Aircraft, and began as a private venture in early 1934. Entering RAF service in 1937, it was a contemporary of the Me 109 and the first combat aircraft to exceed 300 mph. Over 14,000 Hurricanes were built.

Construction followed proven, but antiquated concepts, such as a steel-tubing fuselage strength-truss with wood fairing strips. It was fabric-covered aft of the cockpit and dural forward to the spinner. The wing was an all-metal structure, fabric covered and built in three sections with a long center section. The landing gear retracted inwardly and the wide track made the craft exceptionally stable during taxi, takeoff, and landing, unlike the Me 109. The high cockpit and sloping upper cowling gave the pilot better visibility than in the average contemporary fighter plane. Powered by a 1,030-hp. Rolls-Royce Merlin III 12-cylinder V liquid-cooled engine, the Hurricane Mk. I attained a maximum speed of 324 mph at 16,250 ft. Its loaded weight was 6,600 lbs and range was 425 miles. Service ceiling was 34,200 ft. The Hurricane wingspan was eight feet greater than the Me 109. Armament consisted of eight .303-in. machine guns in the wings.

By September 1939, Hawker had delivered 497 Hurricanes to the RAF. On August 8, 1940, the 2,309th Hurricane had been received by Fighter Command. On the eve of the Battle of Britain, 32 squadrons were equipped with Hurricanes, compared to only 19 squadrons of Spitfires.

In combat with the Emil, the Hurricane proved a disappointment, especially at high altitudes. Although it showed more maneuverability than the Emil at altitudes up to 20,000 ft., it was markedly slower at all altitudes. It was also inferior to the Emil in climbing ability, as were many of the Allied fighters. The craft was very stable, however, and proved to be an excellent gun platform. It was extremely rugged and could absorb considerable punishment, enabling many Hurryboxes to return to base after a mauling. The Hawker design was also handicapped by its greater drag and an inferior rate of acceleration, leaving it in an Emil's gunsight longer than was desirable.

In view of the availability of the Spitfire during the Battle, the Hurricane was usually assigned to tackle the Stukas and larger bombers. However, it took its toll of Emils, as can be verified by many of the surviving Experten. British Battle of Britain Aces Cobber Kain, Douglas Bader, and R.R.S. Tuck all scored heavily while flying the Hurricane.

Supermarine Spitfire: The Messerschmitt's principal adversary during the Battle of Britain. Aerodynamically refined and aesthetically beautiful, the Spitfire was conceived by Supermarine chief designer Reginald J. Mitchell. Using the same approach as Willi Messerschmitt, Mitchell designed the smallest fighter that could accommodate the largest power plant available and have space for pilot, fuel, and guns. Designed in 1934, the prototype was first flown in the spring of 1936, making it the contemporary of the Hurricane, Morane, Dewoitine, and Messerschmitt. The Spitfire was the first all-metal fighter produced in Britain. The narrow track, outward-retracting landing gear was similar to the Me 109's and presented the same problems. Reginald Mitchell worked day and night on the design, despite doctor's orders, because he knew that Willi Messerschmitt was developing the 109. Mitchell died shortly after the Spitfire was completed; it can be said that he gave his life that Britain could have a fighter plane worthy of battling the Messerschmitt.

About 20,350 Spitfires of all Marks were constructed.

The Battle of Britain Spitfire IA was powered by a 1,030-hp. Rolls-Royce Merlin III 12-cylinder V liquid-cooled engine, propelling the 5,784-lb. craft to a maximum speed of 365 mph at 19,000 ft. Normal range was 575 miles and service ceiling 34,000 ft. Armament was eight .303-in. machine guns buried in the wing.

The Spitfire IA was faster and much more maneuverable than the Emil; however, it fell behind in long climbs and dives. Many Emil pilots went into a dive to escape the Spitfire's eight guns, and the British pilots either did not bother to pursue or, if they did, would soon break off because it was impossible to catch the Germans. At higher altitudes Spitfire performance declined while the Emil's did not. The Emil had one more advantage: its cannon armament had a greater range than the British machine guns,

meaning the German pilot could start firing before the British pilot. Later models of the Spitfire also mounted a cannon. The Emil and Spitfire IA were a virtual standoff in performance, and victory depended on the pilot's ability, aggressiveness, and luck!

Curtiss Kittyhawk IA: Flown against the Jagdwaffe over the North African desert by the RAF, SAAF, and RAAF, and battled the Emil, Franz, and Gustav. The American-made Kittyhawk was a development of the Hawk 75 A which had been supplied to France. The first of almost 15,000 Curtiss P-40 types, as it was known in the USAAC, made its appearance in October, 1938. It was basically the P-36 (or 75 A) with a liquid-cooled V engine replacing the air-cooled radial engine.

Although it started life as the Tomahawk, of which Britain purchased over 1,000, refinements in armament and power plant gave the Kittyhawk a better chance under European combat conditions. Britain ordered 2,000 Kittyhawks in 1941, just in time for the fighting over the Western Desert, where it became operational in January, 1942.

Powered by a 1,150-hp. Allison V-1710-39 12-cylinder V liquid-cooled engine, the Kittyhawk IA attained a maximum speed of 362 mph at 15,000 ft. with a loaded weight of 8,280 lbs. Service ceiling was 29,000 ft., and range 700 miles. Maximum rate of climb was 2,100 ft. min. at 5,000 ft. altitude. Armament consisted of six 0.5-in. machine guns in the wing located outside the propeller arc. The craft could carry one 500-lb. and two 100-lb. bombs.

The Kittyhawk was used primarily for ground-support fighter-bomber duties and often given low-level fighter sweeps while the Hurricanes covered the higher altitudes. Its speed was greater than the Emil but less than the Franz and Gustav. Rate of climb was inferior to all Messerschmitts. During interception missions, the Commonwealth Kittyhawks exacted a heavy toll of Stukas and Italian fighters. Rugged and maneuverable, the Kittyhawk was generally out-performed by the Emil and Gustav, but always by the speedy and agile Franz, which made hit-and-run attacks on Curtiss formations.

Despite its inferior performance, the Kittyhawk squadrons in North Africa shot down over 420 Axis aircraft. Famous Commonwealth Aces C.R. Caldwell, N. Duke, J.F. Edwards and many others scored successfully in this Curtiss fighter.

Ilyushin Il-2 Shturmovik: The only plane of its type in any air force, a unique design intended for a single purpose: ground-attack missions to destroy enemy troops and equipment. Although technically not a fighter, it is included here because the Jagdwaffe encountered it so frequently. As the surviving Experten will testify, the Shturmovik was the most difficult airplane to shoot down, taking its toll of Messerschmitts!

The Ilyushin design team began work in 1937, and the Bronirovanni Shturmovik, or armored attacker, prototype made its appearance in the following year. It first took to the air in late 1939, and first saw action in August, 1941 as a single seater. By 1942, the design was modified to include a rear gunner, increased armament, greater maneuverability, and a shorter take off run.

Construction was all metal except for the fuselage behind the cockpit, which was wooden monocoque. The most unusual feature was its strong armor protection. The armor was not bolted in place on a standard airframe, as was done with all other aircraft, but was an integral part of the structure enclosing the engine, radiator, fuel tanks, and cockpit in a single protective cell. This armor weighed almost 1,600 lbs., which was about 15 percent of the plane's total maximum weight! The 1,750-hp. AM-38 12-cylinder V liquid-cooled engine drove the 11,683-lb. Shturmovik to a maximum speed of 263 mph. Obviously designed for low-altitude operation, the Il-2 maximum-efficiency altitude was about 2,500 ft. The basic armament consisted of one 20-mm. engine cannon and two 20-mm. wing-mounted cannon. This cannon's very high muzzle velocity and the tremendous explosive power of the shells give the Shturmovik extra effectiveness against armored vehicles. The rear gunner was provided with a pivoted 12.7-mm. UBT machine gun, an unusually large caliber for the rear gunner in a 2-seater. In addition, two 7.62-mm. Sh KAS machine guns were installed for troop strafing. About 1,400 lbs. of bombs, or eight 82-mm. rockets and four 220-lb. bombs, could be carried under the wing.

It was a frustrating experience for the Experten to attack a Shturmovik because it flew so low and slow. As the Messerschmitt approached, the Ilyushin's gunner would commence firing his big gun. Even if he didn't score a hit it usually was unnerving enough to ruin the Jagdflieger's aim or cause him to break off the attack! Many Experten saw their shells ricocheting off the Shturmovik's armor while the attack plane continued flying uninjured. Reportedly, the newly-arrived Il-2 shot down ten Messerschmitts in the space of a few days in early 1943. On more than one occasion Shturmoviks attacked and destroyed Stukas before proceeding on a mission against German troops and armor! The 35,000

Shturmoviks that were constructed played a very decisive role on the Eastern front. It was truly a time for celebrating when a Jagdflieger bagged a Shturmovik!

MiG-3: Prior to 1943 the only fighter plane which was superior to the Messerschmitt at altitudes above 16,000 ft. Designers Artem Mikoyan and Mikhail Gurevich began work on the design late in 1939, when it became evident that the Western powers had developed high-altitude fighters while the Soviets had concentrated on low-altitude aircraft. The MiG-1 evolved into the MiG-3 by 1941, and this design won the Stalin Prize for its creators. It was one of the few Soviet high-altitude fighters.

Powered by the 1,350-hp. Mikulin AM-35A 12-cylinder V liquid-cooled engine, the 7,695-lb. MiG-3 attained a maximum speed of 407 mph at 22,965 ft. Service ceiling was 39,370 ft. and range 510 miles. It required only 4½ minutes to reach an altitude of 16,400 ft. Armament consisted of two 7.62-mm. Sh KAS machine guns in the upper cowling with 375 rpg, and one 12.7-mm. Beresin BS machine gun on one side. When it became obvious that this light armament was insufficient, field kits were issued to the units to add two 12.7-mm. machine guns under the wings.

The wing outer panels, fuselage rear, and tail was of wooden construction, while the remainder was metal.

Production of the MiG-3 was terminated in autumn of 1941 in deference to the Il-2 after only a few thousand were built. Apparently high-altitude fighters were not part of the Soviet tactical philosophy, and the MiG-3 virtually disappeared from first-line units by 1943.

Bell P-39 Airacobra: One of the most unusual propeller-driven fighter planes of the Second World War. Over 4,750 of the 9,558 American-made Airacobras constructed were sent to Russia by the U.S. under lend lease. This figure was about half the total number of aircraft that the U.S. supplied to the Soviets. Although considered a dismal failure by the Western Allies, the Airacobra was highly regarded by the Russians for its ground-attack ability.

In June, 1936, Larry Bell, R.J. Woods, and H.M. Poyer of the one-year-old Bell Aircraft Corporation began work on a revolutionary, all-metal fighter-plane design. The engine was located in the center of the fuselage, behind the cockpit, with a 10-foot extension shaft running under the cockpit floor and connecting to the propeller via planetary gears. This arrangement was selected to allow space in the nose for a 37-mm. cannon firing through the propeller hub. In addition, the centrally located engine placed this heavy mass near the center of gravity or balance point of the plane which improved maneuverability. Also unorthodox was the tricycle landing gear, the first on any single-engine fighter. First flown in April, 1938, the craft attained a speed of almost 400 mph, however, modifications required by the USAAC, such as the deletion of the turbo-supercharger, leak-proof tanks, four additional machine guns, reduced the performance considerably at medium and high altitudes.

Very few Airacobras saw service in Western Europe; however, the Soviets found that it fit in very well with their low altitude tactical philosophy and so flew it extensively. The vast majority of Soviet Airacobras were the equivalent of the USAAC P-39 Q, the type of Airacobra of which the most were built. Powered by a 1,350-hp. Allison V-1710-85 12-cylinder V liquid-cooled engine, the P-39 Q model attained 376 mph at 15,000 ft. with a maximum weight of 8,300 lbs. Climb to 20,000 ft. took 8½ minutes and service ceiling was 35,000 ft. Range was 600 miles, but could be extended to 1,075 miles with a belly drop tank. Armament consisted of one 37-mm. M-4 cannon with 30 rounds firing through the propeller hub, two cowl-mounted 0.5-inch machine guns with 200 rpg and two 0.5-inch machine guns under the wings enclosed in pods with 300 rpg.

According to the Experten, the Airacobra performed like the Messerschmitt at low altitudes, but lost much maneuverability over 15,000 ft. Remember that an Airacobra shot down Gerd Barkhorn. The 37-mm. cannon was a lethal weapon, and it only took one lucky shot to blow the enemy out of the sky!

Yakovlev Yak-3: Considerably faster, it also had a smaller turning radius, a better climb rate and acceleration than the Me 109G at altitudes up to 20,000 ft. It was developed in early 1943 by Alexander Yakovlev's design team from the previous Yak-1, as a close-support fighter. The Yak-3 made its first appearance in action during the Kursk offensive in mid-1943, and six months later appeared in force all along the front. It raised havoc with many Luftwaffe formations.

As with many Russian designs, the Yak-3 was of mixed construction: an all-wooden wing and a plywood-covered steel-tube-and-wood fuselage structure. The 5,864-lb. airplane was powered with a 1,222-hp. Klimov M-105 PF-2 12-cylinder V liquid-cooled engine which drove it to a maximum speed of 403 mph at 16,400-ft. altitude. Speed increased to 447 mph for those Yak-3 aircraft fitted with the VK-

107 A engine. Range was 560 miles. Armament was relatively light, consisting of one 20-mm. Sh VAK engine cannon with 120 rounds and two 12.7-mm. Beresin machine guns in the upper cowl. A Yak-9 was developed parallel with the Yak-3 and had a similar performance. About 29,000 Yak fighters were constructed.

According to Experten Hartmann and Barkhorn, the Yaks were the most troublesome and dangerous of Soviet fighters, not only because of their high speed, but also because of superior maneuverability. With slats popped out on the Messerschmitt and a firm grip on the controls, the Experten would drop speed down to almost 150 mph and then pull the Me 109 into tight vertical banks up to 4g. This maneuver often out-turned the more maneuverable Yaks, even at lower altitudes. However, as the gravity forces built up in the turn, the Messerschmitt's aileron and rudder controls would become too heavy and the Yak then would gain the upper hand. Of course, all Jagdwaffe pilots were not Experten, and Russian units flying the Yak-3 took their toll of the Luftwaffe. July 14, 1944 was an outstanding day for Yak pilots. In one engagement, eight Yak-3 fighters attacked a 60-plane formation of Junkers Ju-88 bombers and Messerschmitt escort, scoring three Junkers and four Messerschmitts without loss to themselves. On that same day another flight of 18 Yaks engaged 30 Messerschmitts and shot down half of them with only one loss to themselves. These stunning victories so upset Luftflotte Chief Gen. Kesselring that he instructed all of his pilots to avoid confrontation with the Yak-3 because the dwindling Jagdwaffe could not afford the losses!

Lavochkin La-7: The ultimate refinement of an already successful fighter, the La-5. Both types were flown by many Russian aces including Pokryshkin and Kojedub, the La-5 played a vital role over the Kursk salient in 1943. The design was faster than contemporary Messerschmitt variants at altitudes below 22,000 ft., and had a greater initial rate of climb and required a shorter time to make a 180-degree turn. The craft was light on the controls and easy to handle compared to the rather heavy Messerschmitt controls.

After designing the LaGG-3 with engineers Gudkov and Gorbunov, Semyon A. Lavochkin adapted the design to use an air-cooled twin-row radial engine to replace the original V liquid-cooled power plant. This became the La-5 which made its combat debut at Stalingrad in autumn, 1942. The plane was constructed mainly of wood with a Siberian birch structure, and covered with pressure-impregnated phenolic-formaldehyde plywood. The La-7 made its appearance at the front in 1943.

The 7,495-lb. La-7 was powered by a 1,775-hp. Shvetsov M-82FN 14-cylinder radial air-cooled fuel-injected engine, which propelled the craft to a top speed of 430 mph at 16,400 ft. altitude. This engine was fitted with a power boost which increased the horsepower to 1,640 for short periods. Armament was three 20-mm. Sh VAK cannons mounted in the fuselage and firing through the propeller arc.

The Lavochkin design was able to make such tight turns at low altitude that many following Messerschmitts stalled and crashed or skidded into the ground or tall trees!

We see that the Jagdwaffe on the Eastern front did not achieve its phenomenal scores by fighting against antiquated and obsolete aircraft. Numerous Soviet designs were equal or superior to the Messerschmitt on many counts.

Although the previously-discussed American aircraft were of mediocre performance, designed as they were in accordance with the U.S. defense strategy of the mid-thirties, the three American fighters on the following pages were classic designs, and worthy opponents of the Jagdwaffe.

Lockheed P-38 Lightning: The first U.S. Army Air Corps fighter to shoot down a Luftwaffe plane in World War II (a Focke-Wulf patrol plane over the Atlantic Ocean, in February, 1942.) The P-38 was designed in 1937 as a fast-climbing interceptor and evolved into a twin-engine airplane while still on the drawing board when no single engine proved powerful enough to deliver the required climbing performance. The prototype first flew in January, 1939, and in the following month it dashed across the American continent from California to New York in seven hours, establishing a new transcontinental speed record. Almost 10,000 of these twin-engine fighters were constructed during World War II. In the European theater of operations, the P-38 was used as a long-range bomber escort.

The P-38 G, of which over 1,000 were built, made its combat debut in the summer of 1942. This was powered by two 1,325-hp. Allison V-1710-51/55 12-cylinder V liquid-cooled engines, which drove the 19,800-lb. plane to a maximum speed of 400 mph at 25,000-ft. altitude. Normal range was 850 miles at 219 mph and 10,000 feet, however, with the addition of two auxiliary drop tanks it could be extended to 1,670 miles at 211 mph and 10,000 ft. This variant could climb to 20,000 ft. in 8½ minutes. Service ceiling was 39,000 ft. The armament consisted of one 20-mm. Hispano MI cannon with 150 rounds, and four

0.5-inch Colt-Browning MG 53-2 machine guns with 500 rpg. It could also carry 500 or 1,000-lb. bombs for fighter-bomber missions.

The twin engines and large size of the plane restricted maneuverability, reducing its effectiveness against enemy fighters. Efficient at high altitudes, the P-38 encouraged the Messerschmitt pilots to force the Lightning down to about 15,000 ft. where the contest was on a more equal basis.

Republic P-47 Thunderbolt: The heaviest and largest single-engine fighter built until that point. It was conceived by Alexander Kartveli in the summer of 1940, and first flew one year later in May, 1941. The P-47 B first saw action in April, 1943 as a high-altitude bomber-escort fighter.

Powered by a supercharged 2,000-hp. Pratt & Whitney R-2800-21 18-cylinder twin-row radial air-cooled engine, the 13,360-lb. fighter attained a top speed of 429 mph at 27,000 ft. Range was 550 miles at 335 mph at 10,000 ft. Service ceiling was 42,000 ft. The later P-47 C had provisions for an external drop tank which extended the range to 1,250 miles.

Its enormous weight and bulk considerably reduced the Thunderbolts' maneuverability. It was, however, one of the very few airplanes with a higher diving speed than the Messerschmitt, though it had the habit of mushing during the pullout. The Thunderbolt was superior at high altitudes, but at medium and low altitudes the P-47 B couldn't compete with the rate of climb or maneuverability of the Messerschmitt. Armament was very lethal consisting of eight 0.5-inch Colt-Browning machine guns in the wing with 267 rpg.

About 15,600 Thunderbolts were bulit by several plants in the U.S., including Curtiss facilities. Approximately 10,300 were flown by the USAAC and losses were about 520 aircraft, or only little more than 5%. This excellent record can be attributed to the exceptional ruggedness of the P-47, and its ability to absorb even explosive cannon shells and still manage to return to base.

North American P-51 Mustangs: Often called the finest fighter plane of World War Two, it was well-respected by the Jagdwaffe. The design was inspired in early 1940 by the British Purchasing Commission, who gave North American Aviation the general requirements based upon the RAF's experience in the war in Europe. They wanted a prototype in 120 days once the design was approved. North American's president, J.H. Kindeberger, assigned the project to Raymond Rick and Edgar Schmund. Schmund had previously worked as designer for Fokker and

Four of the Experten who devoted their efforts to organize and operate the German Federal Republic, or Bundesrepublik Luftwaffe, are generals: *(top row)* Dieter Hrabak and Günther Rall; *(bottom row)* Johannes Steinhoff and Hannes Trautloft, with an air-minded friend.

On December 15, 1966, the Inspecteur der Luftwaffe, Gen. Steinhoff, congratulated Hptm. Peter Hufnagel for becoming the first fighter pilot in the Bundesrepublik Luftwaffe. The location was Luke Air Force Base, Arizona, where the new Luftwaffe learned how to fly the Starfighter.

Gen. Steinhoff presented the Grand Cross of the German Bundesrepublik with Star to Gen. Trautloft in the summer of 1970, when Trautloft commanded Luftwaffengruppe South.

Oberstlt. Erich Hartmann, Kommodore JG 71 Richthofen, admires a model of the Lockheed Starfighter with Lt. Gen. Robert M. Lee, USAF, on the occasion of Hartmann's visit to the United States in 1961.

Messerschmitt, and it has been remarked in aviation circles that the Mustang bore more than a casual resemblance to the Me 109.

The prototype emerged 117 days later and was fitted with an Allison engine. Production models began arriving in Britain in late 1941, but the RAF was disappointed with the low-altitude engine. After testing four of the planes with the Rolls-Royce Merlin engine, the performance improved considerably. Arrangements were quickly made for Packard to build Merlins in the U.S. More P-51 D variants were constructed than any other: 7,956 of a 15,220 total.

The 1,695-hp. Packard V-165-7 Merlin 12-cylinder V liquid-cooled engine propelled the 10,000-lb. P-51

The Old Puma of the Royal Hungarian Air Force is shown in a photo taken in 1965. Aladar de Heppes moved to the U.S., where he conducted an industrial design service. This patriot died in 1988.

D to a maximum speed of 437 mph. Normal range was 950 miles at 395 mph at 25,000 ft., but this could be extended to 2,080 miles by installing drop tanks. Initial climb was 3,475 ft./min. Service ceiling was 41,900 ft. Armament was six 0.5-inch Colt-Browning MG 53-2 machine guns in the wing with 400 rpg.

According to the Experten, the Mustang was faster and more maneuverable than the Messerschmitt above 20,000 ft., but below 15,000 ft. the Mustang's advantage disappeared. The Me 109 did have one advantage over the Mustang at any altitude: The Messerschmitt could be pulled into a tight turn and just keep pulling; slats popped out and buffeting began, but it kept flying. The Mustang, on the other hand, exhibited high-speed stall/tuck tendencies in this maneuver. Mustangs are credited with shooting down 4,950 adversaries, many of which were Messerschimitt pilots flying at the higher altitudes. The intercepting Jagdwaffe was forced to climb to the high-flying bombers in order to attack them, and that is when the Messerschmitts were bounced by the higher-flying Mustangs.

Focke-Wulf Fw 190: Not an adversary of the Messerschmitt, but it could be considered a competitor because it did in fact vie for victories of Allied aircraft over the skies of Europe. It is of interest to see how this newer design compared with the older Messerschmitt. Designed tightly around an air-cooled radial engine by Dipl. Ing. Kurt Tank in 1938, the FW 190 first flew in the summer of 1939. The type entered service two years later on the Channel coast where it was used for low-altitude hit-and-run missions over southeastern England. About 13,350 Fw 190 fighters and about 6,600 Fw 190 Jabo and close-support aircraft were produced.

The Fw 190 A-8 variant made its appearance late in 1943. A 1,700-hp. BMW 801D-2 14-cylinder air-cooled radial engine propelled the 10,800-lb. plane to a maximum speed of 408 mph at 20,600 ft. Range was 500 miles and service ceiling was 37,400 ft. The armament consisted of two 13-mm. MG 131 machine guns in the wing roots and four 20-mm. MG 151 cannons under the wings in blister fairings, outboard of the landing gear.

The Focke-Wulf fighter's wide-track landing gear required less skill in handling on the ground and in takeoffs and landings. This, the heavy armament, and ease of handling made the Fw 190 a favorite among the younger and inexperienced Jagdfliegern. Below 20,000 ft., the Fw 190 performance was superior to the Messerschmitt, but it had the same high-speed stall/tuck tendencies in a tight turn as the Mustang. Performance began to deteriorate above 20,000 ft., and constant problems were experienced with the engines above that crucial altitude.

Several Experten claim that the Me 109G was a better dogfighter than the Fw 190, although the Focke-Wulf had the edge on maneuverability. They also preferred to contine flying the Messerschmitt even when offered the newer Focke-Wulf. Gerhard Barkhorn led Fw 190 D-equipped JG 6 and refused to fly this plane in combat. Instead, he and his Rottenflieger elected to fly the Messerschmitt while the remainder of his Geschwader flew the issued Focke-Wulf's. Erich Hartmann also preferred to remain with the Me 109.

They all agreed that the Messerschmitt was the pro fighter-pilots' airplane, and once they learned and mastered its flight characteristics they loved the plane and would have no other.

LOSSES

Thus far we have discussed individual victories and unit victories, but not national losses. Accurate figures on losses of either personnel or equipment are most difficult to determine because in many cases complete records were not prepared.

The Jagwaffe casualties for single-engine fighter

The former Experten maintain contact with each other via Gemeinschaft der Jagdflieger; they have many reunions with their former adversaries. In the upper photo Hannes Trautloft (far left) and other former Experten entertain famous French Ace Roger Sauvage (center); in the bottom photo Adolf Galland (center, with vest) and Erich Hartmann (to Galland's left) entertain British flyer Peter Townsend.

This memorial monument, dedicated to the fallen fighter pilots of all nations, was erected by the German Fighter Pilots Association on the banks of the Rhine at Geisenheim. The two eagles symbolize the Rotte.

pilots was about 8,500 dead, 2,700 MIA or POW, and 9,100 wounded in the period from 1939 through 1945. These losses may appear on the low side when compared to the millions who died in the Second World War, but it must be remembered that the figures include only single-engine fighter pilots. The casualties for the entire Luftwaffe through the end of 1944 were about 97,000 killed, wounded, or missing. The single-engine–pilot loss rate was extremely high. For example, JG 26 Schlageter suffered the loss of over 800 pilots killed or missing, and JG 27 Afrika lost about 825 pilots killed or missing throughout the war. A Jagdgeschwader averaged about 120 pilots, sometimes less and at times more. It becomes clear that these units suffered pilot losses equal to over 6½ times their normal complement. In effect they replaced the entire pilot force 6½ times due to deaths and MIA!

Jagwaffe aircraft losses were, of course, much higher, due to bailouts and crash landings in which the pilot survived. About 15,000 Jagwaffe single-engine fighters were destroyed by enemy action, while an additional 7,500 were destroyed under non-combat conditions. About 17,000 single-engine fighters were damaged, one-third due to enemy action.

Total United States Army Air Corps casualties in the European and Mediterranean theaters were about 11,000 pilots killed and 4,000 wounded. The combined aircraft losses of the RAF and USAAC from 1941 through 1945 in these theaters of operation were almost 42,000 planes of all types. The Jagdwaffe alone was responsible for about 25,000 victories of this figure. The remainder were shot down by flak batteries which, in the German military, were part of the Luftwaffe.

During the whirlwind Battle of France, the Armee de l'Air records indicate 201 killed, 231 wounded, and 31 prisoners. It is possible that during this chaotic time, there may have been more unrecorded casualties.

It has been estimated that the Soviet Union lost a total of about 77,000 aircraft and that about 45,000 of these fell as victories of the Jagdwaffe. Germany's Allies destroyed about 16,000 of the total. The remainder were shot down by flak or were destroyed on the ground. Although no casualty figures are available, a close estimate, based upon known casualty/aircraft loss ratios, is about 40,000 pilots killed.

A total of 120,000 enemy aircraft were reported destroyed by the Luftwaffe throughout the war, and 70,000 of this total were shot down by the Jagdwaffe. The remainder fell due to flak or were caught on the ground.

As the figures show, the Soviet aircraft losses were about twice those of the combined Western Allies. This lends credence to reports of the ferocity of the Eastern front aerial combat.

Of the 28,000 men who trained as fighter pilots in the Jagdwaffe, less than 1,400 survived the war, and the road back was an unpleasant experience for these heroes.

Epilogue: Welcome Home

Despite their superhuman efforts, the German fighter pilots could not stave off the overwhelming defeat which engulfed their armed forces. Even the combat leaders, who endangered their careers and very lives in their confrontations with the Oberkommando der Luftwaffe, could not alter the path of incompetent and irrational leadership. All the pleading and rational arguments of Lützow, Galland, Trautloft, and von Maltzahn fell on deaf ears, and their brave Jagdfliegern continued to be blown from the skies. Had the Jagdwaffe been loyally and properly supported by the political and military policy makers, history might have been altered.

After the war was over and peace restored, there was a general feeling among the German population that the Jagdwaffe had been responsible for not stopping the Anglo-American fire-bombing and not halting their advancing armies. The brunt of the blame fell on the fighter pilots, because the policy makers used them as scapegoats to cover their own ineptitude. History proves the fault was not the Jagdwaffe's; instead, it should have received the gratitude of the nation.

Upon returning to civilian life, former fighter pilots faced even more serious difficulties, affecting their families and daily living. When applying for jobs, which they desperately needed, each was of course required to cite previous experience on each application form. Prospective employers invariably refused to hire the applicant once the word Jagdflieger appeared. Except for the more wealthy, and those who left Germany for work abroad, fighter pilots and their families constituted a virtually starving and destitute segment of German society. Germany was beaten and the new government had many reparations to pay, in addition to supporting the armies of occupation. The govenment apparently had no funds to help the Jagdwaffe heroes; therefore, from 1945 to 1949 the fighter pilots had no place to turn.

In 1949, Der Gemeinschaft der Jagdflieger E. V., or German Fighter Pilots Association, was formed to provide employment for the Jagdfliegern and assistance for the dependents of those who had been killed during the war. Germany had been divided by the victorious Allies, and the Association also was to make arrangements for fighter pilots living behind the Iron Curtain to escape to West Germany. In this case, escape was not initiated until the escapee was assured of adequate housing and a position commensurate with the rank he held when on active duty in the Luftwaffe. Through generous contributions to the association by knowledgeable wealthy citizens, through donations from members, and money raised from the publication of *Jagerblatt*, the official organ of Der Gemeinschaft der Jagdflieger, the standard of living of the membership was gradually raised. Once again members were able to take their appropriate place in the community.

In the same year, the Luftwaffe was allowed again to take to the air. The vile propaganda aimed at the Jagdwaffe during the war by inept officials was unmasked and corrected. Former fighter pilots emerged as the most reliable force in the reconstruction of the Luftwaffe and men like Generals Trautloft, Steinhoff, and Kammhuber assumed major commands.

In 1961, the German Fighter Pilots' Association designed and constructed a memorial monument to the fallen fighter pilots of all nations at Geizenheim on the banks of the Rhine River. In the true spirit of comradeship, representatives of the American Fighter Aces' Association and the American Fighter Pilots' Association attended the dedication ceremony. Both U.S. organizations contributed generously to help defray the cost of the monument.

As a breed, the Jagdflieger lived and fought by the soldier's code of chivalry. Testimony to the German fighter pilots' gallantry and clean sportsmanship has poured out from the Allied pilots who flew against them. The Jagdflieger never deserted the fine traditions of chivalry and loyalty and they authored one of the most colorful and incredible chapters in the history of arms.

Appendix

AWARDS

THE IRON CROSS

The Iron Cross is the best known German war medal and has become the symbol of the German military. This famous award was established in March, 1813 by the King of Prussia, Wilhelm III. The basic model was the Cross of the Order of German, or Teutonic, Knights—crusaders who fought the Saracens in the Middle Ages. Wilhelm ordered the famous Prussian architect Schinkel to design a medal of simplicity and beauty. The Iron Cross did not recognize rank, and anyone in the armed forces could earn it.

During the Franco-Prussian War, in July, 1870, King William I revived the award for the duration of the conflict. On the eve of the First World War, in

German Iron Cross—Second Class.

German Iron Cross—First Class.

August, 1914, Kaiser Wilhelm reinstated the Iron Cross again, and on March 16, 1915, he ordered that the award could be given to citizens of allied foreign countries. This order has remained unchanged.

When the Second World War began, the Iron Cross was reinstated a third time. Until this time, it had been a strictly Prussian decoration, but now it was an all-German decoration. The Iron Cross is presented as First Class and Second Class. The First Class is the higher of the two and cannot be awarded unless the recipient has already received the Second Class.

RITTERKREUZ OR KNIGHTS CROSS

The Pour le Merite, or Blue Max, was the highest German decoration of the First World War except for some special medals reserved for nobility and generals. The Blue Max was awarded only to officers and was discontinued when Imperial Germany was dissolved. In September, 1939, at the beginning of World War II, a new version of the Iron Cross was created to replace the Pour le Merite: the Ritterkreuz, or the Knight's Cross of the Iron Cross. Following the example set by the Iron Cross it could be earned by anyone in the German armed forces regardless of rank. The Ritterkreuz was the highest German award during World War II.

The Ritterkreuz was actually a continuation of the Iron Cross First Class and was awarded in four progressively important stages: Knight's Cross of the Iron Cross (Ritterkreuz); Knight's Cross of the Iron Cross with Oak Leaves (Eichenlaub); Knight's Cross of the Iron Cross with Oak Leaves and Swords (Schwertern); Knight's Cross of the Iron Cross with Oak Leaves, Swords, and Diamonds (Brillanten). Two higher forms of this decoration existed, but were awarded only once.

The Ritterkreuz was worn on a black, white, and red ribbon around the neck. It was awarded for conspicuous bravery in action and for outstandingly meritorious leadership. A single act of outstanding bravery was not enough to merit the Ritterkreuz. As with its predecessor, the Pour le Merite, it was awarded only if the recipient exhibited consistent acts of bravery or continuous outstanding leadership. Once the Knight's Cross was awarded and another presentation was in order, the Eichenlaub was presented, followed by the Schwertern and finally Brillanten. Unlike the British Victoria Cross and American Congressional Medal of Honor, the Ritterkreuz was never awarded for one act of bravery in the face of the enemy, regardless of how heroic it may have been.

The Ritterkreuz was awarded 7,500 times and 1,730 of these went to Luftwaffe personnel: 1,483 Ritterkreuzen; 192 Eichenlauben; 41 Schwertern; 12 Brillanten; 1 Golden Oak Leaves; 1 Grand Cross.

Ritterkreuz mit Eichenlaub, Schwerten, and Brillanten— or the German Knights' Cross of the Iron Cross with Oak Leaves, Swords, and Diamonds.

JAGDWAFFE: ORGANIZATION AND AIRCRAFT IDENTIFICATION MARKINGS

The basic tactical element in the Jagdwaffe was the Rotte, consisting of two aircraft. Two Rotten formed a Schwarm and three or four Schwarms made a Staffel. Similarly, three Staffeln formed a Gruppe and three or four Gruppen formed the largest mobile, homogeneous unit in the Jagdwaffe, the Jagdgeschwader.

The sizes of gruppen and Jagdgeschwadern varied depending upon the tactical objective and the number of aircraft and pilots available. Although the Geschwader was under a single command, it did not necessarily operate as a unit from the same base, or even on the same front. The Jagdwaffe was a very flexible organization, and the subunits of Gruppe and even Staffel were often distributed to various assignments hundreds of miles apart, as the tactical situation demanded.

For identification purposes, each Jagdgeschwader was given an arabic numeral preceded by the ab-

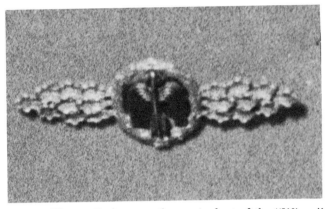

The Jagdflieger Badge was the equivalent of the "Wings" of the RAF and USAF. It consisted of a laurel wreath between oak-leaf wings. Inside the wreath is a winged arrow pointing up.

The Hungarian Military Pilots Badge consisted of a flying eagle with a large crown above.

The Croatian Pilots Badge consisted of an elliptical braid on which was superimposed an eagle clutching a shield. (Croatia joined the German attack on Russia in an effort to gain its independence from Yugoslavia.)

Knights Cross of the Hungarian Order of Merit with Laurel and Swords.

breviation for Jagdgeschwader, JG. Therefore, Jagdgeschwader number 51 would be written as JG 51.

The Gruppen were given Roman numerals which appeared before the Jagdgeschwader identification but separated from it with a slash. II Gruppe of Jagdgeschwader 51 would be written as II/JG 51.

An Arabic numeral was given to each Staffel, and it was also written before the Jagdgeschwader identification thus: 3/JG 51 for Staffel 3 of JG 51. The Staffel is identified relative to the Jagdgeschwader in lieu of the Gruppe.

The reason that it was not confusing to identify the Staffel in this manner is because specific Staffeln are assigned to each Gruppe, and once the pattern is memorized, the Staffel written identification tells at a glance the Gruppe and Geschwader as well. Stafeln 1, 2, and 3 were assigned to Gruppe I; Staffeln 4, 5, and 6 to Gruppe II; Staffeln 7, 8, and 9 to Gruppe III; and Staffeln 10, 11, and 12 to Gruppe IV. Therefore 3/JG 51 tells us that it refers to the 3rd Staffel in the I Gruppe of Jagdgeschwader 51.

With this arrangement, it was necessary to readily identify the various aircraft in the Staffel and a combination of numbers and colors was developed. The planes in each staffel were numbered from 1 to 12. This number appeared on the fuselage side between the cockpit and the cross. Staffeln 1, 4, 7, and 10 used white numbers; 2, 4, 8, and 11 used red numbers; 3, 6, 9, and 12 used yellow numbers.

Similarly, each Gruppe was given an identification symbol located on the fuselage between the cross and the tail. I Gruppe had no symbol; II Gruppe was assigned a horizontal bar; III Gruppe at the onset used a horizontal wavy bar and later switched to a vertical bar; IV Gruppe initially used a round dot, but this was often confused with the British rounded or cocarde insignia and was soon changed to a small Latin cross.

This system told the viewer at a glance the pilot, Staffel, and Gruppe; for example, a plane sporting a white 3 and a vertical bar is aircraft No. 3 from Staffel 7 in Gruppe III, because we know that Staffels 7, 8, and 9 are assigned to Gruppe III, but only Staffel 7 uses white numbers.

The Staffelkapitan generally flew plane No. 1 in his Staffel.

Special symbols were assigned for the Geschwaderkommodore and his staff, while similar, but not identical, symbols were also developed for the Gruppenkommandeur and their Staffs. The Geschwaderstab or Geschwader staff flew in their own Schwarm separated from rather than integrated with the Geschwader. The accompanying illustrations depict the various Geschwader and Gruppe staff markings that appear between the cockpit and the cross on the fuselage side. The symbols were black with white outlines.

LUFTWAFFE UNIT COMMANDER RANK

The personal rank of a unit commander in the Luftwaffe varied considerably, because his personal rank had no direct bearing with his command; for example, a Gruppekomandeur's personal rank could range from a Hauptmann or Major to Oberstleutnant (Captain to Lt. Colonel). The reader will therefore find the following comparison of personal rank and the unit commanded of interest.

Unit or Title	Personal Rank of Commander
Oberbefehlshaber der Luftwaffe	Reichsmarschall
Chef des Generalstabes der Luftwaffe	General der Flieger Generaloberst
Luftflotte	General der Flieger Generalfeldmarschall
Fliegerkorps	Generalleutnant General der Flieger
Fliegerdivision	General Major Generalleutnant General der Fleiger
Geschwader 120 aircraft (Kommodore)	Major/Oberstleutnant Oberst/General Major
Gruppe 30-48 aircraft (Gruppenkommandeur)	Major/Hauptmann Oberstleutnant
Staffel 9-12 aircraft (Staffelkapitan)	Oberleutnant Hauptmann
Schwarm (section of 4 aircraft) Kette (section of 3 aircraft) (Schwarmführer)	Unteroffizier Leutnant Oberleutnant

LUFTWAFFE RANK EQUIVALENTS

Luftwaffe Abbreviation	Luftwaffe Rank	RAF Rank	USAAF Rank
Ofhr.	Oberfahnrich	—	Cadet
Fw.	Feldwebel	Sergeant	Sergeant
Obfw.	Oberfeldwebel	Sergeant Major	Master Sergeant or Warrant Officer
Gefr.	Gefreiter	Lance Corporal	Private 1st Class
Uffz.	Unteroffizier	Corporal	Corporal
Lt.	Leutnant	Pilot Officer	2nd Lieutenant
Oblt.	Oberleutnant	Flying Officer	Lieutenant
Hptm.	Hauptmann	Flight Lieutenant	Captain
Maj.	Major	Squadron Leader	Major
Oberstlt.	Oberstleutnant	Wing Commander	Lt. Colonel
Oberst	Oberst	Group Captain	Colonel
Gen. Maj.	General Major	Air Commodore	Maj. General
Gen. Lt.	Generalleutnant	Air Vice Marshal	Lt. General
Gen. d. Fl.	General der Flieger	Air Marshal	General
Gen. Oberst.	General-Oberst	Air Chief Marshal	—
Gen. Feldm.	General-Feldmarschall	Marshal of the Royal Air Force	5-Star General

LUFTWAFFE ABBREVIATIONS

Adju.	=	Adjutant (adjutant, aide-de-camp)
E. Gr.	=	Erprobungsgruppe (testing Gruppe)
Erg. Gr.	=	Ergänzungsgruppe (replacement training Gruppe)
Fw.	=	Feldwebel (Sergeant)
Gefr.	=	Gefreiter (Lance Corporal, Private 1st Class)
Gr.	=	Gruppe
Hptm.	=	Hauptmann (Captain)
Jabo	=	Jagdbomber (fighter bomber)
JG	=	Jagdgeschwader (fighter Geschwader)
Kap.	=	Staffelkapitan (Staffel Commander)
Kdr.	=	Gruppenkommandeur (Gruppe Commander)
Kdre.	=	Geschwaderkommodore (Geschwader Commander)
KG	=	Kampfgeschwader (bomber Geschwader)
KGr.	=	Kampfgruppe (bomber Gruppe)
LG	=	Lehrgeschwader (training Geschwader operational)
Lt.	=	Leutnant (2nd Lieutenant)
Maj.	=	Major (Major)
NAG	=	Nahaufklarungsgruppe (close reconnaissance Gruppe)
NJG	=	Nachtjagdgeschwader (Night Fighter Geschwader)
Ob.d.H.	=	Oberkommando des Heeres (High Command of the Army)
Ob.d.L.	=	Oberkommando der Luftwaffe (High Command of Air Forces)
Ob.d.M.	=	Oberkommando der Marine (High Command of the Navy)
Obfw.	=	Oberfeldwebel (Master Sergeant)
Oblt.	=	Oberleutnant (1st Lieutenant)
Oberstlt.	=	Oberstleutnant (Lieutenant Colonel)
RLM	=	Reichsluftfahrtministerium (German Air Ministry)
SG	=	Schlachtgeschwader (ground-support Geschwader)
SKG	=	Schnelles Kampfgeschwader (fast-bomber Geschwader)
St. G.	=	Stukageschwader (dive-bomber Geschwader)
TG	=	Transportgeschwader (transport Geschwader)
TO	=	Technischer Offizier (Technical Officer)
Uffz	=	Unteroffizier (Corporal)
ZG	=	Zerstorergeschwader (long-range fighter Geschwader)

MESSERSCHMITT ACES
(PARTIAL LISTING)

Name	Victories	Name	Victories
Adam, Heinz-Günther	7	Boremski, Eberhard von	90
Ademeit, Horst	166	Borngen, Ernst	45
Adolph, Walter	28	Borreck, Hans-Joachim	5
Ahnert, Heinz-Wilhelm	57	Borris, Karl	43
Ahrens, Peter	11	Böwing-Trüding, Wolfgang	46
Aistleitner, Johann	12	Brandle, Werner-Kurt	180
Andel, Peter	6	Brandt, Paul	34
Babenz, Emil	24	Brandt, Walter	57
Bachnick, Herbert	80	Bremer, Peter	40
Badum, Johann	54	Brendel, Joachim	189
Baer, Heinrich "Heinz"	220	Bretnutz, Heinz	37
Balthasar, Wilhelm	47	Bretschneider, Klaus	40
Bareuter, Herbert	56	Brewes	18
Barkhorn, Gerhard	301	Broch, Hugo	81
Bartels, Heinrich	99	Brocke, Jürgen	45
Barten, Franz	53	Brönnle, Herbert	57
Bartz, Erich	30	Brükel, Wendelin	14
Batz, Wilhelm	237	Brunner, Albert	53
Bauer, Konrad	60	Buchner, Hermann	58
Bauer, Viktor	106	Bucholz, Max	30
Becker, Paul	20	Bühligen, Kurt	112
Beckh, Friedrich	48	von Bülow-Bothkamp, Hilmer "Harry"	(+ 6 in WWI) 18
Beerenbrock, Hans	117	Bunzek, Johannes	75
Beese, Artur	22	Burckhardt, Lutz-Wilhelm	58
Beisswenger, Hans	152	Burk, Alfred	56
Belser, Helmut	36	Bürschgens, Josef	10
Bendert, Karl-Heinz	54	Busch, Erwin	8
Bennemann, Helmut	92	Busse, Heinz	22
Benz, Siegfried	6	Carganico, Horst	60
Berres, Heinz-Edgar	53	Cech, Franz	65
Bertram, Otto	21	Christof, Ernst	9
Beutin, Gerhard	60	Claude, Emil	27
Beyer, Franz	81	Clausen, Erwin	132
Beyer, Georg	8	Cordes, Heine	52
Beyer, Heinz	33	Crinius, Wilhelm	114
Bierwirth, Heinrich	8	Crump, Peter	31
Birkner, Hans-Joachim	117	Dahl, Walther	128
Bitsch, Emil	108	Dahmer, Hugo	57
Blazytko, Franz	29	Dähne, Paul-Heinrich	100
Bleckmann, Günther	27	Dammers, Hans	113
Bloemertz, Günther	10	Darjes, Emil	82
Blume, Walter	14	Denk, Gustav	67
Bob, Hans-Ekkehard	59	Dickfeld, Adolf	136
Böhm-Fettelbach, Karl	40	Dietze, Gottfried	5
Bohn, Kurt	5	Dinger, Fritz	67
Bolz, Helmut-Felix	56	Dipple, Hans	19
Bonin, Hubertus von	77	Dirksen, Hans	5
Borchers, Adolf	132	Dittlmann, Heinrich	57
		Döbele, Anton	94
		Döbrich, Hans-Heinrich	70

Name	Victories	Name	Victories
Dombacher, Kurt	68	Gath, Wilhelm	14
Dörr, Franz	128	Geisshardt, Friedrich "Fritz"	102
Dörre, Edgar	9	Gentzen, Hannes	18
Dortenmann, Hans	38	Gerhard, Dieter	8
Düllberg, Ernst	50	Gerhard, Günther	18
Düttmann, Peter	152	Gerhardt, Werner	13
Ebbinghausen, Karl	7	Gerth, Werner	30
Ebeling, Heinz	18	Gienanth, Eugene von	10
Ebener, Kurt	57	Glunz, Adolf	71
Ebersberger, Kurt	27	Golinski, Heinz	47
Eberwein, Manfred	56	Gollob, Gordon M.	150
Eckerle, Franz	59	Goltzsch, Kurt	43
Eder, Georg-Peter	78	Gommann, Heinz	12
Edmann, Johannes	5	Gossow, Heinz	70
Ehlen, Karl-Heinz	7	Gottlob, Heinz	6
Ehlers, Hans	52	Götz, Franz	63
Ehrenberger, Rudolf	49	Götz, Hans	82
Ehrler, Heinrich	209	Graf, Hermann	212
Eichel-Streiber, Dieter von	96	Grasser, Hartmann	103
Eickhoff	5	Grassmuck, Berthold	65
Einsiedel, Heinrich Graf von	35	Gratz, Karl	138
Eisenach, Franz	129	Grislawski, Alfred	133
Ellenrieder, Xavier	12	Grollmus, Helmut	75
Engfer, Siegfried	58	Gromotka, Fritz	27
Ettel, Wolf-Udo	124	Gross, Alfred	52
Ewald, Heinz	84	Grünberg, Hans	82
Ewald, Wolfgang	78	Grünlinger, Walter	7
Fassong, Horst-Günther von	136	Grzymalla, Gerhard	7
Fast, Hans-Joachim	5	Guhl, Hermann	15
Fengler, Georg	16	Günther, Joachim	11
Findeisen, Herbert	67	Guttmann, Gerhard	10
Fink, Günther	46	Haas, Friedrich	74
Fleig, Erwin	66	Haase, Horst	82
Fonnekold, Otto	136	Hachtel, August	5
Fozo, Josef	27	Hacker, Joachim	32
Francsi, Gustav	56	Hackl, Anton	192
Franke, Alfred	59	Hackler, Heinrich	56
Franzisket, Ludwig	43	Hafner, Anton	204
Freuworth, Wilhelm	58	Hafner, Ludwig	52
Frey, Hugo	32	Hahn, Hans "Assi"	108
Freytag, Siegfried	102	Hahn, Hans von	34
Friebel, Herbert	58	Hailboeck, Josef	77
Fröhlich, Hans-Jürgen	5	Hammerl, Karl	63
Fuchs, Karl	67	Handrick, Gotthardt	20
Fuhrmann, Erich	5	Hannack, Günther	47
Füllgrabe, Heinrich	65	Hannig, Horst	98
Fuss, Hans	71	Harder, Harro	22
Gabl, Pepi	38	Harder, Jürgen	64
Gaiser, Otto	74	Hartigs, Hans	6
Galland, Adolf	104	Hartmann, Erich	352
Galland, Paul	17	Hauswirth, Wilhelm	54
Galland, Wilhelm-Ferdinand	55	Heckmann, Alfred	71
Gallowitsch, Bernd	64		
Gartner, Josef	6		

Name	Victories	Name	Victories
Heckmann, Günther	20	Kayser, August	25
Heimann, Friedrich	30	Kehl, Dietrich	6
Hein, Kurt	8	Keil, Georg	36
Heinecke, Hans-Joachim	28	Kelch, Günther	13
Henrici, Eberhard	7	Keller, Hannes	24
Hermichen, Rolf	64	Keller, Lothar	20
Herrmann, Hajo	9	Kelter, Kurt	60
Herrmann, Isken	56	Kemethmüller, Heinz	89
Heuser, Heinrich	5	Kempf, Karl-Heinz	65
Heyer, Hans-Joachim	53	Kiefner, Georg	11
Hilleke, Otto-Heinrich	6	Kientsch, Willi	52
Hirschfeld, Ernst-Erich	45	Kirchmayr, Rudiger	46
Hoeckner, Walter	68	Kirschner, Joachim	188
Hoefemeier, Heinrich	96	Kittel, Otto	267
Hoffman, Gerhard	125	Klein, Alfons	39
Hoffmann, Heinrich	63	Klemm, Rudolf	42
Hoffmann, Hermann	8	Klöpper, Heinrich	94
Hoffmann, Reinhold	66	Knappe, Kurt	54
Hoffmann, Karl	70	Knauth, Hans	26
Hoffmann, Wilhelm	44	Knittel, Emil	50
Hohagen, Erich	55	Knocke, Heinz	44
Holl, Walter	7	Koall, Gerhard	37
Holler, Kurt	18	Koeppen, Gerhard	85
Holtz, Helmut	56	Köhler, Armin	69
Homuth, Gerhard	63	Kolbow, Hans	27
Hoppe, Helmut	24	König, Hans-Heinrich	24
Hörschelmann, Jürgen	44	Körner, Friedrich	36
Hrabak, Dietrich "Dieter"	125	Korts, Berthold	113
Hrdlicka, Franz	96	Koslowski, Eduard	12
Hubner, Eckhard	47	Kosse, Wolfgang	11
Hubner, Wilhelm	62	Krafft, Heinrich	78
Hulshoff, Karl	24	Krahl, Karl-Heinz	
Huppertz, Herbert	68	Kroh, Hans	22
Huy, Wolf-Dietrich	40	Kroschinski, Hans-Joachim	76
Ihlefeld, Herbert	130	Krug, Heinz	9
Isken, Eduard	56	Krupinski, Walter	197
Jackel, Ernst	8	Kühlein, Elias	36
Javer, Erich	12	Kunz, Franz	12
Jenne, Peter	17	Kutscha, Herbert	47
Jennewein, Josef	86	Lang, Emil	173
Jessen, Heinrich	6	Lange, Friedrich	8
Johannsen, Hans	8	Lange, Gerhard	5
Joppien, Hermann-Friedrich	70	Lange, Heinz	70
Josten, Günther	178	Langer, Karl-Heinz	30
Jung, Harald	20	Laskowski, Erwin	46
Jung, Heinrich	68	Lasse, Kurt	39
Kageneck, Erbo Graf von	67	Laub, Karl	7
Kaiser, Herbert	68	Lausch, Bernhard	39
Kalden, Peter	84	Leber, Heinz	54
Kalkum, Adolf	57	Leesmann, Karl-Heinz	37
Kaminski, Herbert	7	Leibold, Erwin	11
Karch, Fritz	47	Leie, Erich	118

Name	Victories	Name	Victories
Lemke, Siegfried	96	Miethig, Rudolf	101
Lemke, Wilhelm	131	Mietusch, Klaus	72
Lepple, Richard	68	Mink, Wilhelm	72
Leuschel, Rudolf	9	Mischkot, Bruno	7
Leykauf, Erwin	33	Missner, Helmut	82
Liebelt, Fritz	25	Mölders, Werner	115
Lieres, Carl von	31	Moritz, Wilhelm	44
Liesendahl, Frank	50	Mors, August	60
Lignitz, Arnold	25	Müller, Friedrich-Karl "Tutti"	140
Lindelaub, Friedrich	5	Müller, Kurt	5
Lindemann, Theodor	7	Müller, Rudolf	101
Lindner, Anton	73	Müller, Wilhelm	10
Lindner, Walter	64	Müller-Dühe, Gerhard	5
Linz, Rudolf	70	Müncheberg, Joachim	135
Lipfert, Helmut	203	Munderloh, Georg	20
Lippert, Wolfgang	29	Münster, Leopold	95
Litjens, Stefan	38	Munz, Karl "Fox"	60
Loos, Gerhard	92	Mütherich, Hubert	43
Loos, Walter	38	Naumann, Johannes	34
Losigkeit, Fritz	68	Nemitz, Willi	81
Lucas, Werner	106	Neu, Wolfgang	12
Lücke, Max-Hermann	81	Neuhoff, Hermann	40
Lüddecke, Fritz	50	Neumann, Eduard	13
Lüders, Franz	5	Neumann, Helmut	62
Lützow, Günther	108	Neumann, Karl	75
Machold, Werner	32	Neumann, Klaus	37
Mackenstedt, Willy	6	Ney, Siegfried	11
Mader, Anton	86	Nordmann, Karl-Gottfried	78
Mai, Lothar	90	Norz, Jakob	117
Makrocki, Wilhelm	9	Nowotny, Walter	258
Maltzahn, Günther Freiherr von	68	Obleser, Friedrich	127
Marquardt, Heinz	121	Ohlrogge, Walter	83
Marseille, Hans-Joachim	158	Olejnik, Robert	41
Matoni, Walter	44	Omert, Emil	70
Matzak, Kurt	18	Ösau, Walter	123
May, Lothar	45	Osterkamp, Theodore (+ 32 in WWI)	6
Mayer, Egon	102	Ostermann, Max-Helmuth	102
Mayer, Hans-Karl	38	Petermann, Viktor	64
Mayer, Otto	22	Peters, Erhard	22
Mayer, Wilhelm	27	Pfeiffer, Karl	10
Mayerl, Maximilian	76	Pflanz, Rudolf	52
Meckel, Helmut	25	Pfüller, Helmut	28
Meier, Johannes-Hermann	77	Philipp, Hans	206
Meimberg, Julius	53	Philipp, Wilhelm	81
Meltzer	35	Pichler, Johannes	75
Menge, Robert	18	Piffer, Anton-Rudolf	26
Mertens, Helmut	97	Pingel, Rolf	26
Meyer, Conny		Plucker, Karl-Heinz	34
Meyer, Eduard	18	Pohs, Josef	43
Meyer, Walter	18	Polster, Wolfgang	5
Michalek, Georg	59	Pragen, Hans	23
Michalski, Gerhard	73	Preinfalk, Alexander	76

Name	Victories	Name	Victories
Priller, Josef "Pips"	101	Schmid, Johannes	41
Pringle, Rolf-Peter	22	Schmidt, Erich	47
Puschmann, Herbert	54	Schmidt, Gottfried	8
Quaet-Faslem, Klaus	49	Schmidt, Heinz "Johnny"	173
Quante, Richard	44	Schmidt, Johannes	12
Quast, Werner	84	Schmidt, Rudolf	51
Rademacher, Rudolf	126	Schmidt, Winifried	19
Radener, Waldemar	36	Schneider, Gerhard	41
Rall, Günther	275	Schneider, Walter	20
Rammelt, Karl	46	Schnell, Karl-Heinz	72
Rauch, Alfred	60	Schnell, Siegfried	93
Redlich, Karl	43	Schnörrer, Karl "Quax"	46
Reiff	48	Schönfelder, Helmut	56
Reinert, Ernst-Wilhelm	174	Schöpfel, Gerhard	40
Reinhard, Emil	42	Schramm, Herbert	42
Reischer, Peter	19	Schrör, Werner	114
Remmer, Hans	26	Schuck, Walter	206
Resch, Anton	91	Schulte, Franze	46
Resch, Rudolf	94	Schultz, Otto	73
Reschke, Willi	26	Schulwitz, Gerhard	9
Richter, Hans	22	Schulz, Otto	51
Richter, Rudolf	70	Schwaiger, Franz	67
Roch, Eckhard	5	Schwartz, Gerhard	20
Rödel, Gustav	98	Schwarz, Erich	11
Röhrig, Hans	75	Seegatz, Hermann	31
Rohwer, Detler	38	Seeger, Günther	56
Rollwage, Herbert	102	Seelmann, Georg	39
Romm, Oskar	92	Seidel	20
Rossmann, Edmund	93	Seifert, Johannes	57
Roth, Willi	20	Seiler, Reinhard	109
Rübell, Günther	47	Semelka, Waldemar	65
Rudorffer, Erich	222	Setz, Heinrich	138
Rüffler, Helmut	70	Seigler, Peter	48
Ruhl, Franz	64	Simon	22
Rupp, Friedrich	53	Simsch, Siegfried	95
Rysayy, Martin	8	Sinner, Rudolf	39
Sachsenberg, Heinz	104	Sochatzky, Kurt	38
Sattig, Karl	53	Soffing, Waldemar	33
Schacht, Emil	25	Sommer, Gerhard	20
Schack, Günther	174	Späte, Wolfgang	99
Schall, Franz	137	Specht, Günther	32
Schauder, Paul	20	Spies, Wilhelm	20
Scheel, Günther	71	Spreckles, Robert	21
Scheer, Klaus	24	Sprick, Gustav	31
Schellmann, Wolfgang	26	Stadek, Karl	25
Schentke, Georg	90	Stahlschmidt, Hans	59
Scheyda, Erich	20	Staiger, Hermann	63
Schiess, Franz	67	Stammberger, Otto	7
Schilling, Wilhelm	50	Stechmann, Hans	33
Schleef, Hans	98	Stedfeld, Günther	25
Schleinghege, Hermann	96	Steffen, Karl	59
Schlichting, Joachim	8	Steffens, Hans Joachim	22

Name	Victories	Name	Victories
Steigler, Franz	28	Wagner, Edmund	57
Steinbatz, Leopold	99	Wagner, Rudolf	81
Steinhausen, Günther	40	Waldmann, Hans	134
Steinhoff, Johannes	176	Walter, Horst	25
Steinmann, Wilhelm	44	Wandel, Joachim	75
Steis, Heinrich	21	Weber, Karl-Heim	136
Stendel, Fritz	39	Wefers, Heinrich	52
Stengel, Walter	34	Wehnelt, Herbert	36
Sternberg, Horst	23	Weik, Hans	36
Sterr, Heinrich "Bazi"	130	Weiss, Robert	121
Stolle, Bruno	35	Weissenberger, Theodor	208
Stolte, Paul-August	5	Weissmann, Ernst	69
Stotz, Maximilian	189	Weneckers	9
Strakeljahn, Friedrich-Wilhelm	18	Werfft, Peter	26
Strassl, Hubert	67	Wernicke, Heinz "Piepl"	117
Strelow, Hans	68	Wernitz, Ulrich	101
Stritzel, Fritz	19	Werra, Franz von	21
Strohecker, Karl	10	Wessling, Otto	83
Stumpf, Werner	47	Westphal, Hans-Jürgen	22
Sturm, Heinrich	157	Wettstein, Helmut	34
Surau, Alfred	46	Wever, Walther	60
Süss, Ernst	70	Wick, Helmut	56
Swallisch, Erwin	31	Wiegand, Gerhard	32
Szugger, Willy	9	Wiese, Johannes	133
Tabbat, Adolf	5	Wilke, Wolf-Dietrich	161
Tange, Otto	68	Willius, Karl	50
Tangermann, Kurt	60	Winkler, Max	21
Tanzer, Kurt	143	Winterfelt, Alexander von	9
Tautscher, Gabriel	55	Wischnewski, Hermann	28
Tegtmeier, Fritz	146	Witzel, Hans	14
Teumer, Alfred	76	Wöhnert, Ulrich	86
Theil, Edwin	76	Woidich, Franz	110
Thyben, Gerhard	157	Wolf, Albin	144
Tichy, Eckehard	25	Wolf, Hermann	57
Tietzen, Horst	27	Wolf, Robert	21
Tonne, Wolfgang	122	Wolfrum, Walter	137
Trautloft, Hannes	57	Wübke, Waldemar	15
Trünkel, Rudolf	138	Wünsch, Karl	25
Üben, Kurt	110	Wünschelmyer, Karl	16
Udet, Hans	20	Würfel, Otto	79
Ulbrich	33	Wurmheller, Josef	102
Ulenberg, Horst	17	Zeller, Joachim	7
Unger, Willy	22	Zellot, Walter	85
Unzeitig, Robert	10	Zimmermann, Oskar	48
Vandeweerd, Heinrich	6	Zink, Fülbert	36
Vechtel, Bernard	108	Zirngibl, Josef	9
Vinzent, Otto	44	Zoufahl, Franz-Josef	26
Vogel, Ferdinand	33	Zweigart, Eugen-Ludwig	69
Vogt, Heinz-Gerhard	48	Zwernemann, Josef "Jupp"	126
Wachowiak, Friedrich	86	Zwesken, Rudi	25

Rank Insignia

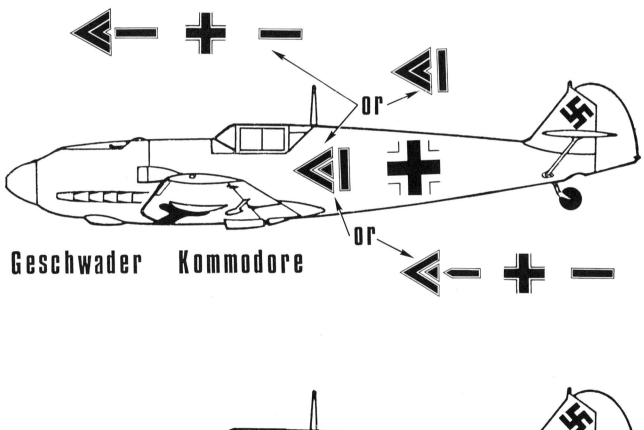

Geschwader Kommodore

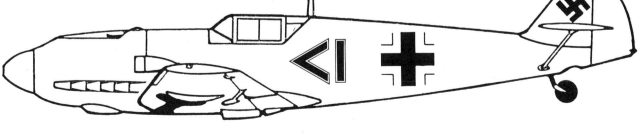

Geschwader Adjutant

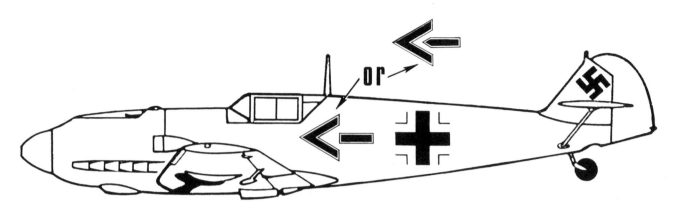

Geschwader Operations Officer

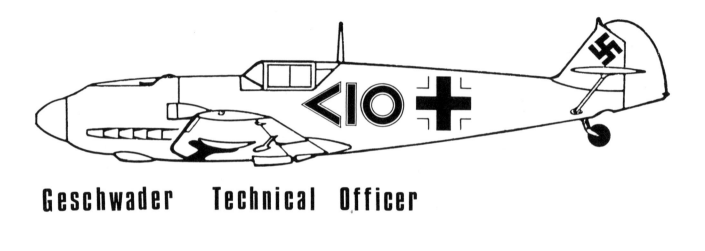

Geschwader Technical Officer

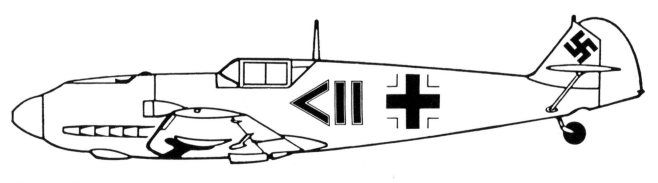

Geschwader Staff Major

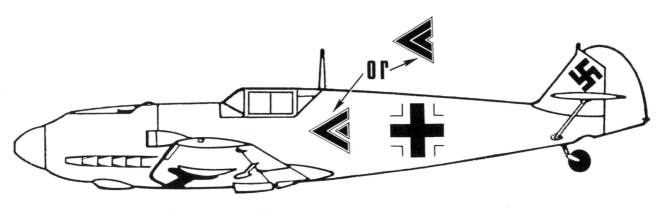

I Gruppe Kommandeur

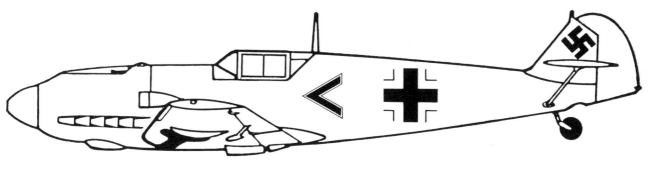

I Gruppe Adjutant

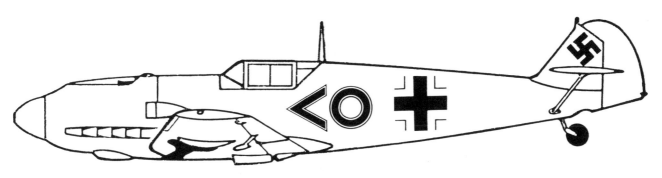

I Gruppe Technical Officer

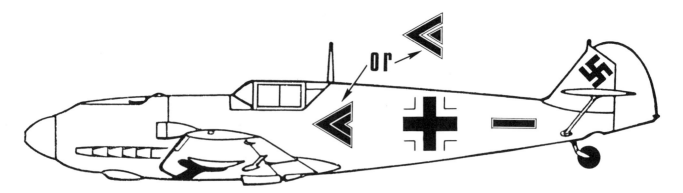

II Gruppe   Kommandeur

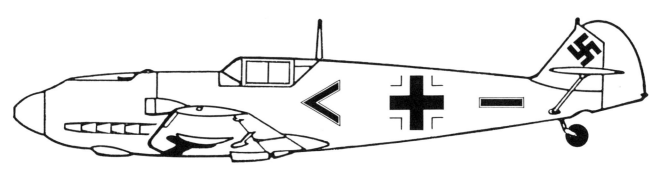

II Gruppe   Adjutant

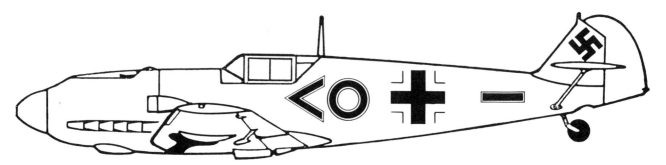

II Gruppe   Technical Officer

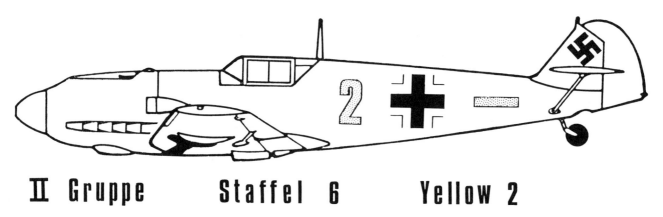

II Gruppe   Staffel 6   Yellow 2

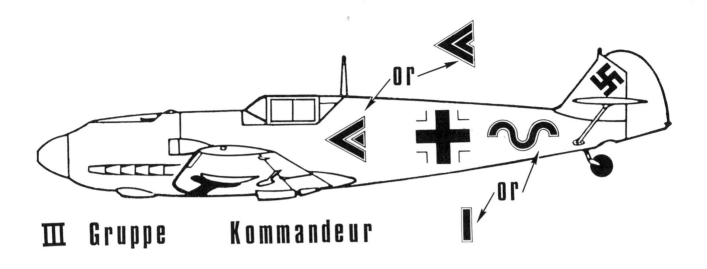

III   **Gruppe**   **Kommandeur**

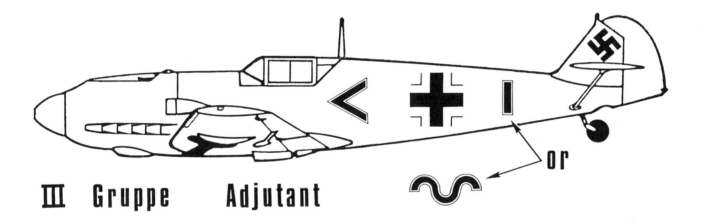

III   **Gruppe**   **Adjutant**

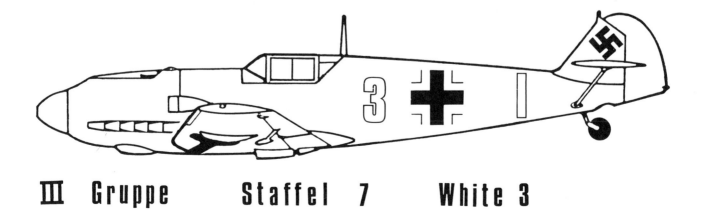

III   **Gruppe**   **Staffel 7**   **White 3**

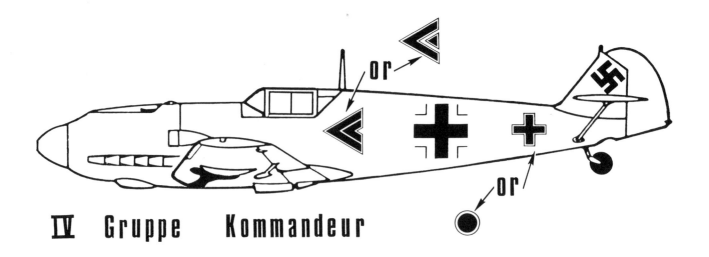

IV Gruppe   Kommandeur

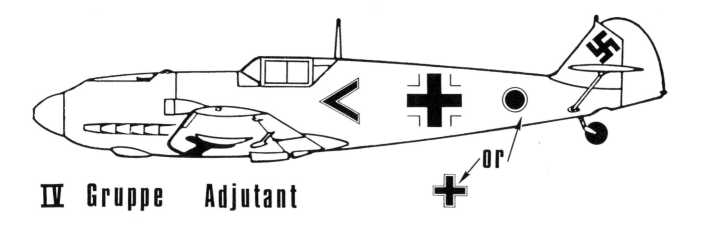

IV Gruppe   Adjutant

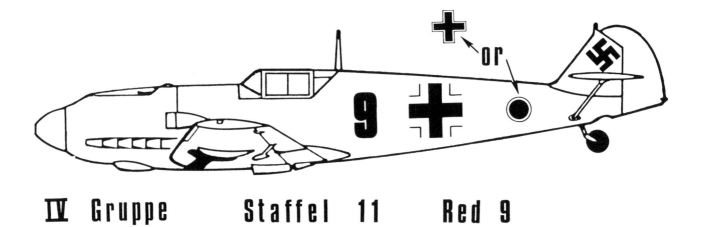

IV Gruppe   Staffel 11   Red 9

Index

Other Bestsellers From TAB

☐ **AERIAL RECONNAISSANCE—The 10th Photo Recon Group in World War II—Tom Ivie**

A fascinating overview of World War II from the unique perspective of the aerial photographer. You'll find dozens of photos chosen from the more than 18,000 taken by these recon photographers, plus details on aircraft, the group's adventures, and more! You'll discover how these secret photos helped turn Germany's last offensive. 208 pp., 366 illus.

Paper $8.95 **Hard $9.95**
Book No. 28900

☐ **IF YOU READ ME, ROCK THE TOWER—Bob Stevens**

A collection of aviation humor by internationally-known cartoonist Bob Stevens—creator of the popular comic "STOP SQUAWK!" in *Private Pilot*. Dedicated to all the airmen of World War II, Korea, and Vietnam, this is a compilation of cartoons, jokes, Air Force jargon, aircraft silhouettes, and barrack ballads—each one more hilarious than the last. And Bob Stevens draws his material from first-hand experience as a former Air Force Pilot and aviation enthusiast for over 40 years. 144 pp.

Paper $8.95 **Hard $9.95**
Book No. 26505

☐ **CHARIOTS FOR APOLLO: The Untold Story Behind the Race to the Moon—Charles R. Pellegrino and Joshua Stoff**

Many books have been written about the astronauts who first set foot on the moon. But the hundreds and even thousands of designers, technicians, and others who made the lunar module possible have been little recognized. Here they are highlighted. You'll witness the political and scientific infighting that surrounded the project. You'll share the frustrations, the sacrifices, the uncertainties, and the humor that affected the ordinary people involved in the project. 256 pp., 40 illus.

Paper $12.95 **Hard $14.95**
Book No. 22923

☐ **AMERICA'S ASTRONAUTS and THEIR INDE-STRUCTIBLE SPIRIT—Dr. Fred Kelly, former NASA Physician, Foreword by Dr. Buzz Aldrin**

Never before has there been an account of the U.S. manned space program that puts its primary emphasis on the astronauts as people or the effect of their careers on their relationships with their families, their friends, and their co-workers. Now, a Navy flight surgeon provides a fascinating and compassionate look at the human side of the space program. 176 pp., 35 illus.

Paper $13.95 **Hard $16.95**
Book No. 22396

☐ **THE DC-3: 50 YEARS OF LEGENDARY FLIGHT—Peter M. Bowers**

The fabulous Douglas DC-3 celebrates over 50 years of flight! And this special anniversary volume lets you relive its fascinating history. It features one of the most extensive photo collections of the DC-3 in the world and covers the distinctions between the many military variants of the DC-3—complete with a photograph of each variant and its reason for existing. 259 pp., 8 Full Color Pages, Fully illustrated.

Paper $16.95 **Hard $19.95**
Book No. 22394

☐ **SWEETWATER GUNSLINGER 201—Lt. Commander William H. LaBarge, U.S. Navy and Robert Lawrence Holt**

By the author of the current bestseller *Good Friday*! Set aboard the U.S. Carrier Kitty Hawk during the Iranian crisis of 1980, this fast-paced novel details the lives, loves, dangers, trials, tribulations, and escapades of a group of Tail Hookers (Navy carrier pilots). As much fact as fiction, it's a story that is both powerful and sensitive . . . by authors who do a masterful job of bringing the reader aboard a modern aircraft carrier and into the cockpit of an F-14! 192 pp.

Paper $11.95 **Hard $14.95**
Book No. 28515

☐ **LIVING IN SPACE—A Manual for Space Travelers—Peter Smolders**

Featuring full-color photographs and drawings from NASA, the Soviet Space Agency, and the European space programs, this is a volume that's guaranteed to provide hours of fascinating reading for anyone interested in space travel. It provides a firsthand glimpse of travel and space living that has never before been available to those not directly involved in the space programs. 160 pp., 200 color photos plus line drawings and black and white photos, 8″ × 10″

Paper $11.95 **Hard $14.95**
Book No. 24180

☐ **GOOD FRIDAY—Robert Lawrence Holt**

"*. . . excitement in the flying scenes and in the fight for power among the Saudi royalty . . . the author does know (his) flying!*
—**The New York Times Book Review**

In this gripping novel, award-winning author Robert Lawrence Holt takes the evening news one step further. Combining both fact and conjecture the author sets up a believable confrontation between the Soviet Union and the Free World over the richest oil-producing nation, Saudi Arabia. You'll find this exciting, realistic work of fiction almost impossible to put down. 224 pp., Hardcover with dust jacket.

Paper $12.50 **Hard $14.95**
Book No. 22399

☐ **THE HUNGRY TIGERS: The Fighter Pilot's Role in Modern Warfare—Frank J. O'Brien**

Now, a former fighter pilot whose impressive service record includes 163 combat missions in Vietnam, provides a fascinating insight into the realities of today's U.S. Tactical Air Forces. O'Brien puts his emphasis on the human element—the "hungry tigers" whose pride, dedication, and sharply-honed skills set them apart from ordinary service men. Includes vivid descriptions of fighter planes. 320 pp., 78 illus.

Paper $12.95 **Hard $14.95**
Book No. 22395

☐ **BLACK CATS AND DUMBOS: WWII's Fighting PBYs—Mel Crocker**

As "Black Cats" the PBYs were stealthy night bombers, painted black and sent out into the night to wreak havoc on the enemy. Affectionately known as "Dumbos," the Catalinas also plucked airmen, seamen, merchant mariners, refugees, coast-watchers, and even the enemy from hostile waters in war zones throughout the world. No record of WWII in the air can be complete unless it includes the contributions of these men and their unique aircraft. 304 pp., 52 illus.

Paper $11.95 **Hard $14.95**
Book No. 22391

Other Bestsellers From TAB